Bereavement in Late Life

Bereavement in Late Life

COPING, ADAPTATION, AND DEVELOPMENTAL INFLUENCES

Robert O. Hansson
Margaret S. Stroebe

AMERICAN PSYCHOLOGICAL ASSOCIATION
WASHINGTON, DC

Published by
American Psychological Association
750 First Street, NE
Washington, DC 20002
www.apa.org

To order
APA Order Department
P.O. Box 92984
Washington, DC 20090-2984
Tel: (800) 374-2721; Direct: (202) 336-5510
Fax: (202) 336-5502; TDD/TTY: (202) 336-6123
Online: www.apa.org/books/
E-mail: order@apa.org

In the U.K., Europe, Africa, and the Middle East, copies may be ordered from
American Psychological Association
3 Henrietta Street
Covent Garden, London
WC2E 8LU England

Typeset in Goudy by Stephen McDougal, Mechanicsville, MD

Printer: United Book Press, Inc., Baltimore, MD
Cover Designer: Berg Design, Albany, NY
Technical/Production Editor: Genevieve Gill

The opinions and statements published are the responsibility of the authors, and such opinions and statements do not necessarily represent the policies of the American Psychological Association.

Library of Congress Cataloging-in-Publication Data

Hansson, Robert O.
    Bereavement in late life: coping, adaptation, and developmental influences /
by Robert O. Hansson and Margaret S. Stroebe. — 1st ed.
        p. cm.
    Includes bibliographical references and index.
    ISBN-13: 978-1-59147-472-2
    ISBN-10: 1-59147-472-8
    1. Bereavement in old age. I. Stroebe, Margaret S. II. Title.
    BF724.85.G73H36 2006
    155.9'370846—dc22   2006009891

British Library Cataloguing-in-Publication Data
A CIP record is available from the British Library.

Printed in the United States of America
First Edition

For Kathleen
—*Robert O. Hansson*

In memory of my mother,
Mary E. Harrold-Swarbreck
For her granddaughter,
Katherine E. Stroebe
—*Margaret S. Stroebe*

CONTENTS

PREFACE

The idea for this volume was born 5 years ago, when we exchanged ideas about bereavement among older people in the context of preparing to lecture on this topic. We found it difficult to gain an overall perspective on research in the field or to access and review the relevant background literature. Information was spread across a wide variety of sources, and no recent article or volume could be found that provided a thorough overview and synthesis. Furthermore, apparently straightforward questions such as "Are older bereaved persons really less susceptible than younger persons to the health consequences of bereavement?" proved more difficult to answer than we had expected. So many issues needed to be taken into account. We concluded that there was a need for an updated review.

Both of us were keen to work on such a project. One of us (Stroebe) has for many years conducted research and theoretical work on bereavement-related coping, risk factors, and outcomes. The other (Hansson) has focused more on the interface of aging and the role of social coping resources in dealing with stressful life events. It seemed time to focus more systematically on the combination: to explore the situation and reactions of those older adults who have become bereaved and to provide a scientific perspective for understanding the phenomena and manifestations specific to this population.

A unique opportunity presented itself; nowhere could we find any attempt to fuse the two independent bodies of theory and research within the fields of gerontology and bereavement. Yet, our acquaintance with the two areas gave good reason to assume that much could be gained from an integration of ideas from the two fields.

We first envisioned this project as a comprehensive review paper, one that would give a state-of-the-art account of scientific knowledge about the experience of bereavement among older persons. This idea was soon abandoned, however, as we quickly found that the issues could not be explored adequately within the constraints of a journal article. Also, we needed more space to explore contributions from the two separate research fields. It seemed important, for example, to examine the applicability of contemporary grief theory, research, and assessment protocols among older populations and to explore the manner and extent to which the circumstances of late life might affect the nature or feasibility of coping and adaptation to the loss of a loved one. At a more fundamental level, it also seemed relevant to question the manner in which cognitive, emotional, and physiological-health processes at the core of the grief experience might change in late life. In this connection, for example, a wealth of developmental and contextual variables could render the bereavement experience more complex, and perhaps less predictable. Finally, we saw an opportunity in this project to develop our own integrative theoretical perspective.

We decided, therefore, to work together on this book—to our knowledge the first scientific monograph to focus exclusively (and in this depth) on bereavement among older adults. We intend the volume to provide the reader with in-depth reviews of contemporary theory and research on bereavement generally and of the intriguing research that has begun to accumulate on bereavement among older adults specifically. Beyond that, however, we hope to engage the reader in our explorations of the connections between aging and the bereavement experience and their implications for theory and intervention in both fields.

ACKNOWLEDGMENTS

We would like to thank Lansing Hays and Ron Teeter, our editors at the American Psychological Association, for their enthusiastic support for our project on aging and bereavement. We wish to thank, as well, a number of individuals who over the years have encouraged and inspired our efforts. We are particularly grateful to Miriam and Sidney Moss, whose research for many years has focused on older people, end-of-life issues, and bereavement; they are treasured colleagues and mentors. We also want to thank Bert Hayslip, who encouraged us in our thinking about late-life developmental issues as they affect the bereavement experience, and Dale Lund, whose research on older bereaved spouses helped to define the most important issues in the field.

Wolfgang Stroebe and Henk Schut stood by us personally and professionally throughout the writing of this volume. Without them, the project would not have been completed. Also, we would like to thank Susan Folkman, Pauline Rohatgi, and Deepika Joshi, who contributed immensely to specific parts of our research.

Finally, our efforts to integrate the perspectives of aging and bereavement would not have been possible without the independent contributions of researchers in both fields, spanning several decades. We want to acknowledge those scholars whose work we have cited. They are to be found in many disciplines (psychology, psychiatry, sociology, anthropology, gerontology, nursing, and many others). We learned much from them. Of course, we are ourselves responsible for the content of the book, and this we happily share between us, reflecting our harmonious and very special collaboration.

Bereavement in Late Life

INTRODUCTION

Most people will at some point experience the death of a loved one, and it can be the most difficult of psychological experiences. In addition to a complex affective and cognitive symptomatology, important physiological consequences have now been demonstrated to include disruptions of normal sleep and appetite, somatic complaints, diminished energy, increased use of medications, and increased hospital visits. A significant subset of bereaved individuals also appears to be at greater risk for problematic, longer term health outcomes (e.g., cardiac, infectious disease) and mortality. Such longer term consequences are consistent with exposure to a major life stress, an absence of adequate coping resources, disrupted self-regulation, and eventual loss-related changes in neuroendocrine and immune functioning (M. S. Stroebe, Hansson, Stroebe, & Schut, 2001).

In this volume, we focus on bereavement experience in later life, a time when the loss of loved ones can become more frequent occurrences, resulting in an accumulation of grief experiences, disrupted emotional networks, loneliness, and financial risk. We have included a broad range of ages (60 years and over) within our classification of late life. We understand that the age at which people might be classified as "old" has increased (to well beyond 60) over recent generations, and that even in very old age, individual differences are prominent. However, many of the developmental processes and contexts relevant to bereavement emerge and begin to influence people during their middle years. Our review of the empirical research therefore focused for the most part on studies involving bereaved persons ages 60 years and over. A number of studies with useful comparisons with younger persons have been included as well.

The various literatures having to do with aging and bereavement have early roots; they are complex, often contradictory, and scattered across many academic and clinical disciplines. Indeed, bereavement researchers and gerontologists seem only infrequently to interact, read each other's journals, or attend each other's professional conferences. There have been exceptions, of course, notable in their small numbers, and we want to acknowledge a few pioneers in this effort. This group includes, for example, Helena Lopata, Miriam and Sidney Moss, Dale Lund and Michael Caserta, Delores Gallagher-Thompson and Larry Thompson, Stephen Shuchter and Sidney Zisook, and Shirley O'Bryant. These individuals introduced many of the most important sociological, psychological, and clinical issues that have shaped the field. Their influence is widely felt.

There is, therefore, a need for a fresh and comprehensive examination of bereavement among older adults. At least five additional concerns suggest the relevance of such an analysis at this time.

1. *Increasing vulnerability.* Aging is associated with diminished physiological status and adaptive reserves and an increasing vulnerability to the consequences of stress. Such factors can complicate an older person's grief experience and inhibit ability to cope.

2. *The aging population.* Since the beginning of scientific and clinical study of bereavement some 60 years ago, society has changed. There are now more older adults, larger numbers of whom are living into very old age and are very different from previous generations. Society has struggled to adapt and provide for their changing needs. But failing to fully understand the experience of loss among older people risks disenfranchisement of that experience.

3. *Research advances.* Adoption of a late-life developmental perspective has resulted in important breakthroughs in our understanding of the dynamics of aging within a number of central life processes, to include cognitive and emotional functioning, coping, adaptation, resistance to disease, and disablement. We believe that similar insights can be achieved with respect to aging and bereavement.

4. *Predictions from traditional bereavement theory.* There is a need to more carefully examine the potential of bereavement theory to increase understanding of this experience among older popu-

lations. One example in this connection is attachment theory, a developmental construct that has guided much of the research and clinical thinking on bereavement at earlier life stages. Predictions from attachment theory have now begun to guide research on the nature, meaning, and course of late-life relationships and of long-term loving and caring. However, the potential implications of attachment style and intensity have not been systematically explored with respect to grief and coping experience among older adults. An exploration of these connections could produce important insights regarding changing "meanings" of loss and the likely nature of subsequent coping and adaptation.

5. *Implications for families, practitioners, and society.* One's increasingly vulnerable health status in late life often results in greater dependency on family or more formal sources for basic needs in daily life or for long-term care. Losing a spouse at this time can disrupt one's closest support network, increasing the complexity of adaptive challenges to be faced. An increased understanding of the influence of aging on this critical life event should benefit both the older adult and any family members or professional practitioners who may become involved in care.

We believe it useful to view the available research on this topic as falling into four, somewhat overlapping traditions.

1. *A focus on risk factors.* The earliest focus on aging and bereavement reflected a concern within the clinical literature to identify risk factors for poor outcome. Studies typically compared outcomes for bereaved persons across varying age classifications, often finding younger widows, for example, to experience grief symptoms and outcomes of greater intensity. Such findings appeared to make sense, after the fact. The death of an older spouse, in contrast, seemed less unexpected, less unfair, and thus less traumatic. A number of reviews of the literature comparing bereavement outcomes subsequently concluded that aging seemed an unlikely risk factor for bereavement, and the question was prematurely foreclosed. From a gerontological perspective, however, conclusions from simple age-group comparisons are problematic. We consider their validity in some depth.

2. *Empirical studies of bereavement experience and outcomes among older persons.* This approach reflects a growing understanding of the complexities of aging, resulting in considerable diversity with respect to risk, coping resources, and the likely intensity and consequences of reactions to the loss of a loved

one. This tradition assumes that age, per se, is a poor proxy for status or adaptive potential, and it incorporates methodologies that allow an examination of age-related processes, even within an older population.

3. *Focus on developmental perspectives.* Important research with a bearing on bereavement in late life has been guided by developmental perspectives and by theory regarding age-related processes of relevance to coping and well-being more generally in later life. Our discussions of this research focus broadly on age-related processes that are protective or that can increase risk or undermine coping. These discussions also emphasize the immense heterogeneity among older people with respect to their experience of developmental processes and their ability to adapt to stressful life events such as bereavement.

4. *Integration of perspectives.* Research in an emerging tradition involves an integration of what we know about human aging into models of coping, prevention, and intervention. This focus reflects the interests of families, practitioners, and institutions that must determine the actual (perhaps unique) needs of older bereaved persons for some form of support or intervention. Theoretical development in this area shows much promise with respect to advancing our understanding of the nature of the bereavement experience itself and how that experience interfaces with the demands of aging.

In this volume, we trace for the reader the assumptions and research emanating from each of these research traditions. In doing so, we argue that the question of whether age, per se, is a risk factor for poor bereavement outcome is too general and imprecise to be meaningful. We believe that the more interesting and important questions for bereavement researchers, clinicians, and certainly for gerontologists should instead focus on how aging and bereavement interact to influence life outcomes, adaptive potential, coping capacity, and successful aging. We argue for a more fine-grained approach, one that takes the experience of bereavement into account on the one hand, and the complexities of the aging process on the other. Such an approach, we hope, will lead to increased understanding of what it means to lose a loved one in old age and of one's potential for adaptation to loss at this time of life.

PLAN FOR THE BOOK

In the first part of the book, we introduce the theory and research base on bereavement. Chapter 1 describes the nature and course of normative bereavement reactions, patterns of symptomatology, the potential for more complicated grief reactions, and implications for care. Chapter 2 introduces the principle of adaptive coping with bereavement and the important theoretical perspectives on this topic. In this context, chapter 2 explores the issues of assumptive worlds and meaning reconstruction, posttraumatic growth, the issue of grief work, the influence of general coping models, cognitive stress theory, trauma theory, and the models of grief and coping currently influencing research. Chapter 3 describes the *dual process model* of coping with bereavement. This model reflects the dynamic nature of coping with bereavement and proposes that a bereaved person will need to oscillate over time between coping efforts oriented toward emotional health and stability (loss-oriented coping) and efforts focused on more practical issues of living, independence, and mastering new skills and roles (restoration-oriented coping). In addition, to provide a conceptual structure for these complex issues, and to establish a basis for considering age-related perspectives, this chapter introduces an *integrative framework* for the prediction of bereavement outcomes.

In the latter part of the book, we introduce the age-related issues that impinge on the bereavement process. Chapter 4 provides some historical background and briefly reviews earlier research on age as a risk factor for poor bereavement outcomes. Particular attention is paid to assumptions and conclusions from this research, to potentially important methodological concerns and confounds in simply comparing outcomes among differing age groups, and to the need to conduct such research within a late-life developmental perspective. Chapter 5 provides a comprehensive review of the research on the bereavement experience of older adults. Emerging patterns of bereavement symptoms and outcomes are highlighted, noting parallels (and inconsistencies) with respect to the experience of younger bereaved persons and a number of important theoretical and methodological breakthroughs resulting from this research on older bereaved populations. Chapter 6, again, focuses exclusively on research on older bereaved persons and on risk factors and resources that appear especially relevant in late life. This chapter examines such factors as the circumstances of the death, the issues of "good deaths," transitions from stressful caregiving, and concurrent age-related stresses such as cognitive impairment, poverty, and changes in support networks. It explores as well the nature of coping resources in old age and the role of gender, religiosity, and culture.

Chapter 7 moves more directly into the gerontological literature, to focus on *protective developmental processes* in later life with potential relevance to bereavement. We introduce the life span developmental perspective and the kinds of maturational, cohort, and individual-history factors that influence developmental change well into old age. Especially important in this connection are the implications of likely changes in (a) emotional responsiveness and regulation and (b) intellectual functioning (reflecting a decrease in neurologic resources, which may be partially offset by acquired expertise in life skills, postformal thinking, wisdom, and strategic coping skills). In counterpoint, chapter 8 deals with the implications of *problematic age-related processes* for the bereavement experience. The most important of these involve an older person's diminishing adaptive reserves, diminishing feasibility of previously successful coping strategies, a narrowing range of adaptive competence to stressful environments, and concerns of comorbidity, crisis, and disablement.

The concluding chapter focuses on integrating perspectives and recommendations for future research on the bereavement experience of older adults. In particular, we offer proposals regarding how late-life developmental issues might be incorporated into the two conceptual models introduced in the early chapters of the book: the integrative framework for predicting bereavement outcome and the dual process model for coping with bereavement. Finally, for the convenience of readers who may not specialize in the field of aging, we provide two brief appendixes: Appendix A discusses assessment and intervention issues specific to working with older adults, and Appendix B provides a list of professional organizations in gerontology (with Web site addresses) and a selective list of primary scientific journals and books in the area.

1

THE NATURE OF GRIEF

The death of a loved one is a particularly devastating life stressor. It can lead to substantial suffering and a symptom picture that includes physical, affective, cognitive, and social disturbance. Health consequences can range from elevated levels of distress, anxiety, or depression to mental and physical illness and premature death. For most bereaved persons, grief runs a relatively normal, if harrowing course. But for others the effects can take the form of complications in the grieving process itself, variously labeled *traumatic*, *complicated*, or *pathological grief*. Given the extreme, enduring effects for some, and the intense suffering for many more people over their period of acute grief, it is not surprising that scientists and clinicians from many related disciplines (e.g., psychology, psychiatry, sociology, epidemiology, physiology) have studied the phenomena associated with bereavement, grief, and mourning and have tried to provide interpretations on a theoretical level.

An important goal for many researchers has been to identify why grief has such different effects on people. What are the characteristics of those who suffer one extreme effect rather than another? What is the role of preexisting risk factors, ongoing life circumstances, the nature and severity of the death experience itself, or varying forms of grieving process? In this chapter we provide some general background on bereavement, defining basic terms

9

TABLE 1.1
Death Rates by Age (All Causes): United States 2000

Age	Deaths per 100,000
All ages	854.0
Under 1 year	736.7
1–4 years	32.4
5–14 years	18.0
15–24 years	79.9
25–34 years	101.4
35–44 years	198.9
45–54 years	425.6
55–64 years	992.2
65–74 years	2,399.1
75–84 years	5,666.5

Note. Adapted from *Health, United States, 2003. Special Excerpt: Trend Tables on 65 and Older Population* (p. 155), by the U.S. Department of Health and Human Services, 2003, Hyattsville, MD: Centers for Disease Control and Prevention, National Center for Health Statistics. In the public domain.

such as *bereavement, grief,* and *mourning,* outlining the consequences of losing a loved person, and indicating how researchers have approached the topic of bereavement.

INCIDENCE AND PREVALENCE OF BEREAVEMENT

Bereavement has been defined as the objective situation of having lost someone significant, a category that includes parents, siblings, partners, and friends (M. S. Stroebe, Hansson, Stroebe, & Schut, 2001). Such loss experiences, however, are by no means restricted to older adults. The national mortality statistics of different countries (with exceptions for nations at war or in the grip of epidemics or famine) can provide a sense for bereavement experience across age groups. The distribution of deaths in the United States in the year 2000 provides a useful example (see Table 1.1; U.S. Department of Health and Human Services, 2003).

Two patterns are suggested by Table 1.1. First, there is a high incidence of infant mortality, a loss with especially devastating consequences for many parents (Gilbert & Smart, 1992; Leon, 1990). Second, we can also see that loss of an older child is not uncommon. Against all expectations that children should grow to adulthood and outlive their parents, we see that although deaths per 100,000 are comparatively low among children from 5 to 14 years, there are still many deaths within this age span. The incidence then rises substantially among subsequent groups of young people, when parents can still be expected to be alive, surviving the death of their child.

It is also clear from Table 1.1 that older people experience the greatest number of bereavements. With increasing age, one's contemporary family members and friends are more likely to die in quick succession.

Widow(er)hood, in particular, becomes increasingly frequent in late life. The percentage of noninstitutionalized persons who are widowed in the age groups 65 to 74 years, 75 to 84 years, and 85+ years is 20%, 39%, and 63%, respectively (Federal Interagency Forum on Aging-Related Statistics, 2004). The conjugal grief reaction can be especially difficult because, in addition to their emotional distress, the bereaved are often required to cope with the simultaneous disruption of their financial security, social status, and primary support networks. For each death reflected in Table 1.1, a range of bereaved persons may be left behind: parents, spouses, children, siblings, and friends. Each of these bereaved persons must come to terms with the death and the consequent changes in their lives.

Causes of death also differ across the life span, with implications for the bereavement experience. Table 1.2 illustrates a remarkable shift across age groups in the highest ranking causes of death in the United States for the year 2000 (U.S. Department of Health and Human Services, 2002). We see younger people dying of more violent causes, with accidents ranking highest through the childhood and young adult years. Homicide also features as a major cause of death within these younger groups. The incidence of suicide is of particular concern; from the age groups 10 to 14 through 35 to 44, suicide ranks high among the four leading causes of death. It is not hard to imagine the disruption that such violent, self- or other-inflicted deaths could cause among the bereaved family and friends. Cancers become the leading cause of death from midlife until early old age (for the age groups 35–44 through 65–74). Thereafter, diseases of the heart displace malignant neoplasms as the leading cause of death. It is clear that these patterns have implications for the planning and provision of both professional and informal care. For example, bereavements among young adults who have lost a partner would more likely involve trauma, compared with bereavements among middle-aged or older adults. In later chapters (4, 5, and 6), we examine the implications of the cause and nature of the death for the experience of bereavement in more detail.

GRIEF REACTIONS

Over time most people manage to come to terms with bereavement experiences in their lives. For most, however, bereavement is associated with a substantial grief reaction persisting over months and perhaps even years after a loss. As Shuchter and Zisook (1993) noted, there is little agreement regarding the time course of normal grief, with the expected duration having increased in recent years (before empirical research showed otherwise, common belief held that acute grief should be over by the end of a calendar year). Intensity of reactions also varies over time, from person to person, and across cultures. The grieving process, therefore, cannot be understood from a static

TABLE 1.2
U.S. Deaths by Age Groups, and Rank Order of
Four Leading Causes of Death (2000)

Age	Four leading causes of death
Under 1 year	Congenital malformations/abnormalities
	Short gestation/low birthweight related
	Sudden infant death syndrome
	Complications of placenta, cord, membranes
1–4 years	Accidents
	Congenital malformations/abnormalities
	Malignant neoplasms
	Homicide
5–9 years	Accidents
	Malignant neoplasms
	Congenital malformations/abnormalities
	Homicide
10–14 years	Accidents
	Malignant neoplasms
	Suicide
	Homicide
15–19 years	Accidents
	Homicide
	Suicide
	Malignant neoplasms
20–24 years	Accidents
	Homicide
	Suicide
	Malignant neoplasms
25–34 years	Accidents
	Suicide
	Homicide
	Malignant neoplasms
35–44 years	Malignant neoplasms
	Accidents
	Diseases of heart
	Suicide
45–54 years	Malignant neoplasms
	Diseases of heart
	Accidents
	Chronic liver disease and cirrhosis
55–64 years	Malignant neoplasms
	Diseases of heart
	Chronic lower respiratory diseases
	Cerebrovascular diseases
65–74 years	Malignant neoplasms
	Diseases of heart
	Chronic lower respiratory diseases
	Cerebrovascular diseases
75–84 years	Diseases of heart
	Malignant neoplasms
	Cerebrovascular diseases
	Chronic lower respiratory diseases
85 years and over	Diseases of heart
	Malignant neoplasms
	Cerebrovascular diseases
	Influenza and pneumonia

Note. Adapted from *National Vital Statistics Report* (Vol. 50, No. 16, pp. 13–15), by the U.S. Department of Health and Human Services, 2002. Hyattsville, MD: Centers for Disease Control and Prevention, National Center for Health Statistics. In the public domain.

or linear perspective; "a full appreciation of the grieving process requires attention to its diverse, multidimensional perspectives" (Shuchter & Zisook, 1993, p. 43).

This leaves us with the difficult question of how to define *normal grief*. Bereavement researchers typically focus on two elements: intensity and duration. Normal grief may involve acute suffering and high levels of distress, but reactions are not experienced as unbearable. In normal grief, although symptoms wax and wane there is gradual movement toward adaptation as time passes. The notion that normal grief is in a sense "healthy" seems fundamental. It is difficult to add to such a definition without becoming prescriptive. As Shuchter and Zisook (1993) noted, "grief is such an individualized process . . . that attempts to limit its scope or demarcate its boundaries by arbitrarily defining [it] are bound to fail" (p. 23).

Grief can be defined as a primarily emotional (affective) reaction to the loss of a loved one through death, whereas *grieving* refers to the processes of coping with bereavement (about which we have more to say in the following chapter). Grief incorporates diverse psychological (cognitive, social–behavioral) and physical (physiological–somatic) manifestations. It is important to note that individual experiences with grief can vary considerably too, in their duration and intensity, in how they are expressed, in consequences for personal and interpersonal functioning, and in changes in life circumstances. Thus, grief should be viewed as a complex emotional syndrome, in which many reactions may be present, but none of which are necessarily so, and not continuously or consistently so across the months and years following loss (Averill, 1968; Averill & Nunley, 1993). In an effort to impose some structure on this complexity, we developed the overview of reactions associated with grief shown in Table 1.3 (see W. Stroebe & Stroebe, 1987, for a more detailed analysis). An excellent review of available quantitative and qualitative measures of grief symptoms can be found in Neimeyer and Hogan (2001). We briefly describe, in the following sections, three core features of grief reactions (depression, anxiety, and loneliness) to illustrate the process of conceptualizing and examining bereavement reactions.

Depression

Bereaved individuals frequently exhibit feelings of sadness, mournfulness, and dysphoria, accompanied by intense subjective distress and "mental pain." Episodes (waves) of depression may be severe and are sometimes (but not always) precipitated by external events (revisiting places that trigger memories, receiving sympathy). Feelings of despair, lamentation, sorrow, and dejection predominate.

Researchers have recently paid particular attention to understanding the commonalities and distinctions between depression and grief (Boelen, van den Bout, & de Keijser, 2003; Neimeyer & Hogan, 2001; Prigerson &

TABLE 1.3
Reactions to Bereavement

Reaction	Symptoms
Affective	Depression, despair, dejection, distress
	Anxiety, fears, dreads
	Guilt, self-blame, self-accusation
	Anger, hostility, irritability
	Anhedonia (loss of pleasure)
	Loneliness
	Yearning, longing, pining
	Shock, numbness
Cognitive	Preoccupation with thoughts of deceased, intrusive ruminations
	Sense of presence of deceased
	Suppression, denial
	Lowered self-esteem
	Self-reproach
	Helplessness, hopelessness
	Sense of unreality
	Memory, concentration problems
Behavioral	Agitation, tenseness, restlessness
	Fatigue
	Overactivity
	Searching
	Weeping, sobbing, crying
	Social withdrawal
Physiological– somatic	Loss of appetite
	Sleep disturbances
	Energy loss, exhaustion
	Somatic complaints
	Physical complaints similar to deceased
	Immunologic and endocrine changes
	Susceptibility to illness, disease

Jacobs, 2001). Are reactions of distress and more severe depression distinct from the grief syndrome, or are they an integral part of it? In earlier research, depression had frequently been used as the indicator of grief reactions, assuming that depression was a valid proxy for assessing grief intensity. Indeed, there are advantages to using a measure of depression; scores on depression and grief scales tend to be highly correlated, and using a depression scale such as the Beck Depression Inventory (Beck, Ward, Mendelson, Mock, & Erbaugh, 1961) would allow levels of symptoms to be compared with those for nonbereaved samples, enabling control group comparisons.

However, it is clear from Table 1.3 that the symptomatology of grief includes more than depression, and there is now growing evidence that depression and grief may represent distinct, though related, clusters of reactions to bereavement. For example, the distinctiveness of symptom clusters within "traumatic" grief and bereavement-related depression has now been demonstrated empirically (Boelen et al., 2003; Prigerson et al., 1995). Consistent with such findings, Wijngaards-de Meij et al. (2005) found different predictors for depression and for grief in a study of parents after the loss of a child. Such studies then suggest not only different clusters of reactions to bereavement but also different causal or etiological factors in the development of symptoms of grief versus depression.

Anxiety

Fear, dread, and foreboding assume many forms during bereavement. Bereaved persons report anxieties about breaking down, about losing their mind, of dying themselves, and of being unable to cope without the deceased. They may be anxious about living alone or about financial matters, and they may worry about any aspects of life that previously had been taken care of by the deceased. Because loss through death entails an irrevocable separation from a loved one, it is understandable that bereaved persons are at increased risk for separation anxiety. In extreme cases, according to the *Diagnostic and Statistical Manual of Mental Disorders* (4th ed.; *DSM–IV*; American Psychiatric Association, 1994), this may be classified as a separation anxiety disorder, the essential feature of which includes excessive anxiety concerning separation from those to whom one is attached. It is interesting to note that the *DSM–IV* only classifies this type of disorder as occurring among infants, children, and adolescents. There are reasons to believe that some bereaved adults, particularly those with insecure attachment patterns (Parkes, 2001b), may also suffer from this type of disorder. Criteria include recurrent excessive distress following separation, nightmares involving the theme of separation, complaints of physical symptoms on separation, and clinically significant distress. The clinical picture resembles that of chronic grief (Parkes & Weiss, 1983), which we describe later in the chapter.

Loneliness

One of the most frequently experienced and most distressing reactions associated with grief is loneliness. Many bereaved persons suffer either ongoing or periodic bouts of intense loneliness, notably at the times when the deceased person would have been present (e.g., evenings, weekends) or during special events that would have been shared (e.g., anniversaries, holidays). Much theoretical analysis and empirical investigation have focused on loneliness, and its centrality in the course of grief and grieving has become quite well understood.

To illustrate, a study by Gallagher-Thompson, Futterman, Farberow, Thompson, and Peterson (1993) suggested that a number of variables central to loneliness were the ones most relevant to survival among the bereaved. These investigators conducted a longitudinal study of older widowed persons (mean age of 68 years) and a comparison group of still-married persons (mean age of 70 years), some of whom died during the 5 years of assessment. During the 30-month period of the study, widowers died more frequently than did widows, still-married men, or control women. The design of the study enabled a comparison of the widowers who died with matched (age, health, socioeconomic status, etc.) widowers who had survived the period of the study. Of all the characteristics that had been measured (and there had been many psychological, social, and physical indices assessed over the course of the study), the characteristics that were significantly more frequently found among the deceased widowers than those who were still alive were the following: Their wife had been their main confidant; they were less involved in social activities; they had smaller social networks; and they actually had expressed a desire for greater social activities. These variables speak of loneliness, and it is not hard to imagine that the deceased widowers' wives had protected and buffered these men against loneliness or even the need for any additional interpersonal relationship as long as they had lived.

PATTERNS OF MOURNING

The terms *grief* and *mourning* are often used interchangeably. However, it is useful to distinguish the two, because they encompass distinct phenomena associated with bereavement. Whereas grief, as we have just described it, denotes the complex emotional response to one's loss, mourning refers to the actions and manner of expressing grief (there is then also some overlap between the constructs). The process of mourning involves social expressions of grief that are shaped by the practices of a given society or cultural group (M. S. Stroebe, Hansson, et al., 2001; also see chap. 6, this volume, for further discussion of cultural issues in bereavement). A still-familiar, although less-frequently observed example from Western culture would be the wearing of black clothes, indicating a period of mourning and respect for the deceased. Interactions with others would be influenced by this form of dressing, and it would be likely, particularly on first postloss interactions, that the prevalent mood would be appropriately somber. Mourning customs continue to evolve, however. In many countries, for example, photos of the deceased are now included in obituary notices, and memorial texts are now regularly placed on the Internet (de Vries & Roberts, 2004).

Patterns of mourning differ across cultures (Parkes, Laungani, & Young, 1997). One contrasting example with our own culture comes from India, a country steeped in mourning traditions. It is important to note that different communities, even within the Hindu religion, follow very different procedures (P. Rohatgi & D. Joshi, personal communication, July 20, 2005). Among the Hindu people, the color of mourning is white, and mourners are normally dressed in white. It is also the Hindu custom for a widow to dress in a white sari for the rest of her life. Traditionally, a widow would never consider remarriage.

There are many further vivid contrasts (as well as some similarities) of the Hindu with Western society. For example, it is the Hindu custom to stay within the deceased person's house for the mourning period of 13 days after the death of a family member. Typically, close friends and relatives will come to offer condolences, bringing simple food (no food is cooked in the house until the period of mourning is over), and the time is spent quietly meditating, listening to the Brahmin priest reciting verses, and planning the final ceremony, when the departed soul symbolically separates from the body and leaves the house. On the 13th day of mourning, it is customary in some families for someone who resembles the deceased in real life to be invited into the house for a special farewell ceremony and to be given shoes, an umbrella, or other items for a journey (symbolizing the journey of the deceased). This is very touching: The family feels the closeness of the departed soul embodied in this person. Indeed, the person will not return to the home for 1 year, for the soul of the deceased is deemed to wander for a year, after which it will have found an ultimate resting place in another form of life (P. Rohatgi & D. Joshi, personal communication, July 20, 2005).

Mourning and grief are mutually dependent. Outward expressions (such as the wearing of black or of white) may influence emotions. In turn, the extent of one's grief can have an impact on the nature and elaborateness of the mourning customs that are undertaken (e.g., the closeness one feels to the deceased will influence decisions to participate in acts of commemoration).

PATHOLOGICAL OR COMPLICATED MANIFESTATIONS OF GRIEF

A range of serious mental and physical health consequences have been associated with bereavement. As noted earlier, some people endure complications in the grieving process itself (pathological or traumatic grief), others reach clinical levels for the diagnosis of anxiety or depression, still others suffer from new or worsening physical ailments or diseases. The major negative consequences are described in the next three sections.

Pathological Grief

Pathological grief has been defined as a deviation from the normative (cultural–societal) experience in the time course or intensity of specific or general symptoms of grief (M. S. Stroebe, Hansson, et al., 2001). Subtypes of pathological grief have been described as chronic, absent, and delayed grief. *Chronic grief* is characterized by long-lasting symptoms and an absence of progress in the process of coming to terms with loss or cognitively "relocating" the deceased person. *Absent grief* is characterized by the nonappearance of symptoms typical of grief. The person continues life as though nothing has happened. The absence of grief should not necessarily be taken to indicate pathology (e.g., a person may simply not grieve for the deceased). Such concern may arise, however, with the occurrence of physical symptoms (in the absence of psychological symptoms), particularly if one's relationship with the deceased had been especially close. *Delayed grief* is characterized by an absence of apparent grieving at first, but later on—perhaps when some other, even minor loss has occurred—symptoms of grief do become apparent and may appear similar to those of normal grieving. The latter two categories, absent and delayed grief, are currently the subject of some debate (e.g., Bonanno et al., 2002; Bonanno, Wortman, & Nesse, 2004), because empirical evidence is thus far weak (and the subtypes difficult, by very definition, to examine). Chronic grief seems more generally accepted.

There are also difficulties in drawing distinctions between normal and pathological grief. For example, as noted earlier, it is difficult to conceptualize "normal" grief, given a need to establish thresholds for each symptom cluster regarding what is normal and what is pathological. Furthermore, definitions of pathological (or complicated or traumatic) grief have been empirically rather than theoretically derived (Prigerson & Jacobs, 2001). Pathological grief is also not a single syndrome with clear diagnostic criteria. It has not yet been classified as a category of mental disorder in the *DSM–IV* (American Psychiatric Association, 1994), although efforts are being made to derive diagnostic criteria for future *DSM* systems. One diagnostic category that is being developed for the new edition of *DSM* follows the traumatic grief (currently termed *complicated grief*) criteria derived by Prigerson and colleagues (see Prigerson & Jacobs, 2001) and resembles chronic grief. However, as noted by Raphael, Minkov, and Dobson (2001), the term *traumatic grief* as currently used does not clearly distinguish traumatic stress or posttraumatic stress disorder (PTSD) phenomenology from bereavement phenomenology and processes. This brings us to disorders that may be related to grieving and to grief complications.

Related Psychological Disorders

Not only is it sometimes difficult to differentiate pathological grief from related disorders such as PTSD, but sometimes disorders may coexist. It is worth noting that, unlike pathological grief, the main coexisting disturbances that have been linked to bereavement have actually been included within categories of mental disorders in the *DSM–IV* (American Psychiatric Association, 1994). The main categories that are discussed in the literature in relationship to bereavement are certain anxiety disorders, in particular, PTSD and separation anxiety; the general category of adjustment disorders; and mood disorders, in particular, major depressive disorder.

PTSD was identified by Horowitz (1986; Horowitz et al., 1997) as a stress response syndrome occurring after particularly shocking and horrific circumstances of death. It is characterized by a reexperiencing of extremely traumatic events, and symptoms include unbidden, intrusive thoughts combined with disbelief, hyperarousal, shock, avoidance of stimuli associated with the trauma, numbness, and a fragmented sense of security, trust, and control (American Psychiatric Association, 1994; Horowitz, 1986; Horowitz et al., 1997). A number of investigators have noted that when providing psychotherapy to survivors of a disaster in which a loved one has been killed, it has often not been possible to facilitate grief or provide grief counseling until the traumatic stress aspects have been dealt with (Raphael et al., 2001).

Adjustment disorders develop in response to psychosocial stressors. In the present case, the stressor would be bereavement, which could incorporate multiple interrelated stressors associated with different aspects of adjustment, such as change in financial status, need to relocate, and the loneliness of the transition to bereaved status. According to *DSM–IV* criteria (American Psychiatric Association, 1994), adjustment disorders are characterized by marked distress, in excess of what would be expected given the nature of the stressor, or by significant impairment in social or occupational functioning. In the case of a major bereavement, an enormous transition and adjustment would likely involve severe distress without this necessarily being classified as "disorder," whereas this classification might have been made had the psychosocial stressor been a more minor one. In fact, *DSM–IV* specifies that bereavement, and not adjustment disorder, is generally diagnosed (but then not classified as a mental disorder, as noted earlier) when the reaction is "an expectable response to the death of a loved one. The diagnosis of Adjustment Disorder may be appropriate when the reaction is in excess of, or more prolonged than, what would be expected" (American Psychiatric Association, 1994, p. 626). Following this *DSM–IV* statement, it is difficult to place adjustment disorder simply as a related psychological disorder, but it is nevertheless important to list this category here, because adjustment difficulties may exacerbate other problems, such as those of separation anxiety or trauma reactions.

Finally, given the overlap and distinction between depression and grief discussed previously, it is not surprising that, among the mood disorders, major depressive disorder (MDD) may coexist with other psychological manifestations. In the *DSM–IV*, MDD is characterized by one or more major depressive episodes (i.e., at least 2 weeks of depressed mood or loss of interest, accompanied by at least four additional symptoms of depression; American Psychiatric Association, 1994). Here too, there is specification for the situation of bereavement: MDD is said not to occur after the loss of a loved one "unless [depressive symptoms] persist for more than 2 months or include marked functional impairment, morbid preoccupation with worthlessness, suicidal ideation, psychotic symptoms, or psychomotor retardation" (American Psychiatric Association, 1994, p. 326).

Physical Health Consequences and Mortality

Extreme physical health consequences are frequently reported in the literature on bereavement (see Table 1.3; for reviews of the research on health consequences, see Parkes, 2001a; W. Stroebe & Stroebe, 1987). Some are associated most closely with recent bereavement and acute grief (e.g., suicides), whereas others extend over a longer time span (e.g., elevated risk of death from natural causes such as certain types of cancer). Bereaved persons suffer excessively from a variety of illnesses, but they also have higher rates than nonbereaved individuals on a broad range of related indicators, for example, for disability and use of medical services, such as consultations with doctors, use of medication, and hospitalization (W. Stroebe & Stroebe, 1987).

The risk of mortality is higher too among the bereaved, and this is manifested across many causes of death (for a review, see M. S. Stroebe & Stroebe, 1993). For example, parents have excessive mortality rates following the death of their child. In a longitudinal study conducted in Denmark, J. Li, Precht, Mortensen, and Olsen (2003) found death of a child to be associated with an overall increase in mortality from both natural and unnatural causes in mothers, and an early increase in mortality from unnatural causes in fathers. These results underline the severity of this type of loss, assumed to be the worst that one can experience. As we show in a later chapter, the implications for older persons are far reaching. The likelihood of losing a child increases with age, so very old adults especially may be confronted with the death of one or more of their children across the years.

RISK FACTORS FOR MENTAL AND PHYSICAL COMPLICATIONS

A major thrust of bereavement research has focused on identifying risk factors for poor outcome. A *risk factor* can be defined as "an aspect of personal behavior or life-style, an environmental exposure or an inborn or inherited characteristic, which on the basis of epidemiological evidence, is shown to be associated with health-related condition(s) considered important to prevent" (Last, 1995, p. 148). Risk factors may be bereavement specific or general. *Bereavement-specific risk factors* are aspects of the bereavement situation that influence the course of adjustment, whereas *general risk factors* are personality or social context variables that affect the health of bereaved and nonbereaved individuals (W. Stroebe & Schut, 2001).

To illustrate, with respect to bereavement-specific factors, the causes and circumstances of death have been investigated extensively. Most people would probably assume that a lack of forewarning of the death of a loved one would have a greater negative impact on health than the impact following a death when there had been forewarning. However, results of empirical studies have been surprisingly inconsistent. Although some studies support the assumption that forewarning helps (e.g., Lundin, 1984; Sanders, 1983), other studies do not (e.g., Bornstein, Clayton, Halikas, Maurice, & Robbins, 1973; Breckenridge, Gallagher, Thompson, & Peterson, 1986). More research is needed to understand such discrepancies and to establish patterns of relative risk by assessing the role of such variables as the (un)timeliness of a death (a factor closely linked to age), psychological (un)preparedness on the part of the bereaved, and the death's (un)expectedness or whether there was any forewarning.

Age is an example of a general risk factor about which we naturally have more to say in subsequent chapters. Age and health are inversely related (higher age being associated with reduced health). A second general risk factor is personality. People who are well adjusted, who feel in control of their lives, should be able to withstand the impact of stressful life events better than those who are poorly adjusted. Research is beginning to pinpoint the types of personality characteristics associated with good adjustment to bereavement. For example, it has consistently been found that people who are emotionally unstable, insecure, have low self-esteem, or are anxious tend to cope less adaptively and adjust more poorly to bereavement (Nolen-Hoeksema & Larson, 1999).

THE COURSE OF GRIEF AND GRIEVING

In addition to identifying risk factors, we need to better understand the course of grief over time following the loss to understand how people ultimately adapt to bereavement and why some people do better than others. Researchers have striven to understand durational fluctuations in terms of stages, phases, or tasks of grief. A new and intriguing direction for such analyses involves the identification of diverse trajectories of grieving (e.g., Bonanno et al., 2004; Levy, Martinkowski, & Derby, 1994). The notion of trajectories refers to different patterns of change in symptoms (grief, depression) across the time following a bereavement. Levy et al. (1994), for example, found five different types of curves in depression: low stable; high stable; high or moderate, descending; ascending; and moderate stable. Such diverse patterns have been obscured when only mean curves have been used to depict the course of adaptation to bereavement.

The early stage theories of grief became unpopular because they were considered to be too rigid. Grief seems not to follow a fixed or universal sequence of stages on the path to recovery. By contrast, phasal conceptualizations have been enormously influential. This recognition has largely been due to the work of John Bowlby, who, in his three-volume monograph *Attachment and Loss* (Bowlby, 1969, 1973, 1980), analyzed processes of attachment and separation with respect to close relationships across time since death. Bowlby's phasal conceptualizations postulated a succession from an initial phase of shock, with associated symptoms of numbness and denial; through yearning and protest, as realization of the loss develops; to despair, accompanied by emotional and somatic upset and social withdrawal; until gradual recovery takes place, marked by increasing well-being and acceptance of the loss. Durations of these phases vary, but the first two are generally suggested to take a number of weeks, whereas the third, the intense grieving phase, may last several months or even years. There also appear to be considerable cultural differences in the duration or even manifestation of these phases across time. It is important to understand that the phases were conceived by Bowlby and others as descriptive guidelines, not prescriptive statements about where a bereaved individual ought to be in the grieving process. Furthermore, there is understanding that the process is not simply resolved or completed by the fourth phase: There is no "returning to baseline," but rather, for most people, there is eventually acceptance of loss and adjustment to the changed situation, relocation of the deceased person so that life can go on without undue suffering, and the attainment of a new equilibrium in daily life.

More recent models of coping have also, at least implicitly, integrated a time-course perspective. These include Worden's (1991) task model, M. S. Stroebe and Schut's (1999) dual process model of coping with bereavement, and Bonanno and Kaltman's (1999) four-component model. For example, in Worden's (1991) model, the first postulated task (accepting the reality of loss) would precede sequentially the fourth task (relocating the deceased and moving on with life). As for the phase models, there is also the understanding that some vacillation back and forth between tasks of grieving will occur over time. These models are described in more detail in chapters 2 and 3.

THEORETICAL APPROACHES

In the preceding section we introduced some of the models that have been proposed to conceptualize the course of grief and associated coping processes. However, we also need to better understand such fundamental issues as why people grieve, the nature of their reactions, and how social and individual factors interact during the process of adaptation. We need general theories, in addition to the coping models, to identify patterns within the diversity of reactions to bereavement, and we need to derive testable predictions with respect to such issues. Indeed, it has already become evident that the coping models can be—and frequently are—embedded within more general theories.

Contemporary empirical research on bereavement, grief, and mourning is more theory-driven than it was in earlier decades, when it was largely "issue-generated" (e.g., to identify health consequences or risk factors). The scientific literature on bereavement now reflects a number of very different perspectives. Theoretical approaches range from those derived from general psychological theories that bereavement researchers have applied to grief (e.g., psychoanalytic or attachment theories) to specific models constructed to explain bereavement-specific phenomena (e.g., stage or phase models). Comprehensive treatments of most of the perspectives can be found in M. S. Stroebe, Stroebe, and Hansson (1993) and in M. S. Stroebe, Hansson, et al. (2001). We describe these theories in somewhat more detail in chapter 2, in the context of understanding processes of coping with bereavement.

IMPLICATIONS FOR CARE

It has become evident that bereaved people do not usually need the help of professional counselors or therapists to come to terms with their grief or to prevent complications (Parkes, 1998). The majority can be said to have no pathological or extreme health indications, and only in a minority of cases will there be a need for referral. Of course, people need the help and support of their family and friends, and some may find comfort in attending bereavement support groups, such as the "widow-to-widow" program. Generally speaking, however, there is little that can be done to shorten or ameliorate the grief itself that is felt on losing a loved person. It becomes important, then, to identify those bereaved persons for whom the grief process, for some reason, has "gone wrong," who are then in need of additional support, and to make provision for appropriate help in cases in which it is most likely to be efficacious (Schut, Stroebe, van den Bout, & Terheggen, 2001).

What is appropriate professional help? Some investigators (Raphael et al., 2001; Worden, 1991, 2002) draw a distinction between grief counseling and grief therapy. *Grief counseling* is defined as the facilitation of the process (tasks) of normal, uncomplicated grieving to alleviate suffering and help the bereaved to reach a healthy completion within a reasonable time framework. By contrast, *grief therapy* is understood to refer to specialized techniques of intervention for bereaved persons with some type or indication of a complicated grief reaction (e.g., chronic or delayed grief), to guide them toward a normal coping process. Such distinctions are especially important when trying to evaluate interventions for the bereaved. For example, a comprehensive review examining the efficacy of grief counseling and grief therapy studies by Schut et al. (2001) concluded that grief therapy programs directed at high-risk persons or, even more effectively, at those with complications, were indeed beneficial. Those providing grief counseling for bereaved persons in general showed no beneficial effects. These patterns were confirmed in another review (Jordan & Neimeyer, 2003).

CONCLUSIONS

It has become evident from our brief review of phenomena and manifestations associated with bereavement that the negative consequences of losing a loved one are substantial for many people. At the same time, we need to keep in mind that bereavement is a normal life event, one that most of us will experience with increasing frequency across the course of our lives. It is an experience that does not routinely call for professional intervention. Also, we must be aware that there are substantial individual and cultural differences in grief and grieving and that manifestations cover a broad range of potential reactions. Already, we see considerable complexity with respect to the phenomena that researchers and practitioners need to understand. In the next chapter, we explore scientific examinations of bereavement coping processes more closely.

2

COPING WITH BEREAVEMENT

A fundamental question for the bereaved and for those who would support them involves how to try to deal with and overcome this worst thing that can happen, losing a loved one. Early clinical theory (to be described in more detail later) held that it was important to engage in *grief work*, the process of repeatedly confronting aspects of one's loss to come to terms with it and avoid detrimental health consequences (M. S. Stroebe, 1992). However, contemporary researchers are divided in their opinions regarding the efficacy of working through loss. For example, Malkinson (1996, p. 115) concluded that "Grieving is crucial, necessary and unavoidable for successful adaptation," whereas Wortman and Silver (1987) argued that "Those who show the most evidence of working through the loss are those who ultimately have the most difficulty in resolving what has happened" (p. 207). How can these apparently conflicting statements be reconciled?

In the late 1980s and 1990s, bereavement researchers began to refine the assumption that grief work was essential to coping with loss. There was an emerging sense, in particular, that to understand how bereavement affects people, we need first to understand the coping process and to clarify the functions of grieving. This new focus was encouraged in great part by the publication of the classic volume by Lazarus and Folkman (1984) titled *Stress, Appraisal, and Coping*, which introduced *cognitive stress theory*, a generic ap-

25

proach to understanding the impact of different types of life events. Applied to bereavement, the coping perspective embraced in this book would assume that how an individual deals with loss and ensuing grief can reduce or amplify the effects of this stressful life event, not only during the early days of acute grief but also as the months and years of bereavement unfold. Coping makes a difference. It can affect levels of emotional distress, as well as the incidence and intensity of physical and mental health disorders (Skinner, Edge, Altman, & Sherwood, 2003).

In this chapter we examine the nature of adaptive coping with bereavement. We examine the major theoretical perspectives that provide the basis for deriving principles of adaptation, understanding moderating and mediating variables, and developing instruments for the assessment of coping. The various theoretical approaches outlined in chapter 1 have adopted different perspectives on coping. Some, though not all, explicitly discuss adaptive coping and provide empirical evidence for the (in)effectiveness of various strategies. We also address issues in the assessment of coping, identifying specific adaptive dimensions that have been empirically tested and illustrating how these dimensions have been measured. An important goal of this discussion is to establish a baseline understanding of coping with bereavement (generally), from which to explore in later chapters how aging might affect the coping process.

ADAPTIVE COPING IN THE BEREAVEMENT CONTEXT

In the scientific literature, the term *coping* is generally understood to incorporate "the person's cognitive and behavioral efforts to manage (reduce, minimize, master, or tolerate) the internal and external demands of the person–environment transaction that is appraised as taxing or exceeding the resources of the person" (Folkman, Lazarus, Gruen, & De Longis, 1986, p. 572). For example, a recently bereaved widow may use a confrontational, emotion-focused strategy whereby she visits the grave each day, lays flowers, and speaks words aloud to the deceased, clinging to the past to try to reduce the pain of separation. She may appraise her new life situation as too threatening to permit relinquishment of the bond to the deceased and as beyond her available resources (e.g., social support) that could facilitate withdrawal from her deceased husband or reintegration into the changed social environment.

Concepts from coping theory then allow us to describe in consensual, abstract terms the widow's experience, her coping behavior, and associated parameters. However, we still do not know whether adopting a confrontational strategy in the way that this widow did actually reduces distress. Whether strategies are actually successful is not part of the traditional definition of coping nor a major thrust of earlier research (W. Stroebe, 2000). It is important, therefore, to define *adaptive coping strategies* as those that actually lead to a reduction in the negative psychosocial and physical health consequences of bereavement and/or to a lowering of grief. In other words, the concept of adaptive coping implies that certain strategies, but not others, would lead to a decrease in negative consequences of grief, short and long term.

The contribution of *coping* to outcome in bereavement must also be viewed within the broader context of other factors that influence the course of adjustment. In Folkman's (2001) words,

> It is important to note that coping may have a relatively small influence on adjustment and recovery compared to factors such as the timing and nature of the death, history, and personality. *Nonetheless . . . coping is important because it is one of the few factors influencing bereavement outcomes amenable to brief interventions.* (p. 564; italics added)

The term *bereavement outcome* encompasses a wide range of negative consequences, including the intensity and duration of grief or depression, pathological grief or psychiatric conditions, physical health, or even mortality. As we saw in chapter 1, researchers have investigated all of these outcomes. It is worth noting, however, that researchers have also begun to investigate positive outcomes, such as *meaning reconstruction* (Neimeyer, 2001) or *posttraumatic growth* (Tedeschi, Park, & Calhoun, 1998). These latter research programs have focused primarily on demonstrating the potential for positive outcomes, to balance and complement the previous emphasis on negative consequences and to emphasize the theoretical and practical importance of such outcomes. They have yet to examine adaptive coping that actually leads to these positive outcomes. For this reason, and because negative consequences are clearly more worrisome, our review focuses on (mal)adaptive processes in the amplification or reduction of negative outcomes to bereavement.

Although the concept of adaptive coping appears straightforward, there remain a number of difficulties associated with its assessment (for an extended critical discussion of established psychometric assessment techniques for measuring ways of coping with bereavement, see van Heck & de Ridder, 2001). Different strategies may be more effective at different times in the course of grief or for coping with different aspects of bereavement; a strategy may be useful in the short term but harmful in the long term; it may positively affect physical health but increase emotional distress. Also, empirical studies conducted to assess effective coping have often suffered from a variety of methodological shortcomings. For example, many assessments have not been conducted longitudinally but simply cross-sectionally. An adequate research design to examine the effectiveness of coping would, for example, require coping strategies to be assessed at a first data collection point, to predict outcome at a second data collection point. It also would need to control for the level of symptoms manifested at Time 1 (to show the impact of the strategy on symptoms at subsequent time points). Sometimes measurement has relied on retrospective self-reports. This makes it difficult to determine the extent to which a person's report of coping earlier on in the grieving process may be biased by the current state of distress or well-being, or in the case of older bereaved persons, simply by poor memory for previous symptoms. Furthermore, definitions of coping strategies or styles often include *outcome* as well as *coping process* variables, for example, the presence of symptoms reflecting the experience and feelings of despair (which is an outcome variable) as well as suppressing feelings of despair (which is a coping variable). To make matters even more complex, there is conceptual overlap between coping and outcome variables (e.g., crying could be considered a strategy, as a "cry for help," or a symptom, as an index of distress).

Such problems make criteria for adaptive coping hard to construct and investigation difficult to carry out. Fortunately, there have been major theoretical developments and some sound empirical investigations to enable derivation of adaptive coping principles.

THEORETICAL APPROACHES TO COPING

Table 2.1 summarizes the main principles of adaptive coping apparent within the different types of theories. As can be seen, many different principles have been derived, at different levels of analysis (e.g., individual vs. interpersonal) and with differing degrees of specificity (e.g., from grief work to identification of specific coping mechanisms). There is considerable overlap across the various theories in what is considered to be adaptive coping.

General Psychological Theories

Although they differ from each other in important respects, theories in this category are all well-known psychological theories that have been applied to many areas of investigation, not just bereavement. These general psychological theories, such as psychoanalytic (Freud, 1917/1957) or attachment (Bowlby, 1969, 1973, 1980) perspectives, describe grief work as the essence of successful coping with bereavement, whereby a relinquishing of the tie or bond to the deceased person would come about through a gradual process:

> This grief work has to do with the effort of reliving and working through in small quantities events which involved the now-deceased person and the survivor. . . . Each item of this shared role has to be thought through, pained through, if you want, and gradually the question is raised, How can I do that with somebody else? And gradually the collection of activities which were put together in this unit with the person who has died

TABLE 2.1
Coping With Bereavement: Theoretical Principles of Adaptation

Type of theory	Main proponents	Principles of adaptive coping
I. General psychological theories		
Psychoanalytic theory	Freud (1917/1957)	Grief work
Attachment theory (and developmental)	Bowlby (1969, 1973, 1980)	Grief work
Evolutionary (and with attachment theory)	Archer (1999)	Grief work
Social constructionism (including CBT therapy principles); family systems theory; cultural perspectives	Neimeyer (2001); Rosenblatt (2001); Walter (1996)	Meaning making; six principles to shape adaptation (inter)personally; biography reconstruction in families; interpersonal interactions
Life span developmental perspective	Baltes, Staudinger, and Lindenberger (1999)	Developmental changes with protective and problematic influence on adaptation
II. General coping (life-event) theories		
Cognitive stress theory	Lazarus and Folkman (1984); Folkman (2001)	Emotion-, problem-focused coping; confrontation avoidance; positive psychological states vs. rumination
Stress response syndrome	Horowitz (1986)	Cognitive regulation (intrusion/avoidance)
Emotion regulation, disclosure, and sharing	Pennebaker, Zech, and Rimé (2001)	Communication; disinhibition; restructuring
Assumptive worldviews	Janoff-Bulman (1992); Janoff-Bulman and Berg (1998)	Revision of assumptions/meanings
III. Broad-spectrum models of grief; phenomena/manifestations		
Psychosocial transition model	Parkes (1993, 1996, 2001a)	Revision of assumptions; working through
Two-track model	Rubin (1981, 1993, 1999)	Two-track processing (transformation of attachment and recovery)
Four-component model	Bonanno and Kaltman (1999)	Appraisal/evaluation processing and emotion regulation (dissociation of negative enhancement of positive)
IV. Specific models of coping with bereavement		
Stage/phase model	Bowlby (1969, 1973, 1980)	Grief work
Task model	Worden (1982, 1991, 2002)	Four tasks (working through)
Cognitive path models	Folkman (2001); Nolen-Hoeksema (2001)	Positive reappraisal; rumination
Dual process model	M. S. Stroebe and Schut (1999, 2001)	Confrontation–avoidance of loss vs. restoration-oriented stressors; positive–negative meaning (re)construction; oscillation (cognitive control/regulation)

Note. CBT = cognitive–behavioral therapy.

can be torn asunder to be put to other people. (Lindemann, 1979, p. 234)

Such a description seems to pinpoint what many people experience in their grieving. Yet, doubts about the adequacy of the grief work notion as a description of "healthy" grieving have been raised on a number of levels (Bonanno & Kaltman, 1999; M. S. Stroebe, 1992; Wortman & Silver, 1987). For example, the term lacks specification. It is difficult to distinguish yearning and pining, aspects of grieving that are associated with negative outcome (Nolen-Hoeksema, 2001), from grief work, involving a constructive confrontation with the reality of loss that could lead to positive outcome (M. S. Stroebe, 1992). Also, empirical studies have failed to confirm that confronting and working through a loss lead to better outcomes or that avoiding confrontation is necessarily detrimental to adaptation (Bonanno, 2001a; M. S. Stroebe & Stroebe, 1991; Wortman & Silver, 1989). Grief work may also apply more to Western than to certain non-Western cultures in which the norm for grieving could call for suppression of emotions of grief, a clearly different strategy that is not apparently associated with bad outcomes (Wikan, 1988). In addition, as noted in chapter 1, there is now evidence that different bereaved individuals may follow quite different patterns or trajectories of grieving over a period of 4 or more years postdeath. Grieving is also a dynamic process of adjustment to many different life changes, all of which need to be worked through but which cannot all be attended to at the same time. The grief work notion does not provide explicitly for such complexity. In addition, grieving is exhausting: A person cannot do grief work unremittingly; "dosage" is necessary. So we need to be aware of the need for emotion regulation and to extend our theory base to incorporate a more dynamic perspective. In the following paragraphs, we explore how contemporary models of grieving have addressed some of these difficulties.

The social construction models have focused on grieving as a process of meaning reconstruction, an approach that has its roots in symbolic interactionism and in family systems theory (see Rosenblatt, 2001). These models add an interpersonal dimension and recognize that grieving occurs in a social context, not in isolation. For example, the meaning of the death is often negotiated between (grieving) family members. Assumptions about the relationship to the deceased are actively explored and adjusted in this process. Bereaved people develop "narratives" about the nature of the deceased's life and death, and these "social constructions" themselves can affect the course and the outcome of grief (Cook & Oltjenbruns, 1998; Neimeyer, 2000, 2001; Neimeyer, Keesee, & Fortner, 1998; Shapiro, 2001; Walter, 1996; Winchester-Nadeau, 1998, 2001).

The meaning reconstruction theories, then, have extended our understanding and analysis of adaptive coping beyond the intrapersonal to interpersonal perspectives. Because bereaved persons do not typically grieve alone and are likely to be influenced in their grieving by the reactions of others surrounding them, this seems a necessary expansion. In general, meaning reconstruction perspectives also provide a far more detailed specification of the range of changes in cognitions and appraisals that need to be incorporated in the grieving process than was possible following a grief work perspective. Neimeyer (1996) eloquently described adaptation to loss as involving the restoration of coherence to the narrative of one's life, a statement that captures the essence of meaning reconstruction in bereavement. We show in later chapters how meaning reconstruction also helps to shape adaptation to losses associated with aging more generally.

Finally, we would include in this category the life span developmental perspective (Baltes, Staudinger, & Lindenberger, 1999). This perspective is introduced in detail in chapter 7 as a context for understanding how developmental processes in late life can have a protective or problematic influence on one's capacity to continue to cope with stressful life events such as bereavement.

General Coping (Life-Event) Models

Like the theories previously described, in this category too we are describing models that have been generated to understand other phenomena as well as bereavement. In this category, however, the models are more limited in that they focus on the coping process: How do people adapt to stressful life events? We introduced Lazarus and Folkman's (1984) cognitive stress theory in chapter 1. This theory has greatly influenced our understanding of coping processes in bereavement and thus deserves more detailed description here. The original cognitive stress model described a set of principles of coping (see italics that follow). It emphasized the relationship between the individual and the environment. *Stress* was understood to be the consequence of a person's processes of *appraisal* of an event, which involves assessment of whether personal *resources* are sufficient to meet the *demands* of the situation. If resources are adequate, little stress will be felt; if resources are perceived as not sufficing to meet the demands of an environmental stressor, then a great deal of stress will be experienced, and *coping* efforts will become directed at solving problems or at regulating emotions. If coping efforts are successful, a favorable *resolution* will be met and a positive *outcome* achieved. If this is not the case, the process of appraisal begins afresh. Following this framework, bereavement would be the life "event," or stressor, that poses demands on the individual. Consistent with the definition of coping, these demands may be seen by the bereaved person as possibly taxing or exceeding the resources available to him or her, thereby endangering health and well-being. The model lends itself to empirical testing, and much research has been carried out using the framework (see Folkman, 2001). Following the theoretical constructs of cognitive stress theory, a range of coping strategies has also been empirically derived and a coping inventory, the Ways of Coping Questionnaire (Folkman & Lazarus, 1988), was developed for systematic assessment of coping strategies.

Two general types of coping strategies seem especially applicable to bereavement: (a) *problem-* versus *emotion-focused coping* and (b) *confrontation* versus *avoidance* (Billings & Moos, 1981; de Ridder, 1997; Lazarus & Folkman, 1984). Problem-focused coping is directed at managing and changing the problem causing distress, for example, dealing with a drop in income after the death by taking employment. By contrast, emotion-focused coping is directed at managing the resulting emotion, for example, trying to suppress worries about the drop in income. Cognitive stress theorists argue that the former is appropriate in situations that are changeable, the latter in those that are unchangeable. Some aspects of bereavement may be best dealt with in an emotion-focused way, because they are not changeable (the deceased person cannot be brought back), others in a problem-focused manner, because they can be altered (one can learn some of the skills that the deceased had provided in a marriage).

In a similar way, confrontation versus avoidance strategies can become complex, given the multiple stressors associated with bereavement. For example, a bereaved person may avoid certain emotional responses (e.g., a widower may try to avoid crying in front of others about his loss) but confront other aspects of the experience (e.g., anger that his wife had died while others survive). Because bereavement involves multiple stressors, some changeable and some not, one cannot simply confront or avoid as a general coping strategy. Different stressors will be confronted or avoided at different times, just as will happen with respect to problem- and emotion-focused coping.

Cognitive stress theory, then, has led to the development of a much finer grained analysis than is provided in the grief work theories. It also, most importantly, pinpoints the mediating role of cognitive (re)appraisal in adjustment to bereavement, a construct that ties in nicely with the meaning reconstruction theories. Folkman (2001) extended the model in the light of results from a bereavement study. We return to this later, in the section on specific models of coping with bereavement.

Cognitive stress theory is typically applied to a broad range of life events. However, the other three theoretical approaches listed in Table 2.1, Section II, can be considered to be more specifically "trauma theories" (it is clear that bereavement can sometimes be a traumatic experience; see M. S. Stroebe, Schut, & Finkenauer, 2001, for a conceptual analysis of overlap and distinctions). But these three theories represent very different, independent bodies of research. The first is Horowitz's (1986) analysis of stress response syndromes. Horowitz described normal human reactions to the abnormal event of a trauma, detailing how normal manifestations may increase in intensity and frequency to an extent that can be diagnosed as posttraumatic stress disorder (PTSD; Kleber & Brom, 1992). Horowitz identified the antithetical reactions of intrusion and avoidance as distinctive features of traumatic reactions. Intrusion is the compulsive reexperiencing of feelings and ideas surrounding the traumatic event, including sleep and dream disturbances and hypervigilance. Avoidance signifies a denial process, including reactions such as amnesia, inability to visualize memories, and evidence of disavowal. The description of a person's intrusion–avoidance pattern (too much–too little) helps to define the extremity of a person's reaction to a traumatic event. The Impact of Event Scale has become a well-established, short, self-report measure to evaluate the intensity of traumatic symptomatology (Horowitz, Wilner, & Alvarez, 1979; for revision of the scale, see Weiss & Marmar, 1997), and intrusion–avoidance is an integral part of the American Psychiatric Association's (1994) *Diagnostic and Statistical Manual of Mental Disorders* (4th ed.; *DSM–IV*) criteria for the definition of PTSD.

There is a subtle but essential difference between Horowitz's (1986) concern with intrusion–avoidance processes and our interest in adaptive coping. Horowitz's purpose was to determine how much impact the traumatic event had, intrusion–avoidance being a "symptomatic" process for classification of pathology. By contrast, here we are interested in whether intrusion–avoidance coping strategies might lead to adjustment to the event.

The second of the trauma theory categories covers emotional and social sharing approaches. Some empirical evidence has shown that engaging in induced written or verbal disclosure about traumatic events and revealing the personal upset associated with these experiences—very often in some form of diary writing—help adjustment and lower mental and, particularly, physical health risk (for a review, see Pennebaker, Zech, & Rimé, 2001). In contrast, simply asking people to talk or write about feelings associated with a loss (this has come to be known as the *disclosure paradigm*) has not been shown consistently to contribute to adaptive coping with bereavement (W. Stroebe, Schut, & Stroebe, 2005).

It seems likely that Pennebaker's disclosure paradigm, previously described, would be effective for subgroups of bereaved persons who have particular difficulty disclosing their grief naturally, or for persons whose disclosure represents ruminating about a loss, a reflection of intense grief. The goal of the writing intervention is to bring about cognitive change—an active working through and rethinking the impact of the loss. This would be in line with Pennebaker's recent theoretical reasoning. He has suggested that disclosure helps individuals to organize the experience, to clarify psychological states to others, and to translate emotional experience into the medium of language (Pennebaker, 1997; Pennebaker, Zech, & Rimé, 2001).

Pennebaker and his colleagues developed a computerized text analysis system, called the Linguistic Inquiry and Word Count (LIWC; Francis & Pennebaker, 1993; Pennebaker, Francis, & Booth, 2001), that computes the number of words in the diaries that respondents write reflecting dimensions such as negative emotion, positive emotion, causation, and insight or self-reflection. The LIWC has been used effectively to predict adaptation to bereavement: In a longitudinal investigation, for example, cognitive change occurring in narratives and measured using the LIWC emerged as instrumental in bringing about recovery from bereavement in a sample of men who had lost their partners to AIDS (Pennebaker, Mayne, & Francis, 1997).

The third approach emphasizes the role of meaning in the process of recovery from traumatic events. Janoff-Bulman and colleagues (e.g., Janoff-Bulman, 1992) argued that the fundamental assumptions that people hold about themselves, the world, and the relation between these two, which normally go unquestioned, can be shattered by traumatic events such as the death of a loved one, especially if the death had occurred suddenly and from a violent, traumatic cause. These assumptions are postulated to reside at the core of our inner worlds, incorporating beliefs that we are worthy, that the world is benevolent, and that what happens to us "makes sense" (Janoff-Bulman, 1992). When death shatters these basic assumptions, the survivor struggles to integrate the experience into these broad, meaning structures. Coping is said to involve rebuilding the inner world, to reestablish meaning, to adjust old assumptions, or to try to accept new ones. Over time, most survivors reestablish an assumptive world that is not completely threatening.

From this perspective, then, effective coping would likely involve a search for meaning and efforts to integrate the event into broader, positive meaning structures (rather than focusing on the malevolence of the world). This would require a confrontational strategy. It would be difficult, though, to distinguish between bereaved persons who effectively dwell on the meaning of what has happened to them and those who do not confront their grief so effectively. Meaning is an illusive concept in general, and findings have been equivocal with respect to adjustment. In fact, like the meaning reconstruction theories described earlier, Janoff-Bulman's (1992) assumptive worldviews perspective focuses more on describing and understanding trauma reactions than on adaptive versus maladaptive coping. Nevertheless, the meaning variables that she has identified can be integrated usefully into a bereavement-specific coping framework.

Broad-Spectrum Models of Grief

Next we turn to grief-specific theories, and first to those that have endeavored to explain a wide range of phenomena and manifestations associated with bereavements. Parkes's (1993, 1996, 2001a) psychosocial transition model is generally comparable with Janoff-Bulman's (1992) analysis. However, Parkes's model provides information about what actually changes in bereavement:

> When somebody dies a whole set of assumptions about the world that relied upon the other person for their validity are suddenly invalidated.

Habits of thought which have been built up over many years must be reviewed and modified, a person's view of the world must change . . . it inevitably takes time and effort. (Parkes, 1996, p. 90)

Parkes's model is closely tied to the attachment theory perspective. For example, he emphasized the need for the bereaved person to change his or her "internal model" of the world and self within it. He also accepted that grief work is an essential part of adaptive coping. Again, he provided further specification of component, interdependent parts of the grieving process, linking these to the duration of grief. First, there is a preoccupation with thoughts of the lost person. Second, there is painful, repetitious recollection of the loss experience, or "worry work," as the irrevocability of the loss is gradually accepted. Third, there is an attempt to make sense of the loss, to fit it into one's set of assumptions about the world (one's "assumptive world") or to modify those assumptions if need be. This model also goes beyond an analysis of the coping process, for example, in its identification of social and other factors that affect the outcome of grief.

Rubin's (1981, 1993, 1999) two-track model of bereavement is also relevant to an analysis of adaptational coping. Its unique contribution is in its differentiation of two tracks within the bereavement response. The model specifies that a bereaved person will need to deal not only with the biopsychosocial reactions to bereavement but also with the implications of one's attachment to the deceased, how this becomes transformed, and how a new relationship to the deceased is established. The two tracks are interlinked. Intense preoccupation with the deceased was said to "set in motion" the bereavement response (Rubin, 1993). Rubin's perspective is compatible with cognitive stress theory, providing a broader perspective but not providing an analysis of cognitive structures or processes as Folkman did (e.g., Folkman et al., 1991). Rubin also suggested a dynamic mechanism associated with the attachment bond, which is an important addition to previous formulations, as is the identification and clear distinction of the two tracks.

One of the broadest, most integrative models was proposed by Bonanno and Kaltman (1999; Bonanno, 2001a, 2001b). In this model, bereavement is considered in terms of four components. The first component involves the context of the loss. This refers to risk factors such as type of death, age, gender, social support, and cultural setting. The second component involves the continuum of subjective meanings associated with loss. These range from appraisals and evaluations of everyday matters and problems to existential concerns about the meaning of life and death. The third component reflects changing representations of the lost relationship over time. As Bonanno and Kaltman (1999) described, "There appears to be an optimal or manageable level of grief that allows for the reorganization of the bereaved survivor's representational world into a supportive and ongoing bond with the deceased" (p. 770). The fourth component reflects the role of coping and emotion regulation processes. This is the most important component for current purposes in that it highlights the range of coping strategies that may "potentially mollify or exacerbate the stress of loss" (p. 770). It draws on emotion theory as well as cognitive stress theory, integrating these perspectives in an analysis of emotion regulation. Bonanno and Kaltman (1999) argued that emotion regulation may at times involve deliberate or strategic processing, at other times, more a spontaneous or automatic regulatory processing not available to conscious awareness nor easily captured by self-report instruments.

Bonanno and Kaltman (1999) identified an important aspect of emotion regulation in bereavement that would enhance adjustment, namely, the regulation or even dissociation of negative emotions and the enhancement of positive emotions:

> These processes foster adjustment to loss because they help maintain relatively high levels of functioning, and thus contribute to retrospective reappraisals that the pain of loss can be coped with and that life can go on after the death of a loved one. (p. 771)

They have provided empirical support for such claims (e.g., Bonanno & Keltner, 1997; Bonanno, Keltner, Holen, & Horowitz, 1995).

The identification of automatic processing is unique to the four-component model. Adaptive ways of grieving may be better understood if such processes are included in analyses. The theory also moves a step closer to specification at the cognitive–structural level with respect to what precisely constitutes adaptive coping. As is shown in the next section, other theorists have suggested cognitive pathways in coping with bereavement that are consistent with the broader approach of Bonanno and Kaltman (1999).

Specific Models of Coping With Bereavement

Finally, we present those models that have been designed to provide a theoretical framework for understanding, quite narrowly, (mal)adaptive forms of grieving. Recent research developments in model building at the bereavement-specific coping level have focused, first, on the specification of cognitive tasks and, second, on processes in coping. Rather than conceptualizing the grieving process in terms of phases or stages (see chap. 1, this volume), Worden (1982, 1991, 2002) portrayed *tasks* that the bereaved person must perform to adjust to bereavement. Task models involve a more precise definition of the stressors that need working through. One advantage of this type of approach is that it represents coping as a more dynamic process, because the griever is portrayed as actively working through grief (rather than passively experiencing it). The former more closely reflects what most bereaved people report. Worden addressed four important tasks: accepting the reality of loss, experiencing the pain of grief, adjusting to an environment without the deceased, and "relocating" the deceased emotionally, which

Worden (2002) described as finding a place for the deceased that enables retained connection as well as moving on with life. The original tasks were slightly reformulated and extended by Worden in the 2002 edition of his book. For example, the fourth task now includes a principle of more general adaptation, namely, to move on with life.

Worden (1982, 1991) emphasized that not all grievers need to undertake these tasks and that they do not occur in a set order. In general, though, completion of the work associated with each task should facilitate adaptation. As noted in chapter 1, this formulation also incorporates an implicit time dimension, for different coping tasks are appropriate at different points in time across the course of bereavement. This is useful when considering the nature of adaptive coping.

At this point, however, we would suggest a number of additional tasks that need to be performed along the lines of, but also further to, Worden's (2002) revisions. These include working toward acceptance of one's changed world, not just the reality of loss. One needs to take time out from grieving, as well as experiencing pain. The subjective environment itself (not just adjustment to the environment) needs to be reconstructed. Finally, we need to specify that bereaved people work toward developing new roles, identities, and relationships, in addition to relocating the deceased.

Along with defining tasks, as Worden (1982, 1991) did, a number of investigators have provided theoretical analyses of components in this process of coping with loss. Here we focus on two components that are major dimensions in general coping research: (a) positive and negative appraisal processes and (b) confrontation versus avoidance.

We noted earlier that cognitive stress theory had recently undergone some revision. The extension accommodates new insights that emerged while Folkman (2001) was interviewing gay caregivers of men with AIDS. These men, many of whom became bereaved during the course of the longitudinal study, alerted Folkman to the role that positive emotions play in coping with caregiving and bereavement. Despite the burden on them, these men gained strength by finding positive things going on even when their daily lives were grueling. Folkman subsequently incorporated questions about positive affect and (re)appraisal into her research to assess their role in coping. This led to the revision of the model, as depicted in Figure 2.1 (Folkman, 1997, 2001; Folkman & Moskowitz, 2000), and to further empirical testing of the adaptive function of positive psychological states during the grieving process. As can be seen in the figure, the revision highlights meaning-based coping and the importance of positive affect in actually sustaining the coping process (columns 5 and 6 in Figure 2.1). Whereas positive affect was not excluded in the original model, in the revised model positive affect has multiple and important roles. For example, meaning-based processes (e.g., positive reappraisals) may lead to positive psychological states. Negative psychological states may motivate people to search for and create positive psychological

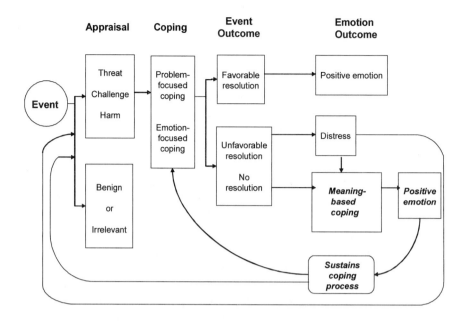

Appraisal   Coping   Event Outcome   Emotion Outcome

Figure 2.1. The revised coping model (Folkman, 2001). From *Handbook of Bereavement Research: Consequences, Coping, and Care* (p. 574), edited by M. S. Stroebe, R. O. Hansson, W. Stroebe, and H. A. W. Schut, 2001, Washington, DC: American Psychological Association. Copyright 2001 by the American Psychological Association.

states to gain relief (coping occurs as a response to distress). Positive psychological states may lead back to appraisal and coping, so that coping efforts are sustained. As Folkman (2001) described,

> [p]ositive affect is included as an outcome of unresolved chronic stress that is prompted by the need to experience positive well-being in the midst of distress, it is maintained by a class of meaning-based coping processes that is distinct from those that regulate distress, and it functions to sustain coping over the long term. (p. 573)

The revised model, then, takes us a step further toward understanding precisely which types of cognitive processes help bereaved persons to come to terms with their loss and how adaptation may come about. The revised model, like the original formulation, is also in a sense a generic model even though it was formulated at the bereavement-specific level. It is applicable across the wide range of stressful life events. As we show in the next chapter, the model also provides the basis for our own bereavement-specific theoretical framework.

Positive affect, then, may further adjustment. Even the occurrence of smiling and laughter during the grieving process appears to be positively related to later adjustment (Keltner & Bonanno, 1997). But, such expression alone appears insufficient. After examining the differential results of studies in which positive affect versus those in which positive reappraisal seems to have been possible, Pennebaker et al. (1997) concluded that it is positive meaning construction and reconstruction that make up adaptive coping.

Just as positive meaning has been linked to good outcome, so has ruminative coping been identified as a maladaptive strategy. *Ruminative coping* has been defined as focusing on distressing aspects and meanings in a repetitive and passive manner (Nolen-Hoeksema, 2001). Controlling for the amount of distress at the outset of evaluation, Nolen-Hoeksema and her colleagues have been able to show that disclosing negative emotions actually has a harmful effect on later recovery (Nolen-Hoeksema, 2001; Nolen-Hoeksema & Larson, 1999; Nolen-Hoeksema, Parker, & Larson, 1994). Those with a more distractive style became less depressed over time.

In an interesting parallel to Folkman's analysis for positive psychological states, Nolen-Hoeksema (2001) suggested pathways whereby ruminative coping may lead to a lengthening or worsening of the impact of loss. For example, it may enhance the effects of depressed mood on thinking. It can also interfere with everyday instrumental behavior, reducing motivation to act that would normally increase the sense of control and lift mood. It can interfere with effective problem solving, because one thinks negatively about oneself and one's life. It can also undermine necessary social support, perhaps because persistent ruminations violate social norms of coping.

In a sense, the research on positive and negative coping strategies represents two sides of a coin. Somehow, these positive versus negative coping pathways need to be combined into a single predictive model. An attempt at such an integration is presented in the following chapter.

A recurring theme in many of these theories is confrontation versus avoidance. It is apparent that grief work would involve confrontation rather than avoidance (although even this is complex). In grieving, a person may avoid "moving on" or other aspects of loss that may need to be attended to, or the person may confront the death in a ruminative way, avoiding constructive reappraisal of one's loss situation. Denial or avoidance of grief has been considered maladaptive, notably in psychoanalytic formulations. Recently, however, investigators have provided evidence that avoidant strategies may be more functional than had previously been assumed. For example, Bonanno et al. (1995) found a dissociation between physiologically measured arousal and indices of psychological upset. Bereaved men who showed high physiological arousal but low psychological confrontation when talking to their deceased partner (in a role-play situation) had good bereavement outcomes, measured at a later point. Although too complete a denial has been associated with negative outcome (Jacobs, 1993), these results suggest that some degree of avoidance may be healthy, just as keeping secrets (Kelly & McKillop, 1996) or suppressing extremely traumatic experiences (Kaminer & Lavie, 1993) may also be.

These studies all point to the possibility that at times it may be adaptive to keep one's grief to oneself and to regulate grieving. The pattern is complex, however. For example, unwanted nondisclosure may have negative consequences: Lepore, Silver, Wortman, and Wayment (1996) showed that bereaved mothers who perceived their social environments as preventing them from disclosing their distress and who had high levels of initial intrusive thoughts about the loss were more depressed in the long term.

How are the adaptive effects of confrontation versus avoidance to be understood? On the one hand, bereaved individuals need to confront and work through the pain of their loss, which is an effortful process. On the other hand, they also need to let the reality of loss sink in gradually, as Janoff-Bulman's (1992) work demonstrated. In addition, both grieving and denial are effortful processes. What research so far seems to have shown is that too much confrontation or too much avoidance is detrimental to adaptation. Both processes may be linked to negative health consequences if undertaken relentlessly, causing exhaustion. Scientific analysis needs to represent the tendency—even necessity—to confront combined with the tendency to avoid, deny, or suppress aspects of grieving as part of the adaptive process, as illustrated in Bonanno and Kaltman's (1999) model.

CONCLUSIONS

Over the course of the 20th century, a major paradigm shift took place, from the early psychoanalytic emphasis on object loss, decathexis, and withdrawal or disengagement to an understanding of grief and grieving as an ongoing process of meaning reconstruction and rebuilding of previously held assumptions. Following this shift, increased attention has focused on how specific cognitive processes might contribute to one's adjustment to loss. Despite such advancements, however, we have noted a number of limitations of various theories with respect to operationalizing and predicting outcome. Finally, a plethora of theories have been advanced to account for various aspects of the bereavement experience, clouding efforts to understand adaptation. Is it possible to derive a specific model of coping with bereavement that will integrate major propositions and overcome some of the weaknesses of theories reviewed so far? We describe one attempt to do so in the next chapter.

3

THE DUAL PROCESS MODEL OF COPING WITH BEREAVEMENT AND DEVELOPMENT OF AN INTEGRATIVE RISK FACTOR FRAMEWORK

M. S. Stroebe and Schut (1999) proposed the *dual process model* (DPM) in an effort to overcome the limitations of earlier theories on effective ways of coping with bereavement. In our review of coping theory in chapter 2, we identified a number of shortcomings associated with specific approaches. There are also a number of additional shortcomings inherent in many of the available theories. These problems for the most part involve theoretical constructs, but limitations on empirical testing and application are evident too. In the following sections, we first summarize the most important of these concerns, then we discuss the parameters of the DPM and how it deals with them. Finally, we place the DPM in broader theoretical context, providing an integrative, conceptual framework that we hope will be useful for understanding patterns of adaptation to bereavement among older persons.

SHORTCOMINGS IN SCIENTIFIC ANALYSES OF COPING WITH LOSS

Although theoretical and empirical research have brought us closer to understanding effective and noneffective ways of coming to terms with a death, inspection of the scientific literature has revealed three types of concerns: First, theoretical constructs need refinement; second, empirical support for postulated (mal)adaptive processes is lacking; and third, (mal)adaptive coping strategies seem not to apply universally. We list the main shortcomings within these categories next.

Theoretical Concerns

- Important terms such as *grief work* are imprecisely defined. For example, following existing formulations it is difficult to differentiate "healthy" working through grief from "unhealthy" rumination.
- The dynamic nature of coping, characteristic of grieving, has not been adequately represented. There is a waxing and waning of deep emotions and a fluctuation in the focus of attention in dealing with loss, rather than a systematic progression through phases or stages of grief.
- Theoretical formulations of patterns of change across time in terms of phases or stages have often been criticized as being too rigid and prescriptive (although a reading of the original texts shows that this was not intended) and for failing to take account of different trajectories of grieving.
- Related to the two preceding points, grieving has frequently been depicted more in terms of a passive process rather than the active, effortful struggle that is a familiar feature of coping with bereavement.
- Theorists have not generally incorporated the concept of "dosage" (in the sense of controlling, limiting the amount) of grieving into their models. Grieving is exhausting if undertaken too relentlessly, and taking "time off" grieving and experiencing positive affect are conducive to adaptation.
- Theorists have not typically been explicit about the range of secondary (i.e., accompanying) adjustments that need to be made when a loved person dies. These associated adjustments may at times be as difficult to cope with as aspects of the loss of the person, per se. In addition to grieving for the deceased, coping can involve a need to take over new tasks, change habits, adjust expectations and plans, and so on. Mastering these secondary changes is an integral part of adjustment to bereavement.
- Following the classic psychoanalytic formulation, the detrimental effects of denial, suppression, and repression have been emphasized, as reflected in the grief work notion. However, processes of at least temporary denial may at times be beneficial (e.g., to give respite and restore energy).

- With a few notable exceptions, researchers have focused too narrowly on intrapersonal processes in coping, neglecting important interpersonal dynamics that could affect outcome.
- There have been few attempts to *integrate* constructs and predictions from different theoretical approaches, specifically with respect to subsuming and organizing the various adaptive coping processes.

Empirical Concerns

- In general, empirical evidence of the efficacy of postulated adaptive processes, notably grief work, has too rarely been provided.
- There has been rather a narrow examination of outcomes in terms of health variables, which disregards other aspects of adaptation (e.g., undertaking new roles; social reintegration).

Application Concerns

- The generalizability of theory across cultures has seldom been addressed. Some non-Western cultures, for example, experience very different ways of coming to terms with loss as compared with Western societies (Wikan, 1988). The same is true for different historical periods (Walter, 1999).
- The notion of grief work seems more applicable to traditional female rather than male ways of grieving. Women appear to be somewhat more likely to focus on and express their grief.
- Substantial individual differences have been identified with respect to ways of (effective) coping, intensity (from "normal" to complicated forms) and course of grief, and level of adjustment. Such differences have been insufficiently addressed in the traditional grief work models.

DESCRIPTION OF THE DUAL PROCESS MODEL OF COPING WITH BEREAVEMENT

A major influence behind the formulation of the DPM was Lazarus and Folkman's (1984) cognitive stress theory. To recapitulate (see chap. 2, this volume), cognitive stress theory enables systematic analysis in terms of characteristics of the stressor, the coping process, and the outcome.

- *Stressors*: In the present context, the major stressor would be bereavement, which incorporates a number of specific stressors (e.g., need for relocation).

- *Demands* on the bereaved person, such as the need to organize the funeral.
- *Resources* available to deal with demands (e.g., mobilizing others' help), which must not be overtaxed or exceeded if well-being is to be maintained.
- *Primary appraisal* (e.g., of the impact of the loss) determines whether the situation (bereavement) is perceived as challenging or stressful.
- *Secondary appraisal* refers to the assessment of one's own strengths in dealing with the stressor.
- *Coping mechanisms* are means of dealing with the stressor (e.g., problem-focused versus emotion-focused coping, the former being appropriate in situations that are changeable, the latter in situations that are unchangeable).
- *Outcome variables* are those related to adjustment (e.g., the level of grief; mental and physical health).

Each of these components can be incorporated into the DPM. However, the DPM also went further, by addressing four additional problems in coping theory.

1. *Coexisting stressors.* Although cognitive stress theory incorporates the possibility that different stressors coexist, it does not describe a process of concurrent appraisal and coping with different stressors, or any form of juxtaposition in dealing with different stressors. Rather, it details processes of appraisal and coping with one particular stressor at a time (cf. Folkman et al., 1991).
2. *Emotion regulation.* Cognitive stress theory says little about emotion regulation in terms of a dynamic process of confrontation and avoidance of the bereavement stressors.
3. *A bereavement-specific model.* Although cognitive stress theory is applicable to bereavement, it is a generic model for understanding adaptation following stressful life events. A bereavement-specific model adds potential to comprehend the particular phenomena and manifestations of bereavement, which have long been known to be highly complex (Averill, 1968). For example, bereavement is an *attachment-related* stressful life event, for which exploration of the nature of the (former and ongoing) relationship with the deceased would be needed. Integration of postulates derived from attachment theory would seem imperative.
4. *Emotion- versus problem-focused coping.* There are problems in applying the emotion- versus problem-focused coping distinction to bereavement. Because bereavement incorporates mul-

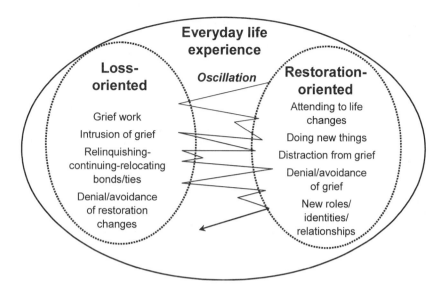

Everyday life
experience

**Loss-
oriented**   *Oscillation*   **Restoration-
oriented**

Grief work

Intrusion of grief

Relinquishing-
continuing-relocating
bonds/ties

Denial/avoidance
of restoration
changes

Attending to life
changes

Doing new things

Distraction from grief

Denial/avoidance
of grief

New roles/
identities/
relationships

Figure 3.1. Dual process model of coping with bereavement. From "The Dual Process Model of Coping With Bereavement: Rationale and Description," by M. S. Stroebe and H. A. W. Schut, 1999, *Death Studies, 23*, p. 213. Copyright 1999 by M. S. Stroebe. Reprinted with permission.

tiple stressors, some of which are changeable (one can develop skills to overcome deficits) and some of which are not (one cannot bring back the loved one), both emotion- and problem-focused coping would seem appropriate. However, the distinction between emotion- and problem-focused coping seems unclear in the context of bereavement. One of the foremost stressors is the emotion of grief itself, because it is hard to control its overt expression, and lack of control presents difficulties for the self and others. The question then arises: How does one deal with this distressing emotion in an emotion-focused versus a problem-focused way? Apparent problem-focused behavior may indeed be emotion-focused. Furthermore, it is difficult to predict the efficacy of emotion-focused coping given that the strategy incorporates the control of emotions as well as their expression, each of which may help or harm.

Three components of the DPM have been postulated to deal with the previously listed limitations. These are the concepts of loss orientation and restoration orientation (which are two categories of stressors) and oscillation (which is a coping mechanism). These components are depicted in Figure 3.1. The DPM is a taxonomy for describing ways that people come to terms with the loss of a loved person. As can be seen in Figure 3.1, it not only incorporates the two types of stressor and the dynamic coping mechanism but also places these in the context of everyday life. It also incorporates description of coping strategies and appraisal, and dynamic emotional regulation between these two, as described shortly. As described next, the DPM was originally developed to understand coping with the death of a partner, but it is potentially applicable to other types of bereavement. For the sake of simplicity, most of our examples are drawn from partner loss.

Loss Orientation Versus Restoration Orientation

A variety of adjustments or psychosocial transitions associated with bereavement have been described by researchers and clinicians (e.g., Lopata, 1993; Marris, 1974; Parkes, 1993). The DPM provides a taxonomy for classifying life changes and losses likely to be experienced and defines two main types of adjustments (loss orientation vs. restoration orientation) that need to be made in relationship to coping processes. Each of these types of stressor is encountered to varying degrees (according to individual and cultural variations), and each requires coping effort. However, this coping effort does not occupy all of the bereaved person's time (we noted how exhausting it is, and how necessary it is to rest from dealing with loss). Coping occurs within one's everyday life experience. The loss may be temporarily put out of mind, for example, when reading an engrossing book, attending to children's needs, chatting to a friend about other matters, or sleeping.

Loss orientation involves concentrating on, dealing with, and processing some aspect of the loss experience itself. The grief work concept of earlier theories falls within this dimension, because focus is on the relationship and bond to the deceased, and because it typically includes yearning and rumination about the deceased, dwelling on life together before loss, and going over the circumstances and events leading up to and surrounding the death. Loss orientation encompasses going over one's memories of the deceased and the implications of the death: looking at old photos, imagining how he or she would react, and crying about the irrevocable separation. Myriad emotional reactions are involved, from painful longing for the deceased to pleasurable reminders, and from relief that the deceased is suffering no more to despair that one is left all alone.

Fluctuations in positive and negative emotions occur not only from time to time (even moment to moment) in any one day but also across the course of bereavement. In the early days, negative affect tends to predominate. However, as time passes, positive affect plays an increasingly important role in the adaptation process. The amount of time spent on loss orientation will also gradually lessen over time, but not in a simple, linear manner; there will be recurrences (e.g., on anniversaries, or when a piece of music jogs the memory).

Thus, the DPM contrasts with phasal models; it proposes not a sequence of stages but rather a waxing and waning, involving ongoing fluctuations over time. The concept of loss orientation is close to attachment theory's focus on the nature of the lost relationship and its understanding of the importance of types of bond, and it also bears some similarity to Rubin's (1981) concept of the relationship track. Attachment and a continued relationship to the deceased are understood to be major components in grieving and determinants of outcome. We integrate these aspects later on.

The construct of loss orientation is compatible with notions from Neimeyer's (2001) meaning construction approach, Janoff-Bulman's (1992) assumptive worldview analysis, and Worden's (1991) task model (described in chap. 2, this volume). These theories emphasized the need for making sense of and finding meaning in the death, dealing with shattered assumptions about the death and the deceased person, and accepting the reality of the loss and relocating the deceased person.

Restoration orientation refers to secondary sources of—and coping with—stress. It is important to note that *restoration* does not refer to an outcome variable (which would imply adaptation to loss) but to the identification of stressors other than loss-oriented ones and to the description of ways of dealing with them. Thus, this analysis focuses on what needs to be dealt with (e.g., being unable to pay the rent from one's lower pension) and how it is then dealt with (e.g., moving to a more reasonably priced home). Restoration orientation is somewhat similar to Cook and Oltjenbruns's (1998) concept of secondary loss in that both conceptualizations identify accompanying life changes that occur as a result of a death. However, Cook and Oltjenbrun's formulation is conceptually narrower, being limited to defining changes in relationships with others during bereavement.

In addition to grieving for a lost loved one, it frequently becomes necessary to make a number of life adjustments that emerge as secondary consequences of the death. These additional sources of stress add to the burden of loss and can cause considerable anxiety and upset. As such, they are part of the loss and grieving experience. It is not difficult to find examples. Many of the secondary stressors involve tasks that the deceased had previously contributed to the partnership, such as cooking, other household chores, dealing with the finances, and so on. Additional, more complex secondary stressors might involve dealing with arrangements for the reorganization of a life without the loved one (e.g., moving into sheltered accommodation), or as time goes on, the struggle to shape a new identity, from "spouse" to "widow(er)" or from "parent" to "parent of a deceased child." As was the case for loss orientation, a variety of emotions can also be involved in restoration coping. On the one hand, a bereaved person may experience anxiety and fear that he or she will not succeed or manage alone, or despair at the loneliness of being with others and yet on one's own. On the other hand, feelings of having

TABLE 3.1
Comparison of Stressor-Specific Models

Phase model (Bowlby, 1980)	Task model (Worden, 1991, 2002)	Dual process model (M. S. Stroebe & Schut, 1999)
Shock	Accept reality of loss.	Accept reality of loss . . . *and accept reality of changed world.*
Yearning/protest	Work through pain of grief.	Experience pain of grief . . . *and take time off from pain of grief.*
Despair	Adjust to environment without deceased.[a]	Adjust to life without deceased . . . *and master the changed (subjective) environment.*
Restitution	Emotionally relocate deceased and move on with life.[a]	Relocate deceased emotionally and move on . . . *and develop new roles, identities, relationships.*

[a]Indicates changes in 2002 to include more restoration tasks. Italics indicate how the dual process model extends the ideas presented in the two other models.

mastered a new skill or having had the courage to go out alone may result in a much welcomed sense of relief and pride.

In formulating the tasks of restoration previously described, the DPM extends our understanding of stressors and coping, relative to formulations in either the phase or task models. Table 3.1 gives a comparative summary of the principles within the three models.

Oscillation

The DPM is most clearly distinguished from all the other bereavement coping models by an emotion-regulation process involving oscillation. Bonanno and Kaltman (1999) included a somewhat similar construct in their theory, and there is some similarity between the two stressor orientations and Parkes's (1993) psychosocial transitions (described in chap. 2, this volume). However, the latter model did not include an analysis of the cognitive processes that regulate attention to losses and gains following bereavement.

Oscillation refers to a process of alternating between loss-oriented and restoration-oriented coping, and between coping and not coping (e.g., in routine, unchanged, everyday life things)—the process of attention to and avoidance of different stressors (and other activities) associated with bereavement (see Figure 3.1). As such, oscillation is consistent with emotion theorists' definitions of emotion regulation (and under the larger category of self-regulation; see Folkman & Moskowitz, 2004), which is the process

> by which individuals influence which emotions they have, when they have them, and how they experience and express these emotions. Emotion regulatory processes may be automatic or controlled, conscious or

unconscious, and may have their effects at one or more points in the emotion generative process. (Gross, 1998, p. 275)

Oscillation is a necessary construct to include in the DPM because it is not possible to attend to both the loss- and restoration-oriented dimensions simultaneously. At times a bereaved person will be confronted by his or her loss, at other times he or she will avoid memories, be distracted, or seek relief by doing other things. Sometimes, too, it is simply necessary to put grief aside for a while and attend to other restoration-oriented stressors, such as trying to master the changes in income and taxes following the death. Oscillation, then, is a regulatory mechanism similar to the confrontation versus avoidance coping strategies described in cognitive stress theory (cf. de Ridder, 1997). However, our formulation involves a dynamic alternating process, whereas earlier coping theorists operationalized confrontation versus avoidance as a way of coping reflecting a state or trait. Our approach parallels and benefits from contemporary theory on emotion regulation in the coping and self-regulation literatures (see Baumeister & Vohs, 2004; Folkman & Moskowitz, 2004).

Oscillation, then, is postulated to be essential for optimal adjustment over time. It occurs both in the short term (transient fluctuations taking place over the course of a day) and also throughout the duration of bereavement. Through this process, a bereaved person will come to explore and discover the significance of what has been lost and what remains, what must be avoided or relinquished versus what can be retained and built on. Although we propose that loss- and restoration-oriented coping occurs in concurrent oscillation, there is usually a shift away from loss, as the duration of bereavement lengthens, and toward restoration-oriented stressors (e.g., forming new relationships). It is interesting to note that Martikainen and Valkonen (1996) reported patterns of excess mortality among spousally bereaved persons in Finland in relation to durations of bereavement that reflect these shifts in orientation. Observed patterns of mortality were interpreted to indicate that stress and grief had short-term effects, whereas the effects of loss of social, material, and task support may dominate at longer durations of bereavement.

A balance between loss and restoration components needs to be achieved after a major bereavement. Attending to loss necessitates distraction from restoration-oriented stressors, and vice versa. Focusing exclusively on loss or restoration orientation would not be conducive to adaptation and would be psychologically (and physiologically) exhausting. We postulate that oscillation has an adaptive regulatory function similar to that proposed in emotion theory (see Mesquita & Frijda, 1992). An extreme focus on either loss or restoration orientation with little oscillation would, then, not be associated with positive outcome. We propose that within these extreme boundaries, "optimal" levels of loss- and restoration-oriented coping will vary across individuals, cultures, and time. In general, as the duration of bereavement extends, in adaptive coping, loss orientation will decrease whereas restoration orientation will increase. These changes occur gradually, with fluctuations. At the present time, we have to be cautious in making further specification with regard to outcome. Future empirical research should help us to establish the nature of "healthy" coping trajectories more precisely.

The process of oscillation between loss- and restoration-oriented stressors is illustrated in the following personal account provided by a 39-year-old widow:

> Maybe it would have been better if it hadn't happened so suddenly. We just weren't prepared, that's all. We hadn't been able to save any money ahead and there wasn't even any insurance money to pay for the funeral—I had to get the whole family to pitch in, you see. The main thing was, I didn't have him any more. (as cited in Sanders, 1989, p. 134)

Kagan (2001), speaking of parental bereavement, also captured the need for oscillation as well as a focus on loss and restoration orientations:

> Readjustment entails a constant interpretation of the grief experienced. It involves changes in perception of self and changes in the relationships with the living family. . . . The process moves from the attachment to the deceased child to an emergence of a new self identity and may continue to progress to the discovery of new meaning in life. (p. 1)

COGNITIVE MECHANISMS IN THE DUAL PROCESS MODEL

In 2001, M. S. Stroebe and Schut published a first attempt to systematize underlying cognitive mechanisms that could be associated with loss- and restoration-oriented coping and the process of oscillation, especially given the fact that oscillation is a very general concept. Again, drawing on earlier cognitive stress research, a starting point for exploration was offered by Folkman's (2001) revised coping model, which incorporates the adaptive role of positive affect and appraisal in the coping process, and Nolen-Hoeksema's (2001) model focusing on the maladaptive function of rumination. As summarized in Figure 3.2, M. S. Stroebe and Schut's (2001) integration of these two processes into one model postulates oscillation between positive and negative cognitive states, *both* when dealing with loss-oriented *and* restoration-oriented stressors. Positive affect leads to adaptive coping, whereas ruminative coping has negative consequences. Of course, in bereavement, negative affect cannot be totally avoided; it is part of grieving, so again, an adaptive process would entail oscillation between confrontation versus avoidance of positive and negative emotions and cognitions having to do with bereavement. Although this analysis needs extension and empirical testing, it does provide a more precise definition of (mal)adaptive cognitive processing than was provided in grief work theories.

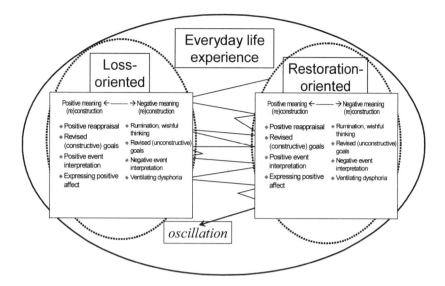

Figure 3.2. Appraisal processes in the dual process model. From *Meaning Reconstruction and the Experience of Loss* (p. 68), edited by R. Neimeyer, 2001, Washington, DC: American Psychological Association. Copyright 2001 by the American Psychological Association.

EMPIRICAL EVIDENCE FOR THE DUAL PROCESS MODEL

As is the case for many of the models already described, the DPM remains in need of much empirical testing. However, both indirect and direct evidence are accumulating. There are suggestive findings from studies of ways of coping with bereavement that support certain tenets of the model, and researchers have begun to use a variety of techniques to directly investigate various parameters of the model. We review these two sources next.

Indirect Evidence

First, as we noted earlier, reviews of empirical evidence for the grief work hypothesis showed mixed results (M. S. Stroebe, 1992; M. S. Stroebe & Schut, 1999). Expression of emotions of grief alone has not emerged as a predictor of good adjustment (see Wortman & Silver, 2001), although reappraising or making sense of loss may promote adjustment (e.g., Davis, Nolen-Hoeksema, & Larson, 1998). More recent studies, notably those of Bonanno and his colleagues (for a review, see Bonanno, 2001a), have found some benefits associated with avoiding grief work, further suggesting that the grief work hypothesis needs revision.

It was an empirical study by Schut (1992; Schut, Stroebe, van den Bout, & de Keijser, 1997) and another by M. S. Stroebe and Stroebe (1991) that first suggested the need for theoretical revision on this topic, and subsequently to the development of the DPM. The Schut study was designed to examine the efficacy of two different types of intervention for bereaved spouses who were moderately to highly distressed approximately a year after bereavement. One of the interventions focused on dealing with emotions, the other on problems. Widows and widowers were randomly assigned to one of the two interventions. The gender patterns were especially interesting to examine, because women are typically somewhat more expressive of emotions such as grief (and more loss oriented), whereas men tend rather to suppress their grief (restoration oriented; Lund, 2001; Walter, 1999). Which gender, then, would benefit from which program? Differential effects were indeed found, with widowers' levels of distress decreasing more following the emotion-type intervention, whereas widows benefited from the problem-type intervention. Such patterns were hard to interpret from a grief work perspective. Rather, they suggested the necessity for these still-distressed persons to avoid those aspects of loss that were, so to speak, the more typical tendencies of each gender and to confront those that were less typical. These bereaved men benefited from counseling that furthered confrontation with grief emotions (loss orientation), whereas their female counterparts gained more from learning how to deal with daily-life problems (restoration orientation). Indirect support was thus provided for the adaptive function of shifting attention from one to the other type of stressor (oscillation) and furthering coping. In the M. S. Stroebe and Stroebe (1991) study, there was mixed support for the grief work hypothesis; although there was some evidence that widowers gained by working through, for widows, working or not working through grief did not make any difference to longer term adjustment.

Bonanno et al. (2004) drew conclusions about differential intervention needs that also seem consistent with the DPM (and the findings of Schut, 1992; Schut et al., 1997), although their study was not set up to examine the model specifically. They reported patterns of resilience and maladjustment during widow(er)hood, using the Changing Lives of Older Couples data set (which is described in detail in chap. 6, this volume). Bonanno et al. (2004) concluded,

> of the individuals who exhibit chronically elevated symptoms and distress after the death of their spouse, some will likely benefit most from focusing specifically on processing the loss (e.g., the meaning of loss). In contrast, others will likely benefit most from dealing with the more pragmatic issues of low-self esteem and coping with the strains of meeting life's daily demands. (p. 269)

Further indirect support specifically for the restoration-orientation conceptualization was provided by Gentry, Kennedy, Paul, and Hill (1995), who described characteristic household patterns in bereavement, identifying different types of adjustment consequent to different types of loss. These investigators concluded that the major types of adjustment following spousal loss concerned household roles, with the widowed person having to adjust to "new acquisition, maintenance, and disposal responsibilities, at the same time when his/her motivation and ability to adjust are minimal" (p. 77). By contrast, the death of a child did not change household structures but affected household communication patterns. They argued that men and women handle their grief very differently, causing a redirection of negative emotions toward the spouse. Escalation of problems due to miscommunication or lack of communication could then result (cf. Cook & Oltjenbruns, 1998). It is not hard to see how this might lead to divorce, but also, conversely, loss of a child can lead to couples communicating better and becoming closer (see Dijkstra & Stroebe, 1998). Taken as a whole, the results of Gentry et al.'s (1995) study nicely pinpoint differences in the types of restoration-oriented stressors following different types of loss.

Empirical Tests of the Dual Process Model's Parameters

Some evidence of individual differences in tendencies to focus on loss- versus restoration-oriented stressors is now available, and links between these patterns and well-being have been established (e.g., Dijkstra, van den Bout, Schut, Stroebe, & Stroebe, 1999; Hogan & Schmidt, 2002; Machin, 2001; V. E. Richardson & Balaswamy, 2001). For example, using a longitudinal design, V. E. Richardson and Balaswamy (2001) examined the predictive value of the DPM in a sample of 200 older widowers. These investigators found loss- and restoration-oriented variables to be important throughout bereavement. It is interesting that they noted that loss-related factors (e.g., circumstances of death) were more important early in bereavement, whereas restoration-oriented factors such as role and identity variables (e.g., dating) became relevant later (which seems neatly in line with the findings reported earlier by Gentry et al., 1995). It should be noted that definitions of the stressors differed somewhat from specifications in the DPM. For example, the specification of restoration-oriented variables in V. E. Richardson and Balaswamy's study included a broad range of social, formal, and individual activities, some of which would be categorized in the DPM as everyday life activities rather than as secondary—restoration-oriented—stressors in need of attention. In a more recent investigation, V. Richardson (in press) replicated the V. E. Richardson and Balaswamy study, again using a longitudinal design and similar variables. The Changing Lives of Older Couples data set was used, enabling inclusion of both widows and widowers. Again, the findings supported the principles of loss and restoration orientation.

Preliminary evidence for the occurrence and adaptive function of oscillation was provided by Hogan and Schmidt (2002). The construct was examined in a sample of 167 bereaved parents. Structural equation modeling was used to test the DPM and other models. Oscillation, which is difficult to operationalize, was measured in terms of dealing with intrusive thoughts of experienced loss and avoiding reminders of the loss. The authors found that bereaved persons do indeed oscillate between dealing with intrusion and avoidance as a means of coping with and processing grief, and that they are both part of the grieving process. The study was cross-sectional and did not allow further tests of the DPM.

Finally, research teams at different locations are beginning to examine the efficacy of intervention programming following DPM principles (e.g., Lund, Caserta, de Vries, & Wright, 2004; Shear, Frank, Houck, & Reynolds, 2005). Shear and colleagues, for example, demonstrated that a DPM-based intervention for complicated grief was more effective than a standard psychotherapy for targeting grief. In addition to such intervention studies, further research on DPM phenomena and manifestations needs to incorporate better ways of measuring oscillation, as well as loss and restoration orientation, and needs to include additional predictions from the model (e.g., with respect to the cognitive pathways). Longitudinal studies using sophisticated techniques that go beyond questionnaire measurement are called for.

EXTENSION OF THE DUAL PROCESS MODEL: PATTERNS OF ATTACHMENT IN BEREAVEMENT

In their original formulation, M. S. Stroebe and Schut (1999) included a consideration of complicated forms of grief in relationship to the DPM, which became basic for subsequent developments. Complications have been described as falling into specific categories, usually defined as chronic grief, traumatic grief (which is still ill defined; see M. S. Stroebe, Schut, & Finkenauer, 2001), and a category including nuances associated with absent, delayed, inhibited grief (cf. Parkes & Weiss, 1983; M. S. Stroebe, Schut, & Finkenauer, 2001). For example, people experiencing chronic grief (long-lasting presence of symptoms of intense grief, absence of progress in coming to terms with loss) would find it difficult to take time off from loss orientation and would neglect secondary tasks (they might be very reluctant to start new relationships). By contrast, those experiencing absent grief (characterized by the nonappearance of symptoms typical of grief) would avoid expression and reminders, tending rather to immerse themselves in work or a new partnership. In either of the two types of complication, there would be too little oscillation occurring. Those experiencing traumatic grief might be expected to have trouble either in alternating between—or coherently dwelling for a period of time on—loss or restoration orientation. Here the problem lies partly with the oscillation itself, this being less balanced, less coherent, or less controlled than in "normal" grief (cf. the intrusion–avoidance symptomatology described as diagnostic criteria for posttraumatic stress disorder; American Psychiatric Association, 1994).

More recently, M. S. Stroebe, Stroebe, and Schut (2005b) extended the DPM to integrate attachment theory propositions. Attachment theory is fundamentally a theory of relationships between people, from infant–caregiver, to romantic relationships, to reactions to the death of a loved one. As such, it provides an excellent framework for understanding individual differences in bereavement (see Bowlby, 1980). The extension of the DPM to incorporate this perspective was fuelled by the analyses of Parkes (2001b) and Shaver and Tancredy (2001), who—independently of each other—drew links between types of attachment (secure vs. the three insecure types) and the different complications in the grieving process outlined earlier. The four styles have been described for infants with generalizations made for adults. It is important to note that although the attachment style category system is useful for the identification of regularities, in reality the descriptive categories are not so clear-cut or as distinctive as outlined here. With this in mind, in brief, the four styles can be typified as follows:

- *Secure attachment*: Normal distress at separation from the caregiver or partner and enthusiastic response on return.
- *Insecure–preoccupied* (also called anxious–ambivalent): Unusual upset and clinging on departure, anger and rejection on return.
- *Dismissing* (also called avoidant): Calmness and avoidance on departure and rejection on return.
- *Disorganized–disoriented* (also called unresolved; fearful): Varies more, with some having contradictory reactions (approaching with head turned away) or disoriented (freezing as if dazed).

Parkes's (2001b) and Shaver and Tancredy's (2001) suggestion was that securely attached individuals would tend to have normal or healthy grieving, experiencing and expressing their emotions to a moderate degree: "more than dismissing individuals but less than preoccupied ones" (Shaver & Tancredy, 2001, p. 80). Furthermore, they would "be able to provide a coherent account of their loss-related experiences (unlike unresolved/disorganized individuals)" (Shaver & Tancredy, 2001, p. 80).

It became evident that these predictions fit the DPM extremely well (for further detail, see M. S. Stroebe, Stroebe, & Schut, 2005a). Secure individuals would be able to oscillate more easily between loss and restoration orientation and would not suffer complications in their grieving, harrowing though their loss may be for them too. Anxious–ambivalent, preoccupied individuals might be more exclusively loss oriented and display more chronic forms of grieving. Dismissing individuals would tend to be the most restoration oriented, delaying and inhibiting their grief, whereas unresolved–disorganized individuals would have a more disturbed, less coherent manner of oscillating between these orientations.

Thus, this extension of the DPM provides not just a description of types of coping that are (mal)adaptive, but a suggestion as to how these patterns are related to styles of attachment. We are beginning to understand what adaptive coping is at a theoretical level, to be able to identify personal and situational factors that contribute to adaptation, and to move toward theoretical integration. Some evidence for the connections between attachment style and coping with bereavement already exists, much of it relating to attachment among older bereaved persons (e.g., Bradley & Cafferty, 2001; Hays, Gold, & Pieper, 1997; Jacobs et al., 1987–1988; Sable, 1989, 1991; Wayment & Vierthaler, 2002). Further research is currently under way to examine the links between the DPM and attachment styles in bereavement (see M. S. Stroebe et al., 2005a).

THE DUAL PROCESS MODEL IN BROADER PERSPECTIVE: AN INTEGRATIVE FRAMEWORK FOR PREDICTING ADJUSTMENT TO BEREAVEMENT

It is important that theory development on coping be kept in proper perspective. The topics addressed thus far in this volume have covered a range of variables and processes associated with adaptation to bereavement. We continue to show in forthcoming chapters that a broad range of factors, over and above coping, contribute to bereavement outcomes. We have proposed a framework for the prediction of bereavement outcomes, which we call the *integrative risk factor framework* (referred to hereinafter as the *integrative framework*; see Figure 3.3; M. S. Stroebe, Folkman, Hansson, & Schut, 2006). Our aim has been to provide order and suggest cause–effect relationships that can be, and sometimes have been, examined through empirical research. The variables described in the integrative framework include the nature of the bereavement stressor, resources, protective and risk factors, coping processes, and health consequences. The framework builds on a schematic description by Lazarus and Folkman (1984), which was formulated within cognitive stress theory (see also Folkman, 2001, for application to bereavement). As such, it identifies the nature of the stressor (Category A in Figure 3.3)—in our case, bereavement—as an event that signals change or threat: "Psychological stress is a particular relationship between the person and the environment that is appraised by the individual as taxing or exceeding his or her resources and endangering his or her well-being" (Lazarus & Folkman, 1984, p. 19). Thus, the extent of stress experienced, which will have an impact on outcome (Category E), depends neither solely on the intra- and interpersonal demands of the situation nor on the intra- and interpersonal resources (Categories B and C) but on the relationship between such demands and resources. The person appraises the personal significance of the event and the options for coping (Category D). Coping is understood as "constantly changing cognitive and behavioral efforts to manage specific external and/or internal demands that are

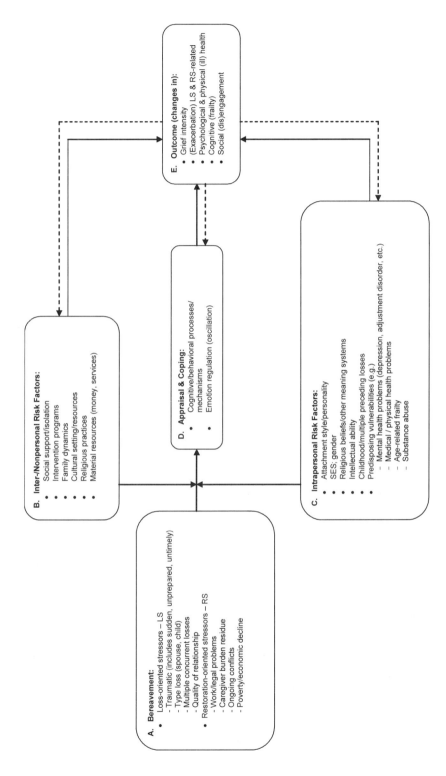

Figure 3.3. The integrative risk factor framework for the prediction of bereavement outcome. SES = socioeconomic status.

appraised as taxing or exceeding the resources of a person" (Lazarus & Folkman, 1984, p. 14).

Various parameters of the DPM are evident in this general integrative framework. For example, following the DPM, coping will entail alternation between appraising and dealing with (Category D) stressors (Category A) related to the loss of the deceased (loss orientation), and also to those changes that are indirect consequences of the death, such as a drop in income (restoration orientation). Likewise, consequences or outcomes of bereavement (Category E) cover aspects of the loss itself (e.g., increase or decrease in grief intensity) and of secondary stressors (e.g., withdrawal from or reintegration in social activities). In this way, the framework is easily able to incorporate a wider range of outcome variables than health variables (a restriction in previous studies noted earlier in this chapter). We believe that each of the other theories listed in Table 2.1 can be discussed within this integrative framework too. For example, the attachment approach would be useful in the specification of intrapersonal resources–risks (Category C), whereas family systems theory (Nadeau, 1998, 2001) would be useful in addressing interpersonal resources–risks (Category B). Furthermore, the framework is applicable across a variety of cultures (we saw this to be a shortcoming of previous formulations), particularly through the specification of societal–cultural factors in Category B.

In particular, with this integrative framework, we have tried to advance the notion that factors relating to adjustment cannot be evaluated in isolation; they need to be understood in relationship to one another. For example, coping will entail oscillation between appraising and dealing with both loss and restoration types of stressors. Likewise, as previously noted, consequences or outcomes of bereavement (Category E) cover aspects concerning the loss itself (e.g., increase or decrease in grief intensity) and concerning restoration (e.g., withdrawal from or reintegration in social activities).

Much research still needs to be done to find out whether and how all of the listed variables are related to bereavement outcome (we compiled the list of factors from variables mentioned in the bereavement research literature), to establish their relative impact on adjustment to bereavement and to see how much variance in reactions can be accounted for. Nevertheless, the integrative framework provides a structure for making sense of the wide variety and types of factors associated with bereavement adaptation. In subsequent chapters of this volume, we often revisit the framework as a conceptual foundation for understanding the bereavement experience of older adults.

CONCLUSIONS

We have seen in this chapter that the DPM addresses the limitations of earlier theories in a number of ways. The three basic components—loss orientation, restoration orientation, and oscillation—further our understanding of healthy grieving as an ongoing, active, fluctuating process that incorporates avoidance as well as confrontation with aspects to do with loss and change. In line with this, denial processes are seen as—sometimes and to some extent—conducive to adjustment, just as positive affect and (re)appraisal are seen as important additional elements to the negative affect and (re)appraisal that are fundamental to grieving.

We noted earlier a predominance in the literature of intraindividual, rather than interpersonal, approaches to coping with bereavement. The DPM lends itself to interpersonal analysis. For example, one would expect to find different grieving profiles (e.g., comparing them with respect to orientations and oscillation in Figures 3.1 and 3.2) for a grieving father compared with a grieving mother. Discrepant patterns of grieving (e.g., if one partner were more loss oriented than the other) could affect the outcomes for both partners. In fact, preliminary evidence has been provided in a study of bereaved parents by Dijkstra et al. (1999), who showed that perceived discordance (in terms of loss vs. restoration orientation) was negatively related to mental health and marital quality among bereaved parents.

It is a strength of the approach that the DPM accommodates consideration of a range of individual and subgroup differences in a way that traditional theories would find more difficult. For example, we are able to specify predicted attachment-style differences that should influence coping with loss of a loved person. Furthermore, gender and cultural differences are more easily understood within the DPM framework; we should expect variations reflecting subcultural and cross-cultural norms about healthy grieving to be reflected in ways of coping. Some people and some cultures will be more versus less loss or restoration oriented (e.g., men are likely to be more restoration oriented in traditional Western culture), but only if there is extreme adherence to one orientation, at the expense of attending to the other, would we predict grief (and perhaps general health) complications.

The specifications previously summarized may be useful for practitioners and clinicians, encouraging a focus on individual differences in grieving. In contrast to the underlying principle of furthering grief work, they emphasize the need for a focus on different patterns of going about grieving, attention to both loss and restoration orientations, and a need for "time-off" from grieving.

We have also seen that the DPM can be placed within the broader perspective of an integrative framework to predict adjustment to bereavement. This extension provides a more comprehensive framework for understanding individual differences in adaptation, including not only the different types of stressors and coping variables that featured prominently in the DPM but also intra- and interpersonal risk factors and a variety of outcome variables. As we show in later chapters, this framework enables us to highlight the unique nature of the bereavement experience among older persons.

It also furthers examination of the impact of different factors in combination and, potentially, it permits assessment of the relative strength of different variables in accounting for individual differences in adaptation. The focus of the framework is on assessing risk (given that bereavement is associated with negative health consequences). However, it will become evident that bereavement among older adults is associated with much that is positive: Older persons have many resources and also show resilience (in a sense, such aspects reflect "the other side of the coin," denoting low risk). It is hoped that researchers will be able to examine parameters of the framework more systematically in the future, to confirm validity.

In the chapters that follow, we begin to explore the nature of bereavement among older adults, patterns of outcome, and age-related variables and processes that appear to make a difference. Then, in the concluding chapter of the book, we revisit the DPM and the integrative framework, to consider their potential application in understanding coping with bereavement among older adults. We examine, for example, ways in which a late-life developmental perspective can be integrated into the dynamics of the DPM (e.g., to accommodate maturation; late-life tasks of development; and developmental changes in cognitive, emotional, and physical status). At the same time, examining the bereavement experience among this particular population will allow us an opportunity to consider the need to extend the spectrum of coping demands specified in the DPM to reflect coping tasks characteristic of late life. Are the coping tasks characteristic of late life—the specific demands that are placed on older adults when they become bereaved—well enough represented in the DPM?

4

AGING AND BEREAVEMENT: INTRODUCTION

Over the years, considerable attention has focused on the impact of aging on bereavement. Perhaps the earliest question of interest to clinical practitioners involved the role of age as a potential risk factor for poor outcome. But more complex questions began to be asked as well. Does aging influence the configuration of emerging grief symptoms, their intensity or expected duration, or the likelihood of longer term complications? Why might symptom patterns vary at different ages? Might aging at some point begin to tip the balance of physical and psychological symptoms more in the direction of the physical? What risk (and protective) factors associated with aging or circumstances in which older adults find themselves might be most relevant?

A number of possibilities were raised. Increased physical frailty among older persons was viewed to increase vulnerability to physical outcomes. Older individuals might also be expected to experience bereavement overload, because in old age, there is heightened risk for multiple and sequential losses of loved family and friends (Kastenbaum, 1969; Moss, Moss, & Hansson, 2001; Parkes, 2001a). In addition, a more general cumulative negative effect might be expected, because of the occurrence of bereavements in close proximity to a wider range of stressful events associated with old age (infirmity, relocation, financial concerns, etc.).

In contrast, the case has also been argued for increased psychological resilience among older bereaved persons. Might successful adaptation to past losses actually lead to the development of a worldview and concept of self that could facilitate adaptation to later losses (Hansson, Remondet, & Galusha, 1993; Wortman & Silver, 1992)? Or might the circumstances of the death advantage older bereaved persons? We have seen (in chap. 1, this volume), for example, that causes of death change across the life span. In the case of spousal bereavement, at least, an older deceased spouse is more likely to have passed away peacefully, after a long and fulfilling life, in contrast to a traumatic, unexpected loss more frequently experienced at younger ages. On the basis of such considerations, a more successful adaptation would, in general, seem more likely for older persons. The impact should be less severe and less enduring, and there should be lower risk of long-term effects.

It is unsurprising, therefore, that theorists and researchers have also differed considerably in their conclusions regarding the existence or likely direction of age differences in bereavement. Bowlby (1980), in his classic *Attachment and Loss* series (Vol. 3, *Loss: Sadness and Depression*), dismissed the importance of conducting age (and gender) comparisons, arguing on the basis of generally low correlations between age and the likelihood of complicated grief that age was not really a risk factor. In a similar manner, Lund, Caserta, and Dimond (1993) concluded on the basis of their extensive research on the bereavement experience among persons age 50 years and older that age "did not predict any of the major indicators of adjustment" (p. 249). Sanders (1989) also concluded from her review of the research on risk factors that age, per se, was not a significant factor.

Other investigators have argued that younger bereaved persons are actually at higher risk for negative outcomes compared with their older counterparts. Parkes (2001a) concluded in his overview of research on bereavement that early bereavements are more often associated with unpreparedness and a sense of untimeliness or tragedy, and that consistent with such observations it is younger widows, for example, who experience a greater need for medical attention or medications. He noted, however, the complexity of such age relationships: Whereas younger widows appear to experience reactions of greater intensity, among older persons multiple loss experiences (including loss of loved ones) may in part account for longer periods of depression.

In a more extensive review of 13 studies on age and bereavement outcomes, Archer (1999) concluded that in those studies in which there were indications of age differences, grief appeared more intense among younger persons, attributable to the perceived untimeliness and unexpectedness of the death. Finally, in a comprehensive review of bereavement risk factors (including age) for both mortality and morbidity outcomes, W. Stroebe and

Schut (2001) concluded, "It is the younger age groups who suffer more severe health consequences as a result of bereavement" (p. 361).

We have, then, quite a range of viewpoints from available research and clinical observation. Some scholars conclude that there are few or no age differences in risk for negative outcome, others argue that younger bereaved persons are at greater risk. Few, however, argue that older adults are at greater risk. How, then, to reconcile such divergent conclusions? We devote the next several chapters of this volume to bereavement research on older adults in an effort to explicate important developmental process and contextual variables characteristic of late-life bereavement experience. Many questions and some answers will result from that analysis. However, the reader should probably understand the source of an important concern in much of the earlier research on age differences in bereavement. The problem is that, even today, most bereavement researchers do not approach the analysis from a gerontological or developmental perspective. Little attention has been paid to the heterogeneity of older populations. Thus, it is not widely understood that age, per se, is actually a poor proxy for vulnerability to stress, illness, or bereavement. In a similar way, age is a poor proxy for recuperative or adaptive potential. In this context, age has not been viewed as important to investigate, and investigators have often simply controlled for it statistically rather than trying to understand its impact. When older bereaved persons are studied, little attention is paid to issues affecting the validity of assessments among older persons, to the increasing interconnections between psychological and physiological process in older persons, or to age-related changes in fundamental cognitive and emotion process at the core of the grief experience. That said, it remains useful to consider the available empirical research to give the reader a sense for its scope and validity and to provide a starting point in the effort to understand bereavement in late life.

In the following sections of this chapter, we examine research comparing older and younger bereaved adults with respect to mental and physical health, and with respect to risk for mortality. We also discuss a number of important conceptual and methodological problems associated with this body of research. Understanding the contributions (and limitations) of the research on age-group comparisons is essential to evaluating the literature to be presented in subsequent chapters on bereavement outcomes and process in older persons.

RESEARCH ON GRIEF REACTIONS AND PSYCHOSOCIAL AND PHYSICAL HEALTH OUTCOMES

Some studies have explicitly set out to examine age differences, others have simply included age as a variable of interest in a more comprehensive examination of risk factors. Outcomes of interest have also ranged across studies. Some have focused on symptomatology specific to grief, others have focused on more general (i.e., non-grief-specific) psychological symptoms such as depression and anxiety, on psychiatric illness or pathological forms of grief, or on physical ill health. Still others have focused on contextual factors in vulnerability, such as deficits in social support. Considered individually, many of these studies were limited in the scope of outcomes assessed. When viewed as a group, there is also a concern that most of the studies focused primarily on current mental or physical symptoms. This narrowness of scope has critical implications for understanding the breadth of bereavement reactions, especially in later life.

Studies have also varied from short-term to long-term investigations of bereavement consequences, and from cross-sectional to longitudinal, involving prospective or retrospective designs. Some of the studies involve only small samples, whereas others present analyses of large-scale, epidemiological (often national) statistics. Most of the studies are on bereaved spouses, but a few investigate bereavement following the loss of other familial relationships as well.

The majority of studies in which a younger and an older age group are compared find more intense grief and more adjustment problems among the younger than the older bereaved. Yet, a number of issues emerge regarding the generalizability of such a conclusion. One such issue reflects the common practice of comparing only two age groups, precluding examination of curvilinear trends. The importance of this issue can be seen in a study by Perkins and Harris (1990), which found the impact of bereavement to be strongest among middle-aged (compared with younger or older) individuals. This finding raises a new concern, however, in that it was one of only a minority of studies in which all types of familial bereavement were included, and not just widow(er)hood (W. Stroebe & Schut, 2001). The weaker effects among the younger group could be due to the relatively high proportion of parent deaths in this group and the higher likelihood in middle-age of losing a spouse or child, which has a greater impact (Leahy, 1992).

Another interesting question raised early on concerned the possibility that younger and older bereaved persons might experience different constellations of reactions. The classic study by Parkes (1964, 1972/1996), for example, observed more psychological symptoms among the younger bereaved but more physical symptoms among the older bereaved. This very important finding is consistent with recent gerontological research on responses to life stress generally, which is discussed in detail in later chapters of this volume.

It is also a concern that many of the most important earlier studies provided no information regarding age differences in bereavement reactions for men compared with women. Many of these studies included only widows (e.g., Ball, 1976–1977; Campbell, Swank, & Vincent, 1991; Maddison & Walker, 1967; Sable, 1991; Vachon et al., 1982; Zisook & Shuchter, 1986). This limits the conclusions about the comparative impact of age on bereaved men compared with women; are findings of heightened impact among the young equally valid for bereaved men and women?

We noted, previously, that most studies have examined spousal loss. Not only does this exclude the growing number of nonmarried partnerships but also other relationships, such as loss of other family members or friends (which are highly significant relationships among older adults; Blieszner & Roberto, 2004). For example, studies of parental loss of a child across the life span are sparse. In this connection, Rubin (1993) reviewed his own and others' research on grieving parents, which included a broad range of age groups among the bereaved parents, both in Israel and in the United States. Rubin (1993) reported that younger parents seem better able than older parents to adapt to the loss of a child, concluding that

> [a]ll parents are changed by the experience, but it is the younger parents who appear less overwhelmed and better able to integrate the loss into a still flexible life structure. Developmentally, older parents appear less resilient and less able to emerge from the severe dislocation of loss of a child. Physiologically and psychologically, consciously and unconsciously, older parents often experience the death of an adult child as one of the most dominant themes and preoccupations of their later life. (p. 299)

We should note, however, that not all researchers agree with Rubin (1993). Some have found grief of heightened intensity among younger parents (cf. de Vries, Lana, & Falck, 1994). Subsequent studies should control for the confounding factor of age of the child, and for cause of death, to further examine these discrepancies (Wijngaards-de Meij et al., 2005). Duration of symptoms was taken into account in only a few of the earlier studies, although it is at the core of our understanding of the nature and course of bereavement. Two studies, however, illustrate the kinds of questions that might be raised. In a longitudinal study spanning 30 months, Thompson, Gallagher-Thompson, Futterman, Gilewski, and Peterson (1991) found that younger bereaved persons appear to have stronger grief reactions soon after loss, whereas problems for older bereaved may be longer drawn out (e.g., Thompson et al., 1991). In contrast, however, McCrae and Costa (1993) concluded from their longitudinal analysis of health and psychosocial functioning (with a 10-year follow-up) that "Widowhood does not appear to have any enduring effect on psychosocial functioning in older men or women" (p. 204). They did find moderate longer term effects among younger widows (although there were too few younger widowers for separate analyses). Such findings suggest a need for investigations of the course of bereavement spanning not only months but also years postloss. Much of the early research on age differences, however, used cross-sectional designs, providing only a single snapshot picture of one's grief and failing to detect any differences between age groups that might be related to duration (e.g., that younger and older persons may adjust at different rates across the months and years following a bereavement). The good news is that comprehensive, longitudinal research is now being conducted; we describe this in later chapters.

More basic methodological shortcomings also cloud interpretation of some studies. For example, some investigators did not include nonbereaved older and younger control groups. This is particularly important, because when the outcomes assessed in bereavement studies reflect general emotionality, psychological health, or physical health, care must be taken to distinguish between expected effects of bereavement and the separate or interactive effects of aging. Including younger and older nonbereaved controls provides the needed baseline rates for such comparisons. For example, if younger persons are in general more emotionally expressive (a finding that is supported by gerontological research to be reviewed in a later chapter), might that artificially inflate their scores on grief-specific measures? It is clear that no comparison of bereaved and nonbereaved individuals' responses is possible when grief-specific measures are used, leaving a problem of interpretation. Such assessment problems, then, suggest a need for multiple-measure strategies and for the inclusion of control groups. There is reason, also, to broaden assessments to include the context of the death and to consider relevant circumstances prior to the death. For example, as we noted in chapter 1, there are important age-related differences reflected in causes of death, with the deaths of younger persons tending to involve greater trauma. Predeath and cause-of-death variables were seldom assessed in the earlier studies but have been included in some recent studies, to be discussed in a later chapter.

Age Patterns in Bereavement and Mortality

Studies of the mortality of bereaved persons across the adult age groups complement and to some extent overcome the shortcomings of the studies on psychosocial and physical health (see M. S. Stroebe & Stroebe, 1993, for a review). Control groups (e.g., widowed to married) are typically included, and samples are large. Most, though not all, of this research has focused on spousal bereavement.

Early analyses of national, cross-sectional statistics by Shurtleff (1955) and others (see Kraus & Lilienfeld, 1959) showed excessive rates of widowed mortality compared with those for age- and sex-matched married individuals. In addition, they showed a relatively higher risk of death among younger widows and widowers compared with their older counterparts. The pattern seems even more extreme for widowers than for widows, younger widowers being at the highest risk of all groups, even compared with other marital status groups.

There are, however, limitations to interpretation in these large-scale cross-sectional mortality surveys as well. As in the morbidity studies, confounding artifacts could at least partly account for the patterns previously described (Kraus & Lilienfeld, 1959; M. S. Stroebe & Stroebe, 1993). For example, younger and healthier widowed persons remarry more frequently than older or unhealthier widowed persons, so that the younger widowed category becomes composed of less healthy individuals (and that pattern would be reflected at time of measurement). Age at widow(er)hood has an even more detrimental effect on widows' than widowers' remarriage chances (Wu, 1995). Given these selection patterns, excess mortality rates among the younger widowed may in part reflect differential selection of the fittest out of the widowed and into the married category. Remarriage among widowed persons has been found to be associated with better health status and longevity (K. Smith, Zick, & Duncan, 1991). Unfortunately, cross-sectional surveys do not provide information about the duration of bereavement or the implications of remarriage (early on or later) for mortality risk.

Cause of death can also be a confounding factor in studies of bereavement-related mortality. We have seen (in chap. 1, this volume) that younger people more frequently die from accidents compared with their older counterparts. This raises the possibility that both members of a couple may have been involved in the same accident. Should one partner survive the accident just a little longer than the other before dying from sustained injuries, he or she will be classified within the "widowed" marital status, and his or her death inappropriately attributed to this widowed status. It is thus important in mortality studies to obtain cause of death for both partners.

Longitudinal surveys have overcome many of the artifacts present in cross-sectional surveys in that they can incorporate into analyses such variables as age and health at time of widow(er)hood, as well as remarriage events. Such surveys have provided additional information on age patterns in mortality among the bereaved, particularly with regard to the duration of bereavement and mortality. Here, too, most surveys have focused on conjugal bereavement. Results generally support the patterns observed in the cross-sectional studies. The majority of studies have found excessive mortality rates among bereaved persons compared with nonbereaved controls, though not necessarily for all subgroups. In addition, these studies have identified the recently bereaved as those most at risk (Martikainen & Valkonen, 1996; Parkes, Benjamin, & Fitzgerald, 1969; M. S. Stroebe & Stroebe, 1993).

Although not always reaching statistical significance, the large-sample studies show excess mortality among the younger widowed (e.g., Helsing & Szklo, 1981; Jones & Goldblatt, 1987; Kaprio, Koskenvuo, & Rita, 1987; Mellström, Nilsson, Oden, Rundgren, & Svanborg, 1982; Schaefer, Quesenberry, & Wi, 1995). The smaller numbers involved in the younger age groups, in which mortality is a rarer event, may have precluded attainment of statistical significance in many studies.

In the first of the large-scale longitudinal studies, Helsing and Szklo (1981; see also Helsing, Comstock, & Szklo, 1982; Helsing, Szklo, & Comstock, 1981) examined mortality among a sample (N = 4,032) of widows and widowers between the ages of 18 and 75-plus years in the United States, matching it with married spouses. They found the relative risk of mortality for bereaved spouses to be higher in the younger age groups, although this did not reach significance. Significant excesses for widowers 55 to 64 and 65 to 74 years of age were found. Nonsignificant excesses for younger widowers and widows under age 65 were found in the second year. It is noteworthy, given the selection artifact previously described, that mortality rates for widowers who remarried were much lower than among those who did not remarry, whereas no significant differences were observed between widows who did or did not remarry.

In a study in the United Kingdom, Bowling (1988; Bowling & Charlton, 1987) based mortality analyses on the total population figures from English life tables (N = 503). In this study, significantly higher mortality rates were found in the first 6 months for widowers age 75+, whereas no significant effects were found for younger widowers and for older or younger widows.

Manor and Eisenbach (2003) also reported trends by age for mortality after spousal loss. Their study, conducted in Israel, used death records from 1983 through 1992 and identified 4,402 men and 11,114 women who became widowed. The typical pattern of excess mortality in the first 6 months of bereavement was observed (about 50% excess for women, 40% for men). Although risk was relatively excessive for all the bereaved across the age groups, among men it declined linearly with age, whereas for women it varied little across the age range (from 50 to 79 years).

Quite a few studies have now found a relatively higher mortality risk for widowers compared with widows, relative to their same-sex, nonbereaved controls (for a review, see M. S. Stroebe, Stroebe, & Schut, 2001), and it seems likely—following the patterns found in most studies—that younger widowers are a particularly high-risk group. Few studies, however, have investigated the gender by age interaction as Manor and Eisenbach (2003) did, and it is also possible that some curvilinear relationships have gone undetected.

A few mortality studies have focused specifically on suicide among younger and older bereaved persons. These studies, too, underscore the potentially devastating impact of bereavement. For example, Luoma and Pearson (2002) found highly excessive suicide rates of widowed compared with other marital statuses in a study in the United States. National suicide mortality data were analyzed from the years 1991 to 1996, for 5-year age groups. Replicating findings of earlier studies (Buda & Tsuang, 1990; Kreitman, 1988; J. Smith, Mercy, & Conn, 1988), these investigators found particularly high rates for young widows and widowers. Studies on aging and mortality, and on aging and bereavement-related suicide, are discussed in more detail in the next chapter.

Summarizing the Age-Difference Studies

Accumulating studies on age differences in bereavement, not available to earlier reviewers, now permit a more extensive evaluation of early assumptions in the field. We have noted certain shortcomings within much of the research and gaps in knowledge in general. We describe in the sections that follow some of the most important conceptual and methodological issues that should be addressed in future research.

Conceptual Issues

Studies across a broad range of psychosocial and physical health indices and on mortality show with reasonable consistency that younger bereaved persons—at least spouses—are more vulnerable to the consequences of losing a loved one than are their older counterparts. Yet, there remain important questions regarding how to interpret age-related patterns (reflecting a lack of attention to the heterogeneity of older populations, to age-related changes in life circumstances and coping resources, etc.). In addition, an interaction of age and gender has been found in a number of different studies: Younger widowers seem the most highly vulnerable group among the widowed; however, there remain unresolved questions about the possibility of curvilinear relationships. There is cause for concern regarding the impact of bereavement on the health and well-being of all bereaved persons, older as well as younger (and for other relationships too, such as parents). It must also be remembered that age and health are negatively related. Even if older adults are relatively less affected by bereavement, they are *in general* more vulnerable, and they will, in considerable numbers, experience the wide range of debilities previously described. They will enter a bereavement from a more problematic health baseline.

We noted in the introduction to this chapter two competing assumptions regarding the bereavement reactions of older persons: that age-related vulnerabilities and the potential for bereavement overload might increase their risk for poor outcome, and that older adults might prove resilient, given a lifetime of experience in coping with life stressors. The studies discussed in this chapter (for the most part, simple age-group comparisons) appear more consistent with the latter of the two assumptions but provide little insight regarding age-related mechanisms, protective factors, or risk factors. We devote the remaining chapters of the book, therefore, to those issues. In chapter 5, we provide a comprehensive and critical review of current bereavement outcome research with older bereaved persons. In chapter 6, we examine the research on mechanisms and contextual factors related to bereavement outcomes among older persons. In chapters 7 and 8, respectively, we review current gerontological theory and research pertinent to understanding *protective developmental processes* (and resilience) and *problematic age-related processes* (and risk for poor outcome).

Methodological Issues

The studies reviewed in this chapter provided information about many phenomena associated with bereavement. Perhaps most important, they testify to the wide range of negative consequences, given the loss of a loved one. Despite the value of many individual studies and the body of research as a whole, however, conclusions drawn from simple age-group comparisons are of questionable validity and limited usefulness. We have already noted some concerns. But a few others are worth mentioning here.

Many of the early studies reviewed used only a limited range of outcome variables, overlooking the potential role of bereavement (in later life) in the longer term processes of disablement, cognitive decline, economic decline, and social disengagement, as well as the potential for adaptive coping process. Also, variables studied have seldom been derived from a systematic theoretical framework. In particular, much of the empirical research on age differences in bereavement has not yet incorporated a developmental perspective. For example, we describe research, in chapter 7, demonstrating age-related differences (in adulthood) in capacity for self-regulation. Older adults appear to exhibit greater emotional control, mood stability, and emotional maturity, and such differences could affect one's feeling, expression, and communication of the emotions incorporated in grief. Failing to incorporate such a developmental perspective in bereavement research, then, makes it difficult to establish how much of the variance in bereavement reactions is due to age-related person or situation variables.

It is also a core principle, among gerontological researchers, that age is a poor proxy for either vulnerability or adaptive potential. Many of the outcome variables that have been associated with bereavement tend to exhibit increasing individual differences with increasing age. In fact, there is often greater variability within an age group than between age groups on factors such as psychological vulnerability, physical status, social status, social engagement, economic security, and the degree of emotional or social disorganization caused by a death. Within older populations, more specifically, there are vast differences in successful aging. Some older persons retain high status, resources, and potential (Rowe & Kahn, 1997); relational competence (Hansson, Daleiden, & Hayslip, 2004); and coping strategies (Freund & Baltes, 2002). The more important issue, then, would involve how these variables interact with bereavement among older persons rather than in comparison with younger persons.

Studies of age differences have also often failed to examine the contexts in which bereavement is experienced. Are there differences between age groups, for example, with respect to access to social support or in cultural tradition? As we discuss in chapter 6, the contexts of bereavement are often different for older and younger persons. Does it matter that most younger widowed persons work, whereas their older counterparts are mostly retired? Further differentiation on this point can be made with respect to gender differences in bereavement. For example, Lund and Caserta (2001) suggested that elevated bereavement distress among men in their 70s (compared with bereaved older women) may reflect concurrent stress associated with the adjustment to retirement. There is an emerging consensus that older and younger adults may respond in similar ways to stress but that they are frequently called on to cope with different kinds of life stressors, including those stressors associated with bereavement (Lazarus, 1996). Our discussions of the dual process model of coping with bereavement (in chap. 9, this volume) further explore the nature of contextual stressors for younger and older bereaved adults.

Other selection biases in sampling also introduce a confound when interpreting the research previously reviewed. One such issue involves the purposeful exclusion of institutionalized individuals from the sample. This is also an issue in many large public health and epidemiological studies. It is likely that older widowed persons, being alone and frail, would be more likely than their younger counterparts (or still-married controls) to have entered institutions, thus eliminating from studies a large number of older widowed persons who would exhibit highly problematic mental and physical symptoms. A related issue in longitudinal studies concerns subject attrition. For example, Norris (1985) examined the characteristics of dropouts over the course of a longitudinal study among older adults and found that those in poor condition initially (well-being, health, social, and life event measures, etc.) were the ones to drop out. Attrition is also likely to be greater among the oldest respondents. These trends then threaten the validity of any comparisons of the experience of those older bereaved who do remain in a study (the healthiest and most adaptive of their age group) with a younger group of bereaved respondents (which presumably still includes its least healthy and adaptive members).

Many early studies of age and bereavement also failed to consider the importance of cohort or generational effects in limiting the generalizability of findings. Succeeding generations of older adults in Western cultures are now older, healthier, better educated, and wealthier, and such patterns are expected to continue. Our definitions of *old*, therefore, have had to change (to distinguish between young-old, middle-old, and very-old). The nature of family and social structure and the availability of support networks have evolved as well, with the modernization of societies. Likewise, health experience and causes of death have changed. Health experience in old age now reflects greater complexity, including chronic and progressive illness to be managed rather than cured. We therefore need to look beyond simple comparisons of younger versus older persons, and we need to be cautious about making generalizations from patterns found for earlier generations to predictions about patterns just a few decades later.

We raised the possibility of nonlinearity earlier in this chapter, with respect to bereavement outcomes. However, research on emotional experience across the life span adds broader insight into this issue. Carstensen, Pasupathi, Mayr, and Nesselroade (2000), for example, found that a curvilinear relationship best characterized certain aspects of emotional experience. She noted that by assessing emotion at only two age points (and often at different age points in different studies), individual researchers may have tapped different parts of a nonlinear trend across the life course. Inferences about linearity could thus be false and mask more complex, curvilinear relationships. A researcher's choice of age points to be compared is especially problematic if there is no theoretical basis for predicting precisely where along the life span the developmental changes in emotional experience are to be expected.

Finally, most early studies of age differences in grief failed to consider divergent patterns of grieving among younger and older adults (e.g., the possibility of "peaks" in grieving at different durations of bereavement, or different patterns of symptomatology or coping strategies). A recent focus in the field on mapping trajectories of grief over time (which vary across individuals and which may prove to vary across age groups) could advance our understanding in this respect (Bonanno et al., 2004). Bonanno and colleagues identified a variety of distinct patterns in depressive symptoms across time in bereaved older persons (it would be useful to extend this investigation to include grief-specific symptoms). Some survivors appeared resilient, some experienced severe depression that subsided by 18 months, some were not initially depressed but later experienced depression, some were chronically depressed before bereavement and suffered even higher intensities afterwards, and some, finally, were stressed caregivers who experienced relief after the death. Such findings again suggest that age comparisons are too simple and assume a degree of homogeneity within age groups that does not exist. These data (including more extended time analyses) are discussed in greater detail in chapter 6.

CONCLUSIONS

We must be cautious when drawing conclusions about the relative impact of bereavement on older versus younger persons. When conclusions are based on simple comparisons of grief intensity and symptomatology across a young sample and an old sample of bereaved persons, their validity must be questioned. We would argue that the question of *which* age group is at greater risk for poor outcome is not especially meaningful.

Originally, researchers had good reason to include the age variable in their studies. The early clinical literature sought to identify risk factors for poor bereavement outcome. It is time, however, to broaden the focus of our investigations. The more interesting and important questions for bereavement researchers, clinicians, and gerontologists concern how aging and bereavement interact to influence life outcomes, adaptive potential, coping, and successful aging.

The early research on aging and bereavement tended to be fragmented; it lacked integrative perspective and direction. We believe that a more fine-grained approach is needed, one that takes the experience of bereavement into account on the one hand and the complexities of the aging process on the other. In the following chapters we try to enhance our understanding of bereavement among older adults by viewing it within a coherent theoretical perspective on late-life development.

5

AGING AND BEREAVEMENT: OUTCOMES

Much of the empirical research on bereavement has focused on conjugal loss, an event that is associated with increasing age. Older bereaved persons have therefore been included in many of the studies that influenced thinking on the nature of bereavement in general. However, significant research on the specific implications of aging for bereavement began only in the 1980s.

In this chapter, we examine the research specific to older adults with respect to bereavement outcomes. We note those areas of outcome in which age appears to make a difference (and where it does not). We also address methodological confounds in some of the research, including measurement and sampling issues, changing symptomatology in old age, and so on. As the chapter unfolds, we also ask the reader to note four recurring themes. First, older persons are highly diverse in their reactions to bereavement. Second, they generally exhibit extraordinary resilience. Third, the context (circumstances) of an older person's bereavement is critical to understand and is likely to vary considerably from that of younger bereaved persons. And, finally, important insights have resulted from a broadening of assessment strategies when studying older persons (e.g., beyond the usual focus on clinical outcome measures).

DIVERSITY AMONG OLDER ADULTS

As they age, older people become increasingly heterogeneous as a group with respect to experience and adaptive potential. Human beings begin life with a unique genetic potential and then are differentially influenced by a lifetime of developmental and environmental factors. As a consequence, older populations tend to exhibit increased variability in physical and health status, vulnerability to stressors (including bereavement), adaptive reserves, and coping styles (Rowe & Kahn, 1987). Studies on older adults illustrate the issue of diversity in bereavement experience. Lund et al. (1993), for example, assessed symptoms and adaptive process in a group of bereaved persons (mean age of 67 years) across the 2 years following the death of a spouse and found a wide range of reactions, both in the short and longer term. Some respondents were devastated by the experience, whereas others seemed able to rise to the challenge, learn new coping and life skills, and make needed adjustments. There appeared also important instances of within-person diversity in the experience. For example, an older widow might acknowledge coping quite well in some areas of her life but continue to experience symptoms of loneliness or depression and a diminished ability to accomplish routine activities of daily living such as shopping.

Bonanno et al. (2004) examined the diversity of bereavement experience in a more formal manner, using prospective data on depressive symptoms, beginning prior to the death of a spouse. These researchers identified five bereavement patterns within their sample of bereaved older persons (mean age of 69 years). Respondents classified as being in the *common grief pattern* (11%) had low preloss depression scores but then experienced a grief-related increase in depressive symptoms, which then abated within 18 months. Those in the *resilient pattern* (46%) had low preloss depression scores and remained low throughout the 18 months. Those in the *chronic grief pattern* (16%) had low preloss depression scores that then increased at 6 and 18 months. Respondents in the *chronic depression pattern* (8%) had high preloss depression scores that remained high throughout the 18 months. Respondents in the *depressed-improved pattern* (10%) had high predeath depression scores that abated at 6 and 18 months. Subsequent analyses (Boerner, Wortman, & Bonanno, 2005) followed these groups out to 48 months postloss. The resilient and common grief groups continued to experience relatively low levels of depression out to 48 months, and the chronic grief group appeared to improve by 48 months. However, the chronic depression group continued to experience relatively high symptom levels, and the depressed-improved group began to exhibit elevated symptom levels.

RESILIENCE AMONG OLDER ADULTS

Older bereaved persons are likely to experience both emotional and physical distress. However, a majority of older bereaved adults also appear to be highly resilient, finding the resources with which to cope with their distress and adapt to their new circumstances. Lund, Caserta, and Dimond (1989, 1993), for example, found 82% of bereaved spouses reporting that they were managing their lives with some success at 2 years postloss in terms of health, life satisfaction, and available social support. In that research, 72% reported having learned important new skills since the loss, and only 12% sought professional help.

A qualitative study by P. S. Fry (1998) reinforced Lund's conclusions. Fry interviewed older bereaved men and women 4 months after the death of a spouse, and then again at 12 months. Content analyses of reported reactions at 4 months suggested emotional reactions commonly found in other bereaved populations. These included loneliness, yearning, feelings of pain and physical symptoms, self-blame, survivor guilt, a loss of meaning, disruptions of family activity patterns, loss of control, and so on. Follow-up interviews at 12 months postloss, however, focused on the bereaved persons' understanding of their own adaptations to the death and processes associated with recovery. Again, content analyses revealed theoretically interesting processes given respondents' ages, which ranged from 65 to 83 years, and the loss of a marriage that had endured for an average of 38 years. These involved a growing sense of one's potential and a process of self-discovery. Most respondents had adapted with some success, learning (or relearning) along the way their potential strengths and possibilities and gaining a degree of confidence. In addition, there appeared a growing sense of personal control and autonomy, as well as a growing motivation to extend personal gains and engage afresh in social interaction. As a continuing, realistic backdrop, however, there recurred occasional waves of emotional distress, feelings of confusion, loneliness, and depression.

CONTEXTS OF BEREAVEMENT IN OLD AGE

Bereavement research has most often focused on the personal (emotional, physical) consequences of a loved one's death. However, it is also critical to understand the contexts of bereavement in later life (e.g., the bereaved person's status and life circumstances). Among long-married women, for example, the death of a spouse may result in a degree of life disorganization and dislocation, reflecting a loss of meaningful social roles with their various rights and responsibilities, income, personal status, support systems, and opportunities for rewarding interaction. Availability of needed support, emotional and instrumental, may be constrained by support systems inappro-

TABLE 5.1
Percentage of Widowed Persons Age 65 or Older in the U.S.

Age (years)	Percentage widowed		
	Total	Men	Women
65+	31.6	14.3	44.3
65–74	20.0	8.8	29.4
75–84	39.3	18.4	53.3
85+	63.5	34.6	78.3

Note. Not including institutionalized persons. Adapted from *Older Americans 2004: Key Indicators of Well-Being* (p. 71), by the Federal Interagency Forum on Aging-Related Statistics, 2004, Washington, DC: U.S. Government Printing Office. In the public domain.

priate to one's needs, by a culture focused on couple-companionate relationships, or by the traditions of earlier generations in which women were not encouraged to develop skills for building relationships beyond the family. The transition from wife (the known) to widow (the unknown), therefore, can be highly stressful and, as might be expected, often results in loneliness (Lopata, 1993, 1996).

Further context is provided by the family circumstances of older persons. They are more likely to be women (see Table 5.1), many of whom live alone. They are unlikely to remarry. Many are childless, and given the importance of adult children to support systems in late life, these older persons are less likely to receive needed emotional or financial support (O'Bryant & Hansson, 1994).

In addition, the issues of death and bereavement seem more immediate for older persons. They will likely have experienced more deaths of family and friends. There is also the possibility that the grief experienced by older persons will be disenfranchised (Moss & Moss, 1989). This may occur when an older person's grief-related symptoms (e.g., loneliness, fatigue, somatic symptoms) are misattributed by others to old age. When the deceased is someone younger in the family (e.g., a grandchild), older family members may also be relegated to the role of secondary griever, as bereavement support focuses primarily on their adult children (Moss et al., 2001).

Their age and place in the family also expose older adults disproportionately to the death of an adult child, a sibling, or a grandchild (Moss & Moss, 1994). The loss of a child is widely viewed to elicit more intense and problematic grief, complicated by feelings of unfairness, survivor guilt, lost opportunities for generativity and legacy, and a realistic concern for the loss of one's own potential support network. Relationships with siblings represent a lifetime of shared meanings, identity, and experience. Yet, they are not always viewed as an attachment bereavement and may not elicit usual forms of support (Moss & Moss, 1994).

Such concerns have begun to stimulate bereavement research focused specifically on these relationships. For example, in a longitudinal study spanning 3 years, de Vries, Davis, Wortman, and Lehman (1997) examined the experience of men and women (mean age of 70 years) who had lost an adult child to death within the last 10 years. At both times of measurement, the bereaved parents reported significantly higher levels of depression compared with a sample of control participants. Reports of perceived physical health did not differ between the groups at the first measurement, but the health of the bereaved group worsened significantly at Time 2 compared with controls. Within the broader population of older persons who have lost a child, however, we should remain aware of cultural differences likely to affect the intensity and course of symptoms. It is instructive, for example, that Goodman, Rubenstein, Alexander, and Luborsky (1991) found older Jewish American women to experience greater symptoms of loneliness and depression and less of a sense of mastery and control after the death of a child. Such findings were interpreted to reflect a cultural tradition in which Jewish mothers remain intensely involved with, interdependent, and protective of even their adult children, and such a tradition makes it more difficult to achieve acceptance or perspective on the death.

Of related interest, a study of grandparents (mean age of 66 years) who had experienced the death of a grandchild identified a number of intriguing themes underlying grandparents' grief, themes that differentiate the experience from that of others in the family system (P. S. Fry, 1997). In addition to emotional distress, they experienced a sense of survivor guilt, regrets over not showing the deceased more love, and a need to restructure relationships with remaining family, especially remaining grandchildren (e.g., spending more time, having more personal emotional contact, sharing and reassuring often, becoming more tolerant).

OUTCOME STUDIES ON OLDER ADULTS

Bereavement outcome studies on older adults over the last three decades have generally paralleled those on younger persons. Studies have systematically assessed *nonclinical consequences*, to include personal functioning, loneliness, well-being, coping, personal control, social functioning, and social participation. They have also explored an array of *clinical consequences*, to include complicated or traumatic grief, depression, and suicide, as well as physiological health and mortality outcomes. Many of these studies are one-time, correlational analyses, but many are also longitudinal in their design, allowing insights into the course, development, and resolution of symptoms over time. Some of these studies are guided by theoretical concerns regarding the nature of the bereavement experience as it interacts with aging process. Other studies focus on issues of more immediate concern to practitioners. The comprehensive body of research, then, allows insights into the nature of the bereavement experience among older persons, but also a consideration of the similarities and differences in bereavement experience across the life span.

The Nature and Course of Bereavement Outcomes
Among Older Persons

Earlier studies often relied on the use of psychiatric and physical symptoms as indicators of bereavement-related distress. Subsequent research, however, has broadened and deepened our view into the consequences of bereavement among older persons. In particular, a number of longitudinal investigations have tried to delineate bereavement symptomatology among older persons, with an eye to person and situation variables that might influence adjustment and the efficacy of potentially useful intervention strategies. As we see in subsequent sections of this chapter, the implications of late-life bereavement can also include loneliness, social withdrawal, diminished health and nutritional behavior, economic and housing dislocation, and increasing dependency, both on family networks and on more formal institutions.

Lund et al. (1989), for example, examined the effects of spousal bereavement on well-being among bereaved men and women (in relation to a sample of matched, nonbereaved controls) over a 2-year period. Participants (mean age of 67 years) were assessed at six points in time using measures of depression, life satisfaction, and perceived health. At Time 1 (3–4 weeks postbereavement), there was a significant bereavement effect on depressive symptoms. Depression scores among the bereaved then decreased over each subsequent measurement over the next year and a half, with a small increase at the 24-month assessment. At Time 1, 16% of bereaved and 5% of controls reached clinical range. Of interest, however, is that at no time during the study did bereaved participants' depression scores return to the level of the control group. There were no significant bereavement effects for either life satisfaction or perceived health over the 2 years postloss.

Another longitudinal study of older adults (mean age of 68) who had recently lost a spouse illustrated a commonly found pattern of reactions (Gallagher-Thompson et al., 1993; Thompson et al., 1991). These researchers assessed grief-specific emotions, depression, mental health symptoms, physical symptoms, and mortality risk over a period of 30 months postbereavement. Compared with a sample of matched controls, bereaved respondents reported elevated levels of general psychological distress, grief-specific distress, and physical illness at 2 months postloss. For example, 30% of bereaved respondents reported experiencing mild to severe depression at 2 months postloss, but at 30 months that percentage had dropped to 18% (not significantly different from controls). By the end of the first year of bereavement, differences for symptoms of psychopathology and depression and for physical complaints were no longer significant. Scores for more specific grief symptoms, however, continued to be elevated throughout the 30 months. Mortality rates also suggested an increased mortality risk for widowed respondents, especially within the first year, and especially for male respondents. Gallagher-Thompson and colleagues identified a number of insights from this study, in addition to an apparent pattern for the time course in adjusting to loss of a spouse in old age. For example, it seems clear that time of measurement matters in comparing respondents or outcomes. It is important, also, to use a broad measurement strategy, with measures of general psychological and physical distress, but also grief-specific measures of emotional and cognitive symptoms. Finally, they proposed that theoretical formulations for bereavement should distinguish between grief-specific reactions and depressive reactions, as a successful resolution of general distress may nevertheless be accompanied by lingering aspects of the grief-specific symptoms.

Research by Byrne and Raphael (1994, 1997) addressed more directly the issue of how bereavement-specific symptoms would be associated with more general psychological symptoms over time. A sample of widowed men over age 65 was assessed at 6 weeks postdeath (Time 1), and then again at 6 months (Time 2) and 13 months (Time 3). Bereaved respondents completed a measure of bereavement-specific phenomena, as well as measures of depression, anxiety, loneliness, distress, somatic symptoms, insomnia, and social dysfunction. At first assessment, more than 75% of widowers reported characteristic grief symptoms (nostalgia, intrusive thoughts, sadness, preoccupation with the deceased, yearning, etc.). More than 50% of respondents also experienced crying, a sense of the presence of the deceased, searching for the deceased, and a desire to talk about the deceased. Of particular interest, however, at Time 1 a summary score of grief-specific symptoms was significantly related to depression, anxiety, distress, somatic symptoms, insomnia, and social dysfunction. Six months later, scores on the grief-specific symptoms remained significantly related only to anxiety, distress, insomnia, and social dysfunction. At 13 months, grief scores remained significantly related only to anxiety and distress. Over the 13 months, widowers reported significantly greater distress than a sample of matched, married controls. However, this effect reflected primarily their elevated anxiety scores (Byrne & Raphael, 1997).

A program of longitudinal research on older widows by Bennett (1997a, 1997b) raised a number of additional concerns, both methodological and conceptual. This research followed a sample of widows (mean age of 73 years) and a matched control sample of married women for a period of 8 years, with repeated assessments of anxiety–depression, life satisfaction, social engagement, and physical symptoms. At 4 years, compared with controls, the widows reported increased anxiety and depressive symptoms and lower life satisfaction but no change in levels of social engagement or satisfaction with their social networks. Both widows and controls had experienced significant increases in health symptoms and use of medications. At the 8-year follow-up, scores on the anxiety–depressive measure declined among widows but remained higher than married controls. Widows also continued to report lower life satisfaction. However, widowed status was unrelated to levels of social engagement or physical status. For all groups (and almost all were now over age 75), there was a main effect of time of measurement (over 8 years) on physical symptoms and status. In the context of this research, Bennett (1997b) suggested several important concerns with respect to interpreting assessment data from older persons. One concern, for example, is that a high percentage of older adults report elevated depressive symptoms, which may provide a floor effect for measured symptoms in the population. Also, there may be an increased risk among older persons that depressive and physical symptoms are even more closely linked than in younger populations, and that one may mask symptoms of the other. Furthermore, there is the general concern about confounds of aging, per se, in bereavement studies of older persons, in that some of the measured changes in older widows may simply reflect aging process. A related issue involves the time of assessment, when looking for short-term versus long-term effects, and the increased risk that any longer term effects among older persons are more likely to reflect aging process. Also, the increased risk of mortality among older populations, reflecting both aging and disease process, raises questions about selective dropouts from longitudinal studies. In Appendix A we provide a more detailed discussion of assessment issues among older persons and an introduction to the emerging literature on the development and validation of instruments specifically for older adults. One such instrument, the Geriatric Depression Scale (Sheikh & Yesavage, 1986), for example, directly addresses the need to remove the influence of physical symptoms from assessments of clinical depression.

Loneliness and Social Engagement

One of the most common and distressing consequences of conjugal bereavement in later life is loneliness. Unique emotional ties to the person lost, shared understandings and interaction patterns, and validation of one's self as worthy of love cannot easily be replaced (Lopata, 1996). Lopata found that older American widows in her studies experienced both emotional loneliness (for a specific attachment figure) and social (more general) loneliness. Of interest, however, these findings were not replicated in her subsequent studies of widows among non-Western cultures in which one's attachment to husband was less prominent and the extended family played a greater role (Lopata, 1996).

In their studies of older widows, Lund et al. (1993) also found loneliness to be the most commonly reported and most distressing consequence of the loss of a spouse. Reports of loneliness continued over 2 years, even among respondents who acknowledged being surrounded by supportive others.

A longitudinal study of loneliness by van Baarsen, van Duijn, Smit, Snijders, and Knipscheer (2001–2002), however, found considerable variability among older widowed men and women (mean age of 74 years) across a 2½-year period following their spouse's death. Approximately one third of respondents' emotional loneliness scores remained low and stable, one third ascended in the short run but then dropped to near baseline levels, and one third ascended in the short term but then continued rising across the 2½-year period of the study. To a smaller extent, such differences were found across time also with respect to social loneliness. For most respondents (70%), however, social loneliness remained fairly stable and low.

A longitudinal study by Utz, Carr, Nesse, and Wortman (2002) examined more directly the effect of widow(er)hood on the kinds of social participation that would be expected to ameliorate loneliness among older persons. This study assessed both informal social participation activities (e.g., visiting or calling friends and relatives) and formal social participation activities (e.g., volunteering, attending club meetings or religious services). Participation by widowed respondents was assessed at predeath baseline and again at 6 months postdeath and was compared with parallel assessments among a matched control group of still-married persons. Analyses indicated that the soon-to-be widowed group already had significantly lower levels of informal social participation at predeath baseline (associated with spouse's poor health and care needs), but after the death they appeared to reengage. There was, then, a significant increase in informal social participation compared with controls. Levels of formal social participation remained stable across time for both groups. Finally, among these older widowed persons there were interactions of marital status and income, education, and race, with persons of minority and lower socioeconomic status reporting less social participation.

Physical Health

Bereavement studies on older persons have broadly included assessments of physical health outcomes. However, many of these studies were limited in that they failed to account for prebereavement health status or the possible confounding effects (pre- or postloss) of medications (Murrell, Himmelfarb, & Phifer, 1988). This represents a huge oversight, because according to the Federal Interagency Forum on Aging-Related Statistics (2004), among noninstitutionalized American adults age 65 and older,

- 31% of men and 39% of women suffer from arthritis,
- 18% of men and 14% of women have diabetes,
- 25% of men and 18% of women have had cancer,
- 10% of men and 8% of women have suffered a stroke,
- 47% of men and 52% of women have hypertension,
- 37% of men and 27% of women have heart disease,
- 16% of men and 19% of women experience vision loss, and

- 18% of men and 31% of women have at least one chronic physical disability.

An older person's previous poor health status can present a coping deficit, with the potential to alter the course or effectiveness of adaptation to future life crises. This point was illustrated by Murrell et al. (1988) in their analyses of longitudinal data on older men and women (mean age of 67 years) who had experienced the death of a spouse, parent, or child. Assessments occurred at five points in time, at intervals of 6 months. The death occurred between assessments at Time 1 and Time 2. Respondents indicated the extent to which the death had changed their lives, the undesirability of that change, and the extent to which they experienced preoccupation with the death. Measures of health included a self-report index of symptoms, a checklist of the 10 most common serious health conditions among older persons, reports of new illness, reports of seeking medical services, and, where necessary, notation of the subject's own death. A general pattern of findings emerged across the subsequent health measures when regression analyses were used, accounting for predeath health status. In both the short and long term, once predeath health status was entered into the analysis, the bereavement impact measures made only negligible contributions to subsequent health experience. Thus, one's previous health status provided the strongest prediction of subsequent health. Finally, one further finding involved a trend to improved health over the 2½ years. The researchers speculate that this may reflect a period of poor predeath health reflecting the stress of dealing with the impending death of an attachment figure, after which improvement is possible with some degree of successful adaptation.

Researchers have also begun to examine the effects of bereavement on normally occurring functions important to long-term health. For example, Rosenbloom and Whittington (1993) investigated whether bereavement would be associated with nutritional problems, considered to play a critical role in the health of older persons. Widowed participants (mean age of 70 years), compared with matched married controls, experienced poorer appetites and less enjoyment of mealtimes (72% of the bereaved reported feelings of loneliness at mealtimes and also that eating had become a chore). Widows consumed a greater proportion of snacks with high fat or sugar content, and an assessment of their overall diet quality (by a registered dietician) was significantly lower. Widows were less likely than married controls to take nutritional supplements. As might be expected, then, the widows (only) reported significant unintentional weight loss. Of interest, also, widows completed the Grief Resolution Index (Remondet & Hansson, 1987), a brief measure of the extent to which they had adapted to the emotional distress specific to bereavement. Scores on this measure significantly predicted enjoyment of meals, diet quality, appetite, loss of interest in eating, and number of pounds lost.

The impact of late-life bereavement on social rhythm stability and sleep impairment has also been examined. Theory would suggest that losing a long-time spouse in late life can disrupt the level and timing of one's routine life activities and one's social and circadian rhythms. Such disruptions are typically associated with sleep impairment, with implications for physical and mental health. In this connection, L. F. Brown et al. (1996) compared the experience of three groups of widowed men and women, age 55 to 85 years (approximately 6 months postloss), and a sample of nonbereaved controls. The widowed groups had previously been classified as experiencing major depression, minor depression, or no depression. The control group exhibited no significant psychiatric disorder. Participants completed comprehensive psychiatric interviews and measures of sleep quality, social rhythm stability, and a 14-day sleep diary. Results indicated that problems with social rhythm stability and sleep quality increased across the four groups as depression scores increased. Brown et al. concluded from this cross-sectional data that spousal loss may be a factor in disruption of social rhythms and sleep patterns and in depression. Further insight is provided by longitudinal analyses of disrupted sleep and bereavement outcomes (S. J. Richardson, Lund, Caserta, Dudley, & Obray, 2003). Richardson and colleagues found that over a 2-year period postbereavement, widowed persons who experienced persisting sleep disruption also experienced greater difficulty in bereavement-related adjustment.

Researchers have also explored the role of bereavement in later life on the experience of physical pain. For example, Bradbeer, Helme, Yong, Kendig, and Gibson (2003) assessed pain experience among independently living adults (mean age of 73 years), including widowed persons. Pain measures focused on experience of activity-limiting pain, strength of one's most severe pain, and strength of current pain. A composite bereavement index reflected the length of one's widow(er)hood (from 1 to 30 years, with higher scores reflecting a more recent death of spouse). Finally, a composite index of mood disturbance was created from measures of depression, positive mood, and negative mood. Analyses indicated that recency of one's loss was significantly related to experiencing activity-limiting pain and experiencing moderate-to-severe current pain. Widowed persons were three times more likely to report current, strong pain, compared with persons of the other marital status groups. The researchers further hypothesized that the relationship between bereavement and pain experience would be mediated by current level of mood disturbance. This expectation was confirmed in a path analysis in which a direct path model (widow[er]hood $\rightarrow$ pain) accounted for only 1% of variance in pain severity, but an indirect model (widow[er]hood $\rightarrow$ mood disturbance $\rightarrow$ pain) accounted for 17% of variance in pain.

Mortality

Earlier in this chapter we noted findings of excess mortality following conjugal bereavement but also trends suggesting that older bereaved respondents were actually at less risk compared with younger persons (M. S. Stroebe & Stroebe, 1993). Of interest, also, is that causes of death among the very old, at least, are more likely to reflect normative patterns of age-related physiological decline and disease process, leaving little variance to be accounted for by events such as bereavement. For example, Bowling (1994) assessed over 500 men and women in England (39% under age 70, 61% age 70 and older, and over 15% age 80 or older). Participants were interviewed approximately 5 months after the loss of a spouse, with follow-ups at 2 years, 5 years, and 13 years to determine length of survival and mortality. At 13 years, 62% of respondents were themselves deceased. For the overall sample, at 11 years, death rates were not significantly different from the expected rates by age and sex for the population of England. Among those who died in that period, causes of death generally reflected the causes of their spouses' deaths, which also paralleled the experience of the broader population. Mortality in the sample was associated with increasing age (being an older man or woman), gender (being a younger or an older male), and functional health (measured at 6 months postloss). The oldest men (age 75+) were at greatest risk (and were at continued risk out to 6 years). Self-ratings of health at 6 months predicted length of survival within the 13-year period but did not predict mortality. Bowling speculated that this reflects a diminished sensitivity among deaths occurring later in the 13-year period (by which time many of the very old respondents were nearing death from causes not directly related to their bereavement). In a similar way, those bereaved persons judged by interviewers to be depressed at the 6-month assessment were more likely to die within the first 2 years. Also, those judged to have experienced some relief by the death (e.g., from caregiving burdens) were less likely to die within 2 years. These associations were not significant over longer periods of time, and they were no longer significant when analyses controlled for age and sex. These findings are consistent with results of McCrae and Costa's (1993) longitudinal study, described earlier, in which mortality among widowed persons after 10 years was significantly related to age, gender, and level of education but not to having become widowed.

Interpreting mortality rates in late life, then, is enormously complex, given a concern that mortality predictors may become less stable over longer periods of time. Meinow, Kareholt, Parker, and Thorslund (2004) examined the predictive validity of mortality risk factors over time among a Swedish sample of 421 older adults. Respondents were age 75 or older (in 1986) when they participated in a comprehensive assessment on health, demographic, and psychosocial variables. The date of each respondent's death over the next 15 years was available from public records. Analyses then focused on length of survival after baseline assessment, allowing the calculation of relative risk of death (associated with any given predictor variable) at any given time (although data are presented only for Years 1, 2, and 15 postloss). These analyses were conducted for the entire sample and then separately for subjects age 75 to 84 and age 85+ at the time of baseline assessment, to permit consideration of effects of aging. Results indicate that the largest mortality risk reflects number of health symptoms at baseline assessment. At Year 1 follow-up, the odds of mortality for persons with 1 to 2, 3 to 6, and 7 to 10 serious physical health symptoms at baseline were 11, 13, and 27 times that of the reference group (who reported no symptoms). However, physical symptoms also represented the *most variable* risk over time in that persons with 7 to 10 serious health symptoms at baseline were only three times more likely than the symptom-free reference group to die in the Years 2 to 15 postloss. This latter figure was similar to the average mortality rate for all years in the study (which is the most commonly reported mortality figure in research). The psychological and social variables (life satisfaction, social contact, mental status), however, did not show significant variability in these time analyses, revealing fairly similar risks for mortality at Years 1, 2, and 15, as well as for the average of 15 years. These variables were associated during Years 1 and 2 with 1½ to 2 times mortality risk, but then declined considerably during the remaining years of the study.

Use of Services, Dislocation, Moving

There is complexity, also, in the relationship of losing a spouse in late life to increased needs for formal health services and supportive housing. Some earlier studies found a relationship between bereavement and increased use of health settings (Wolinsky & Johnson, 1992). However, findings have been mixed, and there remains some controversy regarding mechanisms. Cafferata (1987) proposed that, rather than simply reflecting threatened health status among the newly widowed, one's disrupted living arrangements may also play a role. Many frail older adults are able to maintain health function and minimize demands for formal health services only because they are embedded (with a spouse) in a family network that can provide support services informally. Indeed, the size and accessibility of family support networks are critical to deferring or preventing a need for institutionalization of older persons (Hansson & Carpenter, 1994). For each older person in a nursing home, there is another (with similar health status) living with family members.

In this context, Wolinsky and Johnson (1992) drew on a large national probability sample of adults age 70 and older (the Longitudinal Study of Aging, or LSOA) to assess the role of recency of one's loss (annually over a 2-year period postloss) on the use of formal health services and need to move into a nursing home. The study provided numerous measures of health (ability to conduct physical and cognitive activities of daily living, lower and upper body limitations) and multiple measures of use of formal health care services (physicians, hospitals, and entry into a nursing home). Results indicated that recency of one's loss was unrelated to health status or to visits to physicians or hospitals. However, subjects widowed between the baseline and follow-up assessments experienced twice the risk compared with the nonwidowed for being moved to a nursing home. Analyses of such risk for each year postloss then produced an intriguing pattern. The time of significant risk was during the second year postloss. The researchers conclude from these analyses that widowed older persons at risk can often continue to cope for about a year before being overwhelmed by the demands of living alone; then they seek more supportive housing and care arrangements. In one final analysis, Wolinsky and Johnson (1992) attempted to confirm the sequencing between conjugal loss and first entry into a nursing home. They identified every person in the sample who had lost a spouse during the study. In every case, widow(er)hood preceded institutionalization.

Bradsher, Longino, Jackson, and Zimmerman (1992) also analyzed data from the LSOA to assess the role of functional disability and loss of a spouse in predicting residential moves (excluding institutionalization) on the part of independently living older persons age 70 and older. Many older persons at some point also move to more appropriate housing (e.g., more physically accommodating or nearer to adult children) as current arrangements become problematic. These researchers found decreasing functional ability to be associated with an increasing likelihood of residential relocation. However, there was also a significant interaction between losing a spouse and functional disability on likelihood of a move. The researchers concluded that becoming widowed significantly increases the probability of needing to move under conditions of declining function.

Depression

Studies of the consequences of bereavement have often relied on generic measures of distress, emphasizing especially measures of depression (Neimeyer & Hogan, 2001). This is also the case for studies of bereavement in late life. Depression was discussed earlier in this chapter in the context of comprehensive studies of the course of bereavement. Recent research, however, has revealed great complexity in the relationship between bereavement and depression among older persons. In this section, we discuss that research. However, it is useful, first, to provide some perspective on the nature of depression in later life generally, as a basis for evaluating the experience of older bereaved persons. We draw here from two comprehensive reviews on depression in older adults (Blazer, 2003; Gatz & Fiske, 2003).

Prevalence

The incidence of depressive symptoms in community samples of older persons appears similar (or lower) to that in middle age (see review by Blazer, 2003). The incidence of *clinically relevant depressive symptoms* after the age of

65 years ranges from 10% to 15% among men and from 16% to 22% among women. Age is associated with higher incidence, and women experience higher incidence in all age groups (Federal Interagency Forum on Aging-Related Statistics, 2004). Major depression in late life is fairly uncommon in community samples; prevalence estimates in the United States and in Europe tend to be within a range of 1% to 4%. Rates are higher among women, among those who are hospitalized, and especially among those in long-term care institutions (nursing homes). Studies of the course of major depression in older adults find patterns and likelihood of remission to be similar to persons of younger age (Blazer, 2003).

The issue of medical comorbidity is a particular concern in this research (Blazer, 2003). The incidence of depressive symptoms is higher, for example, in patients with chronic pain, heart disease, stroke, hip fracture, and diabetes. Thus, medical and functional problems can influence the course of depression, but the reverse also seems true; depression may exacerbate mortality risk following heart attack, lead to weight loss, influence the course of functional disability over time, and be a risk factor for osteoporosis. Depression is a significant factor in predicting hospital and outpatient services in old age, and also in predicting both nonsuicide and suicide mortality (Blazer, 2003). Psychological and social factors also play an etiological role among older persons, as in the broader population. Chronic and uncontrollable experience of negative life events, daily hassles, and abuse are indicated as risk factors. Social engagement, religious involvement, and available social support are demonstrated protective factors (Blazer, 2003).

The use of depression as an outcome variable in studying older adults has thus proved quite useful. We review, later in this chapter, its use in studies of bereavement in late life. Caution is in order, however, when trying to interpret depression findings among older persons. The following concerns are adapted from Gatz and Fiske (2003):

- Among older adults, depressive disorder may be expressed through symptoms not included among standard diagnostic categories or instruments.
- Depression in old age is more likely to co-occur with physical symptoms, such that psychiatric distress may be misattributed to physical disorders normally associated with aging.
- However, physical complaints may be misattributed to depression.
- Cognitive declines associated with aging or with a disorder may undermine memory for past symptoms.
- Population studies may underestimate the incidence of depression in old age because they often exclude institutionalized older persons, who exhibit a significantly increased incidence of depression.

- Conclusions that depression is less prevalent in old age may fail to consider that people who have experienced major depression are less likely to live to old age.
- Age-related estimates of incidence may be confounded by a cohort effect. For example, a higher incidence of depressive symptoms among people born since the 1940s may result in higher rates in a future generation of older adults.

Bereavement-Related Depression

Bereavement is an important predictor of depression among older adults (Harwood, 2001; Parkes, 1997; Rosenzweig, Prigerson, Miller, & Reynolds, 1997). We describe here four studies that illustrate emerging patterns of findings but that also illustrate the complexity of depression findings across studies. Because samples and measures often vary considerably across these studies, symptom trajectories also tend to vary a little, but with an underlying pattern of immediate elevation of depressive symptoms postloss, and then eventual return to baseline for most within 2 years. A substantial number of older respondents appear to reach criteria for designation of high-depressive symptomatology, especially among women and the very old.

An influential prospective study by Mendes de Leon, Kasl, and Jacobs (1994) assessed community-living adults age 65 to 99 over 3 years. After the baseline assessment, 139 subjects lost a spouse to death. Depression data (using the Center for Epidemiological Studies Depression Scale; CES-D) were available for 98 widowed and 633 nonwidowed subjects from each time of measurement. Several interesting findings emerged. Widow(er)hood was associated with higher depression scores in the first year postloss, although most had returned to baseline by Year 2. The researchers identified those subjects with CES-D scores of 20 and above (reflecting high depressive symptomatology). At baseline, the percentage of widowed-to-be subjects meeting this criterion was 14% (about twice as high as married controls), and at final follow-up, that percentage was 23% (about three times that of married controls). Recency of bereavement in these analyses was also related to intensity of symptoms. Of interest, however, is that widowed persons also had higher depression scores at the baseline assessment, prior to the death of a spouse (perhaps reflecting the stress of caregiving and anticipated death of the spouse). The researchers divided subjects on the basis of age (young-old, age 65–74; and old-old, age 75 and older). Among men, the depression response to bereavement was generally similar to the pattern previously described. Among women, the old-old widows had elevated baseline depression scores relative to all other groups. However, their symptoms did not change postbereavement. Among the young-old women, however, depression scores increased significantly postloss and then remained high for the duration of the study.

In a similar study, Turvey, Carney, Arndt, Wallace, and Herzog (1999) analyzed data from a longitudinal study (two waves of assessment, 2 years apart) to examine effects of conjugal bereavement on depression in old age. Subjects were age 70 or older at the first assessment. Subjects whose spouse had died prior to the first assessment were classified as long-term widowed; those whose spouse died between assessments were classified as short-term widowed. Wave 2 assessment included a version of the CES-D measure of depressive symptoms (setting a criterion cutoff score of six symptoms) and a measure of syndromal depression from the Composite International Diagnostic Interview (CIDI). Depression status was compared across three age groups (70–79, 80–89, and 90 or older) and across sexes. Older respondents and women were significantly more likely to have six or more symptoms on the CES-D measure. Women were more likely to be classified with syndromal depression. Newly bereaved were more likely to meet thresholds for depressive symptoms and for syndromal depression, compared with the long-term widowed and also compared with control samples of still-married and divorced persons. Again, recency clearly mattered; at 1-month postloss, 33% of bereaved respondents scored at or above the threshold for symptoms from the CES-D, but at 2 to 3 months that figure dropped to 13%, after which it appeared to stabilize. Of potential concern, 12% of subjects continued to experience at least six CES-D symptoms out to the final assessment (at 19–24 months).

A study by Byrne and Raphael (1999) examined the incidence of depressive symptoms and major depressive episodes (MDEs) in older men (age 65–90 years; mean age of 75 years) and a matched sample of still-married controls, at 6 weeks and again at 13 months after the death of a spouse. Depressive symptoms were assessed with the CIDI. At 6 weeks postloss, 12% of widowers and no controls met the criteria for a current MDE. At 13 months, only 2% of widowers and no controls met the criteria. Of some concern, however, is that bereaved men were more likely at 6 weeks postloss to experience certain depressive symptoms, including depressed mood, weight change, sleep disturbance, guilt, poor concentration, and thoughts of suicide. Thoughts of death and suicide remained elevated at 13 months. None of the widowers had sought treatment for such symptoms during the study.

Finally, Carnelley, Wortman, and Kessler (1999) assessed the impact of bereavement on depression in older women (mean age of 66 years) over a 3-year period, using two waves of data from a prospective nationally representative sample. Analyses focused on the experience of 64 women whose spouse had died between the two assessments and a group of still-married controls. Two measures of depression were used: the CES-D symptoms scale and a classification of major depression based on interview questions reflecting criteria from the *Diagnostic and Statistical Manual of Mental Disorders* (3rd ed., rev.; American Psychiatric Association, 1987). Bereaved subjects were classified into three groups with respect to their time since the death (0–12 months, 13–24 months, or 25–33 months). Consistent with the studies previously described, bereaved subjects as a group exhibited higher

CES-D symptom scores at the second assessment compared with controls; 12% of the bereaved were classified with major depression compared with 3% of controls. However, there was again an effect of time since the death, wherein depression was not significantly elevated among subjects in their third year postloss. In addition, subjects widowed during the first year of the study exhibited higher CES-D symptoms at first assessment (prebereavement baseline), compared with controls and compared with those widowed in Years 2 and 3 of the study. Finally, at the follow-up assessment, bereavement was found to have differentially affected depression scores among widows whose husband, prior to the death, had or had not been seriously ill. When the husband had not been ill, widowhood significantly predicted both measures of depression. Among those whose husbands had been ill (who had warning, perhaps had already begun to grieve and to express depressive symptoms), widowhood was not associated with increased depression at Time 2. Somewhat parallel findings were also found relating to a widowed person's own level of physical functioning or disability prior to bereavement (Telonidis, Lund, Caserta, Guralnik, & Pennington, 2004–2005). These researchers analyzed longitudinal data (over 18 months) from a sample of (moderately to severely) physically disabled widowed women (mean age of 75 years) and a matched comparison group of nonwidows. Findings suggested an improvement in physical functioning among widows (across the 18 months of the study) but a slight decline in functioning among nonwidows. Telonidus et al. speculated that this finding may reflect a situation in which a large proportion of subjects from both groups may have been involved in caregiving for an old and frail spouse but that the death freed the widows from the physical demands of caregiving, resulting in decreased problems in meeting the physical needs of everyday living.

Complicated–Traumatic Grief

Older bereaved persons have been included in much of the recent research that has tried to differentiate complicated grief from bereavement-related depression. This work has been directed primarily to assessing the validity of the construct of complicated–traumatic grief and has not been guided by late-life developmental theory. It does, however, provide some insight into the generalizability of these ideas to older populations.

A study by Prigerson et al. (1995), for example, included a sample of widowed persons (mean age of 68 years). At 3 months postloss, participants responded to a comprehensive assessment of grief and emotional and functional well-being, with follow-up assessment 18 months later. A factor analysis of baseline measures produced two clusters of symptoms. The first of these, termed *bereavement-related depression*, included measures of hypochondriasis, apathy, insomnia, guilt, loneliness, depressed mood, and self-esteem. The second factor, termed *complicated grief*, included measures of yearning, preoccupation with the deceased, crying, and disbelief. Scores derived from these factors were then used to predict functioning at the 18-month follow-up assessment. Complicated grief scores were found to predict a global measure of functioning, depressed mood, sleep quality, and self-esteem. Depression scores predicted degree of medical illness. Subsequent analyses found that scores on the Inventory of Complicated Grief (reflecting the themes identified in this research) also predicted suicidal ideation over a 17-month prospective study of older bereaved persons (Szanto, Prigerson, Houck, Ehrenpreis, & Reynolds, 1997).

Suicide

Suicide is a common consequence of untreated depression in older persons, as it is among the young. However, although constituting only 13% of the population, persons over age 65 account for 18% of all completed suicides in the United States. White men over age 85 are at particular risk (National Institute of Mental Health, 2003). Important age-related risk factors for depression and suicide include the experience of severe physical illness (e.g., cancer, AIDS, multiple sclerosis, spinal cord injury), disability, bereavement, and social isolation (Szanto et al., 2002).

In this context, a longitudinal study by G. Li (1995) illustrated how gender and death of a spouse interact in determining risk for suicide in late life. This study examined the causes of death over 12 years for a large sample of married and widowed persons who were age 60 or over at the beginning of the study. During those 12 years, among the entire sample, widowed persons in general were 1.4 times more likely to complete suicide compared with married persons. Of particular interest, however, widowed men were three times more likely than married men to commit suicide, whereas the differences in suicide rates among widowed and married women were negligible. After controlling statistically for socioeconomic status, age, church attendance, and smoking, the relative suicide risk of widowed to married men was 5:1, whereas the risk among widowed and married women was nearly identical.

KEY POINTS FROM THE OUTCOME STUDIES

A number of methodological and substantive issues emerging from this review of the outcome research on older bereaved persons deserve further emphasis.

Methodological Issues

- Researchers have defined "old" in quite disparate ways for purposes of sampling. Some studies include a broad grouping of persons age 55+, others specify under age 70, over 70, and so on. Other studies simply control statistically for age. As a result, findings are limited with respect to their contribution to our understanding of developmental influences on bereavement experience over this 30 to 40 year span.

- The timing of postbereavement assessments seems critical, given the nonlinear course of symptomatology. Comparing findings across studies must take this into account.

- Bereavement should be studied with a broad sampling of potential outcomes, including general (but also bereavement-specific) measures of distress and coping, and guided by theory that predicts differential rates of adaptation across measures.

- Interpretations of depression outcomes should reflect an appreciation for the nature of depression in late life. Concerns here reflect, for example, elevated reports of depressive symptoms in old age and a closer linkage between depressive and physical symptoms (raising the possibility that one may mask the other).

- In the very old, symptoms noted in longer term assessments are increasingly likely to reflect aging process rather than bereavement status. Very-old widowed persons are more likely to die from causes not directly related to bereavement.

- Longitudinal studies that include the very old should attempt to estimate any effects of selective dropout, given increased mortality rates with age, and of the likely exclusion of institutionalized older persons from study samples.

- Longitudinal bereavement studies are more easily interpreted when they include (a) matched control groups of nonbereaved persons and (b) a prebereavement assessment of mental and physical health status, as this variable is one of the clearest predictors of postbereavement outcomes.

Substantive Issues

- The *nature* of bereavement experience among older adults generally parallels that of younger persons, involving a mix of affective, physical, cognitive, behavioral, and social symptoms and consequences. Research on health, depression, complicated grief, and suicide is as relevant to older bereaved populations as it is to younger ones.

- The *course* of bereavement reactions among older adults is also similar to that of younger persons in that intense symptoms are to be expected in the first months postloss, after which (with some important exceptions) they begin to subside as the individual adapts. Among both young and old bereaved adults, however, individual differences have been observed with respect to trajectories of symptoms over time.

- There are large individual differences in vulnerability; in the intensity, disruptiveness, and duration of symptoms; and in resiliency. Many older adults adapt with manageable difficulty to the loss of a loved one, but others are devastated. Such differences reflect a range of dispositional and contextual factors.
- The predictive validity of many risk factors appears to decrease with increasing age, because increasing portions of variance in most measures of physical and emotional status in late life are accounted for by natural aging, disease process, and age-related social and contextual variables.
- There has been, to date, insufficient attention in the research on (a) the influence of developmental process on bereavement and, in contrast, (b) the influence of the bereavement experience on developmental process in late life. The research tends not to be conceptualized in terms of late-life developmental theory.

CONCLUSIONS

In this chapter, we have focused on providing the reader with a sense for the nature and course of the bereavement experience of older adults. Individual outcome studies raised issues having to do with measurement, design, lack of attention to individual differences, and so on. But, in general patterning of symptomatology, course, and intensity, bereavements among older persons appeared quite similar to those of younger bereaved persons. It remains a concern, however, that similarities and differences noted between the age groups raised important problems of interpretation, because most studies were not guided by predictions from theory on late-life development. In the next three chapters, therefore, we explore risk factors, resources, and developmental processes that can have a protective or problematic influence on bereavement experience among older adults.

6

AGING AND BEREAVEMENT: RISK FACTORS AND RESOURCES

In chapter 3, we introduced the integrative risk factor framework for the prediction of bereavement outcomes. That framework differentiates between *loss-oriented* stressors and *restoration-oriented* stressors, drawn from the dual process model and known to intensify risk for poor outcome. It also differentiates between *interpersonal* and *intrapersonal* risk and resource factors believed to influence appraisal, coping, and eventual adjustment to a loss. The integrative framework, and the research base on which it rests, are viewed as relevant across the life span. However, many of the most important risk and resource factors (e.g., the circumstances of the death; personal and contextual protective and coping resources; and societal influences such as family, culture, and gender) have recently been studied in some detail among older bereaved adults. In this chapter, we examine that research and the insights it has generated with respect to risk and resource factors important to adjustment in late-life bereavement and widow(er)hood.

CIRCUMSTANCES OF THE DEATH

One notable program of research, the Changing Lives of Older Couples (CLOC) study, has begun to address the interaction of aging with contextual factors that affect bereavement (for a recent review, see Carr, Nesse, & Wortman, 2005). The CLOC study is a comprehensive longitudinal study on stress, health, and well-being that began in the 1980s and is conducted at the University of Michigan's Institute for Social Research, with funding from the National Institute on Aging. Respondents in this study of community-living couples (with a husband age 65 or over at the time of first assessment) have undergone comprehensive psychological, social, biographical, and well-being assessments, including assessments of grief reactions in the event of a bereavement. Several bereavement papers published from this research are especially interesting and are described in the following section.

Timing of the Death

One of the CLOC studies focused on the timing of a spouse's death: Was it sudden, or was there forewarning and an opportunity to prepare for the transition? Evidence on the topic is mixed. Many studies have found sudden conjugal bereavement to be associated with negative outcomes, some have found forewarning to be associated with negative outcomes, and some have found no effects (Carr, House, Wortman, Nesse, & Kessler, 2001). However, Carr and colleagues noted that most earlier research on this topic was conducted on younger and middle-age adults, and therefore was more likely to reflect experience with "off-time" or violent deaths. Death in older couples, in contrast, more often results from chronic illness and is likely to be more predictable, allowing the couple some time for communication, planning, and anticipatory emotional adaptations. Even the context of caregiving in old age is likely to differ, with a dying spouse more likely to reside in a nursing home, thus shifting the intense burden of care duties to institutional staff. Carr et al. drew on the CLOC sample to assess the effects of suddenness and forewarning of a spouse's death on psychological adjustment at 6 and 18 months postloss. In all, 210 men and women (mean age of 70 years) who had lost a spouse were available for subsequent assessments over that period. Dependent variables included depression, anxiety, and a measure of grief symptoms (shock, anger, yearning, intrusive thoughts). Participants also indicated the number of months' warning they had prior to the death. Analyses controlled statistically for participant's age, sex, income, education, and baseline mental and physical health. Overall results indicated that forewarning had little effect on mental health (depression or anxiety) at 6 or 18 months postloss. A sudden death, however, was related (in the short term only) to incidence of intrusive thoughts, a component of the grief measure. A prolonged warning was associated with greater experience of anxiety at both 6 and 18 months postloss, presumably reflecting the accumulation of stressful experience associated with chronic illness and foreknowledge of the outcome.

A study by Barry, Kasl, and Prigerson (2002) presents an intriguing contrast to that of Carr and colleagues. Participants in Barry et al.'s study, conjugally bereaved men and women (mean age of 63 years), received a baseline interview at about 4 months postloss, with a follow-up approximately 5 months later. Assessments permitted the classification of participants who were experiencing complicated grief, major depressive disorder, or posttraumatic stress disorder. The predictor variable in this study also focused on the issue of forewarning, but rather than simply quantifying length of warning in months, it involved a more personal appraisal. Participants indicated how well prepared they had felt for the death. Analyses statistically controlled for age, sex, time since the loss, and previous psychiatric history. Results indicated that feeling less prepared for the death was significantly related to complicated grief at 4 months and 9 months postloss and to depression at 9 months. Lack of preparedness was not related to posttraumatic stress disorder. Barry et al. speculated that significant findings for complicated grief, reflecting difficulties of separation, suggest an attachment reaction rather than a stress reaction, at least at the initial assessment.

Emotional Closeness

In another CLOC study, Carr et al. (2000) assessed important qualities of the marriage prior to the death as they related to bereavement adjustment. Results indicated that marriages that were emotionally close tended to result in greater yearning at 6 months postloss, whereas those characterized by conflict led to less yearning. Dependence on the deceased spouse for instrumental tasks (e.g., home maintenance) was associated with increased yearning and anxiety.

In a somewhat related study, Prigerson, Maciejewski, and Rosenheck (2000) analyzed 3-year longitudinal data from men and women (in their 60s) with respect to the interaction of marital harmony and widow(er)hood on health service use and estimated health costs postloss (on the basis of the number of physician visits and hospitalizations). At the preloss baseline assessment (controlling for baseline demographic and health status), high marital harmony appeared protective and was associated with lower total health costs. This would be expected, given widely demonstrated emotional and support benefits of marriage. Among persons widowed between assessments, however, those widowed from a harmonious marriage experienced overall health costs 32% higher than those experienced by persons widowed from a nonharmonious marriage. Prigerson and colleagues proposed that such findings may reflect the increased disruption and trauma associated with losing a particularly close and valued partner and the mediating effects of complicated grief symptomatology.

Good Death

In another analysis of CLOC data, Carr (2003) explored the characteristics of a "good death" in old age and effects on psychological distress among bereaved spouses. Attachment theory and stress theory suggest a number of such characteristics (e.g., the deceased's acceptance and peace with death, relative lack of pain, timeliness of the death, quality of relations with spouse, dying at home with family rather than in a nursing home, being of little burden to caregivers, and having had the opportunity to lead a full life). It might be argued, further, that there are positive aspects to sudden deaths but also to anticipated deaths. For example, sudden deaths may involve less pain for the deceased but also less opportunity for the couple to discuss the death and its implications for family, whereas anticipated deaths allow more time for family communication and resolution of unfinished business but involve increased pain and stressful caregiving burden. Among the bereaved at 6 months postloss, four measures of bereavement-related distress were related to various indicators of quality of the death. Continued yearning at 6 months was higher if the spouse had died in pain and higher if the marital relationship was positive in the last days. Continuing experience of intrusive thoughts was higher if there had been high pain but lower if one had been with the spouse at the time of the death. Anger was lower if the relationship had been positive just before the death and if one was highly religious but was higher if the bereaved interpreted the death as being caused by substantial negligence on the part of medical staff. Loss-related anxiety was higher if the deceased spouse had been in great pain but lower if the spouse had been placed in a nursing home for some period prior to death.

Suicide

The issue of a "good" death might also be explored among older bereaved persons whose spouses have died by suicide. We saw in the previous chapter that suicide in older adults is associated with depression and that depression can be a consequence of painful, chronic, or disabling illness. It is not unreasonable, under such circumstances, to consider the position of the death with dignity movement that suicide among older individuals may sometimes be an adaptive reaction for the person in pain (Hillyard & Dombrink, 2001). The most powerful counterargument, however, involves the devastating consequences for the bereaved who have lost a loved one to suicide. In this context, Farberow, Gallagher-Thompson, Gilweski, and Thompson (1992) conducted a longitudinal study comparing bereavement reactions among individuals (mean age of 62 years) who had recently lost a spouse to suicide or to natural causes with reactions of a still-married control group. Findings showed that, in comparison with controls, bereavements from both natural causes and suicide were associated with an intense sense of loss and with similar symptom patterns reflecting grief and psychological disturbance (depression, anxiety, hostility, and so on). In both bereaved groups, symptoms abated over the 2½-year duration of the study to a point not significantly different from controls. However, differences appeared in the trajectory with which symptoms declined. Persons bereaved by natural causes began to exhibit improvement (in grief, depression, and symptoms of psychopathology) after only 6 months, with another drop after 18 months, but significant change among those bereaved by suicide appeared only in the final year of the study. Farberow et al. concluded, then, that the components of the bereavement experience are similar in nature and intensity among bereavements of suicide or natural causes but that the course of the bereavement is different, with suicide survivors needing perhaps a year longer to adapt, extending their period of greatest vulnerability and risk for secondary consequences.

CAREGIVER STRAIN AND TRANSITIONS

Most deaths in old age result from lingering, chronic conditions or disease. The experience of bereavement in late life, therefore, is more likely to occur as a transition from extensive caregiving. This raises a number of contextual and relationship issues with the potential to ease or compound grief reactions.

Are the Consequences of Caregiving and Bereavement Additive?

Long-term caregiving, like bereavement, involves for most people considerable stress and adaptive challenge. It would appear reasonable, therefore, to assume that these events in sequence could result in an accumulation of stressors and a potential compounding of negative consequences. Alternatively, a relatively successful experience with caregiving might be expected to result in increased coping skills and a sense of increased mastery and purpose. Such outcomes, then, might be construed to increase one's coping resources for dealing with the subsequent death of a spouse.

A number of recent studies appear consistent with the latter of these views. Wells and Kendig (1997), for example, found that widowed persons (in a sample of community-living people age 65 or older) who had been spouse caregivers were less likely to be classified with depression, compared with either married-current caregivers or widows who had not formerly served as their spouse's caregiver.

In a similar study, Robinson-Whelen, Tata, MacCallum, McGuire, and Kiecolt-Glaser (2001) assessed the consequences for a group of bereaved caregivers (mean age of 70 years) for 3 years after the death of their patient, incorporating comparisons across time with a matched group of continuing caregivers and a group of noncaregiving controls. At the prebereavement assessment, the two caregiver groups experienced greater depressive symptoms than controls but did not differ from one another, and this pattern continued for 3 years postbereavement. In a similar way, the two caregiver groups reported greater loneliness compared with controls but did not differ from one another on this measure. However, loneliness decreased across the 3-year period for the caregiver groups while remaining stable among controls. At the prebereavement assessment, perceived stress was highest in the caregiver-bereaved group. Perceived stress in this group decreased after the death to a level comparable with the continuing caregiver group. However, stress among caregivers never dropped to the level of controls. Robinson-Whelen and colleagues concluded from these patterns that the consequences of caregiving in late life are substantial and extend into the years after bereavement.

Finally, a study by Chentsova-Dutton et al. (2002) involving caregiving spouses and children (mean age of 63 years) found depressive symptoms to be highest at 2 months preloss and again at 2 months postloss, after which they decreased significantly over the next year to the level of population controls. This pattern, then, suggests that the event of the death does not significantly increase depression when participants have already dealt with a lengthy period of caregiving.

The Emotional Burden of Caregiving

A number of studies have more directly investigated factors related to the burdens of caregiving. For example, Schulz et al. (2001) classified recently widowed persons (mean age of 80 years) as having been strained or not-strained caregivers (on the basis of the patient's predeath health status, disability, and needed help with activities of daily living and the caregiver's reported level of strain associated with caregiving). Assessments were conducted annually, and analyses compared caregivers' status during those assessments immediately before and after bereavement. Among the caregiver-strained group, depressive symptoms were significantly higher prebereavement and remained unchanged postbereavement. Among the caregiver-not-strained bereaved group, prebereavement depression was low but increased postbereavement to approach the experience of the caregiver-strained group. Prior to bereavement, the caregiver-strained group (only) also experienced elevated problems with health-risk behaviors (forgetting own medications, missing medical appointments, etc.), but after the death such problems decreased to near the level of not-strained caregivers. These data then suggest that more strained caregivers are at greater risk but that for such persons the death eases the burden. Schulz et al. proposed that such a pattern may reflect (a) relief for the end of the patient's suffering and from highly demanding caregiver responsibilities, (b) the predictability of the death, and (c) the likelihood that during the caregiving period, family support systems would develop and be helpful at the time of the death.

Ferrario, Cardillo, Vicario, Balzarini, and Zotti (2004) also examined the implications of emotional burden among caregivers for older cancer patients. These caregivers, mostly wives and daughters (mean age of 56 years), experienced considerable emotional burden, given the nature and progression of the disease. As is often the case, over 50% felt they were the only person available to assume responsibility, and over 50% reported becoming isolated from their own friend networks. At 12 months postloss, emotional distress associated with bereavement remained elevated and was related to reported level of emotional burden emanating from caregiving and from the nature of one's relationship to the deceased (with significantly greater distress reported by spouses than by adult child caregivers).

The components of caregiver burden have been examined as well with respect to subsequent bereavement reactions. For example, Beery et al. (1997) found that depressive symptoms among bereaved spouses (mean age of 68 years) were related not only to the extent that caregiving responsibilities had caused emotional burden but also to changes in how well they cared for themselves, maintained eating habits, and remained involved in recreation and work activities.

Traumatic Exposure in Caregiving

Prigerson et al. (2003) have shown that a caregiver's risk may sometimes extend beyond the consequences of caregiver burden to reflect traumatic exposure. This research assessed caregivers (nearly all 65 years or older) of cancer patients for approximately 2 years. Patients were now receiving hospice services and were near death. Caregivers indicated the extent to which they had witnessed their loved one in extreme distress (e.g., in severe pain, unable to eat, dehydrated, choking, vomiting, falling, in confusion). Witnessing such events was common among these cancer caregivers (especially among spouse caregivers compared with adult children) and were associated with feelings of helplessness. Caregivers who had more frequently witnessed these forms of traumatic patient distress were themselves more likely to meet criteria for major depressive disorder and for complicated grief. They also reported diminished mental and physical health and social functioning and increased caregiver burden. Of particular interest, these effects on depression and quality of life appeared to be independent from the effects of caregiver burden. Consistent with such findings, a recent study from Denmark (Elklit & O'Connor, 2005) estimated 27% of a sample of recently widowed persons (average age of 74 years) to meet criteria for posttraumatic stress disorder classification at 1 month postloss.

Cognitive Impairment

Caregiving can be especially difficult, also, when an older patient is cognitively impaired, as occurs with Alzheimer's disease. For, example, a study by Schulz et al. (2003) found that half of the caregivers (mean age of 65) for elderly persons with dementia reported devoting over 40 hours per week to providing care, and nearly 60% felt a need to be on duty 24 hours a day. In addition, 48% had to reduce their hours at work, and 18% had to leave the workforce completely to attend to their caregiving responsibilities. The chronicity and unpredictability of Alzheimer's disease are major contributors to stress; patients may survive for up to 20 years. In the course of the illness, caregivers must increasingly provide for the patient's basic needs, cope with the patient's diminishing cognitive competencies, and come to terms with the loss of the relationship. It is understandable, then, that caregiving for an older family member with dementia takes a toll. Alzheimer's caregivers are widely viewed to experience grief reactions. Recent psychometric work suggests at least three components of such reactions, reflecting (a) the burden of self-sacrifice, (b) deep sadness and longing for how their life once was, and (c) uncertainty about the future, which is made more difficult by their isolation from others who might provide comfort and support. Each of these components is associated with elevated caregiver strain and depressive symptoms, and with perceptions of effective social support (Marwit & Meuser, 2002). Participants in the study by Schulz and colleagues had been caregivers for periods ranging from 2 to 5 years. At the time of death, depressive symptoms increased among caregivers, but within 4 months these returned to levels experienced during caregiving. Here, too, then, the death was viewed as a relief; 90% of caregivers felt the death brought relief to the patient, and 72% indicated that it was also a relief to themselves.

Relationship to the Deceased

Several studies have also compared the dynamics of caregiving and bereavement for spouses and adult children. Seltzer and Li (2000), for example, analyzed longitudinal data from wives and adult daughters as they entered the caregiving role, made the decision to institutionalize the patient (father), and experienced bereavement. Reactions differed, reflecting structural and life span related variables. For example, because spouses tend to assume initial responsibility, daughters are likely to become involved only when the spousal caregiver has become incapable or has died. Thus, the care recipient is usually older when daughters become involved. Daughters are more likely, then, to place the recipient in an institution. Adult daughters are also at a life stage at which they are more involved with other people, their own families, social roles, and occupations. Among spouses, however, a greater proportion of one's identity and existence is mingled with that of the care recipient. It is consistent, then, that Seltzer and Li found older wives (mean age of 70 years) to be more affected than daughters (mean age of 58 years) by entry into caregiving and also by the bereavement. Upon becoming a caregiver, wives were more likely to decrease outside leisure and social involvements and to perceive diminished family and social satisfaction. Upon bereavement, however, wives, but not daughters, experienced increasing social involvement and feelings of personal growth. For neither group did depressive symptoms change significantly after bereavement.

Bernard and Guarnaccia (2002, 2003) also explored the implications of one's relationship to the deceased for bereavement reactions. Their research compared bereavement reactions among older husbands (mean age of 64 years) and adult daughters (mean age of 41 years) after caring for breast cancer hospice patients. Analyses indicated that at 90 days postloss, intensity of one's grief did not differ between the two groups, although in both groups, age was negatively related to grief adjustment. For both groups, grief was lower if the patient died at home (perhaps reflecting notions of a "good death" compared with deaths in a critical care hospital or institutional hospice environment). Finally, among husbands only, grief scores at 90 days postloss were significantly predicted by prebereavement symptoms of anxiety or depression, emotional strain, and physical health strain associated with caregiving. This pattern may reflect a diminished adaptive capacity among older caregivers, from whom intense social support may be withdrawn after some normative amount of time, whereas adult daughters are more likely to be immersed in and receive support from their own families.

CONCURRENT STRESSORS

It is also relevant that among older adults, psychological health can be affected by small life events (e.g., daily hassles) as well as by major stressors like bereavement. For example, Murdock, Guarnaccia, Hayslip, and McKibbin (1998) compared the experience of recent widows (mean age of 70 years) with a married control group. These researchers assessed general psychological distress, major life events over the past year, demographic and health status, and small life events experienced over the previous month. The measure of 46 small life events included such things as the breakdown of household appliances or systems; unwanted pests in the house; allergies, pain, or illness; disruptions or conflicts in family life; having to attend a funeral; and so on. In this study, the experience of small, disruptive life events during the last month contributed significant variance to general psychological distress, even after the effects of poor health, education, lack of social support, and major life events (including death of a spouse in the last year) had been controlled statistically. The findings from this study on older widowed women paralleled and supported earlier findings from a similar study on both men and women (Zautra, Guarnaccia, Reich, & Dohrenwend, 1988). Zautra and colleagues have suggested that the usefulness of considering small life events lies in part in the more current and detailed information they provide about the individual's experience during important transitions and the potential for recurring and cumulative contributions to stress.

Researchers have studied extensively the personal and social coping resources available to the bereaved. As we have already seen, such resources may include one's baseline physical and mental health, integration into a supportive personal or cultural network, education, income, personality, and coping styles. These issues have received much attention also as they affect older bereaved adults. For example, a study by Gass (1987) examined the potential influence of available coping resources on participants' appraisal of the difficulties they faced in their bereavement experience. Participants were women (mean age of 71 years) in their first year of spousal bereavement. The study widely construed one's potential coping resources (to include measures of social support, comforting religious beliefs and rituals, perceived control, good prior emotional health, the absence of concurrent losses, adequate finances, and so on). Analyses indicated that among these widows, those with greater resources (a) appraised their bereavement experience as less likely to involve additional losses, complications, or threats beyond the death itself and (b) exhibited significantly higher scores on measures of physical and psychological well-being.

Economic Resources

Only a few decades ago, the threat of poverty was considered a primary risk factor for the aging population as a whole, and by implication for adjustment to late-life widow(er)hood (Lopata, 1993). Many countries, however, have made significant advances in this respect. In the United States, the percentage of people over age 65 living in poverty declined from 35% in 1959 to 11% in 1998 (approximately the rate for the broader working age population). This national estimate, however, masks important variance across subpopulations. For example, the percentage of people over 65 who live in poverty rises with increasing age and is higher for women and ethnic minorities (Federal Interagency Forum on Aging-Related Statistics, 2004).

The death of a spouse in late life often contributes to change in economic status. In the first year postloss (the period of greatest risk for physical and psychological consequences of bereavement), the percentage of widows living in poverty rises to 22%. Economic status prior to the death is an important predictor of poverty after the loss, but approximately 60% of those in poverty in the first year postloss are not poor in the year prior to the death. And most are not simply hovering above the poverty line prior to the death; declines in income are substantial (Hungerford, 2001) and, over a 5-year period postloss, are twice as large among women as among men (Zick & Smith, 1991). Fortunately, many widows who fall into poverty during that first year exit this status over the next few years as they become eligible for survivor benefits, seek employment, or receive contributions from or move in with family (Bound, Duncan, Laren, & Olenick, 1991).

Women appear most vulnerable to the economic consequences of conjugal loss (Lopata, 1993; Wortman, Silver, & Kessler, 1993). They are more likely to have been dependent on their spouse for current income, health insurance, a survivor's share of private pensions, and so on (Blieszner, 1993). It is consistent, then, that insufficient income in widow(er)hood (especially among women) is associated with increased depressive symptoms (van Grootheest, Beekman, van Groenou, & Deeg, 1999).

Interpersonal Resources

Helena Lopata's early studies (in the 1960s and 1970s) of the support systems of American widows provided an impetus and baseline for much of the research to follow on this topic (see reviews in Lopata, 1993, 1996). In her research on older widows in Chicago, Lopata cataloged over 60 kinds of support, classifying them into four broad support systems (economic, service, social, and emotional) and examining the source (family, community, medical, government) and quality of such support. She demonstrated the ways in which widowhood disrupts and disorganizes the life and functioning of older women, and the importance of available support. Lopata's research also showed the interrelations among support systems; the role of personal abilities, education, and income in reducing vulnerability; the constraints imposed by the culture regarding appropriate roles and behavior for older widows (e.g., in romantic relationships or the workplace); and how the assumptions underlying these systems were often bound by one's culture and time in history.

Following Lopata's early work on the topic, descriptive research has focused on the practical circumstances of widow(er)hood in late life, producing a number of important insights (for a review, see O'Bryant & Hansson, 1994). For example, it is now clear that most older widowed persons are women, many of whom live alone. Widows tend to have fewer financial resources than married people, and thus receive more financial support from family. Adult children often become involved as well in decision making in practical, financial, and health matters. Given traditional patterns of gender-divided household tasks in a marriage, which do not encourage cross-role skill development, widows also appear to receive more types of assistance from their adult children than do married counterparts. Housing often becomes problematic, and there are pressures to relocate. Given a preference for independence, however, older widows may move close to but not in with their adult children. Because adult children are so important in parental support, widows without children appear to be at increased risk. Long-term caregiving, then, is often complex, generally involves an adult child (usually a daughter), and can be rewarding but stressful for all parties (O'Bryant & Hansson, 1994).

Social Support Issues in Late Life

Across the life span, social support is associated with positive health outcomes. Besides providing a level of instrumental and informational resources needed for survival, social support is viewed to foster relational closeness, encourage emotional expression, and facilitate feelings of mastery and self-efficacy (Antonucci, Langfahl, & Akiyama, 2004; Charles & Mavandadi, 2004). In healthy people, the socioemotional process inherent in social support is associated with reduced physical health symptoms, a more responsive immune system, and greater resistance to infection. Among people at increased risk because of age or chronic illness (e.g., arthritis, lung disease, cardiovascular disease, or cancer), social support is associated with better functioning and survival (Charles & Mavandadi, 2004).

Older adults tend to become more dependent on family and social support with increasing age and frailty. As previously suggested, however, the support environment for older adults can be complex, depending in part on the size and stability of the support network, the goodness of fit between network resources and recipient needs, and relations among network members. Adding to the complexity, the impact of bereavement is often felt throughout the entire family network, undermining its ability to respond to the needs of those most directly affected (Hansson & Carpenter, 1994; Stylianos & Vachon, 1993).

People within family and support networks usually appear highly motivated to provide needed assistance to older family members. However, a variety of factors having to do with the dynamics of personal relationships, stressful demands of the situation, and the aging of the network itself may undermine efforts to provide support that adequately matches an older person's needs.

With increasing age, for example, support networks often narrow and decrease in size or competence as members themselves become frail, relocate, or die. Support needs become more complex, with a greater emphasis on medical care and the need to coordinate services from a number of providers, some from outside the immediate network. Family members are often willing to enter into intervention or caregiving roles. However, they may have little understanding of the realistic nature of aging or the demands of long-term care, and at some point they may come into conflict regarding the equitable allocation of caregiving responsibilities. In this context, it can be difficult for both caregiver and the older care recipient to establish ground rules, assert their own needs, and communicate feelings or concerns about rights and privacy. The chronic and progressive demands of caring for an older person, then, can result in caregiver strain and burnout (Hansson & Carpenter, 1994).

A number of studies have now been conducted to more formally assess the role of social support in adjustment to bereavement. On balance, the research finds main effects for social support—it appears to help all people. In contrast, there is little evidence of a stress-buffering effect of support; that is, it is not consistently found to be protective or to foster recovery from symptoms specific to grief (see reviews in W. Stroebe, Stroebe, Abakoumkin, & Schut, 1996; W. Stroebe, Zech, Stroebe, & Abakoumkin, 2005). From an attachment theory perspective, support from other people cannot replace the deceased, alleviate one's yearning or loneliness, or lessen the need for loss-oriented coping. It may, however, help with restoration-oriented coping tasks, and among older adults for whom there will arguably be many more restoration tasks to be faced, social support would be expected to take on a different character completely.

The research described here further illustrates the complexity associated with social coping resources that may influence outcomes among older bereaved persons. For example, Siegel and Kuykendall (1990) examined two forms of social ties with respect to consequences of nonconjugal bereavement (parents, siblings, children, grandchildren, nieces/nephews). Participants in this cross-sectional study, men and women age 65 and older, provided biographical data and completed a measure of depressive symptoms (the Center for Epidemiologic Studies Depression Scale; CES-D). The social ties of interest were marital status (married, a proxy indicator for social connectedness and support, or widowed) and church or temple membership (an indicator of available and relatively stable institutional support). Results suggested the importance of social resources but also showed significant and interesting differences between men and women. Among women, poor health was associated with increased depressive symptoms. Among men, however, depressed mood was associated with being older, being widowed, poor health, and having experienced a nonconjugal loss within the previous 6 months. In addition, among men only, there were a number of significant interactions. The relationship between experiencing a nonconjugal loss and depression was higher if they were widowed or were not a member of a church or temple. And the highest depression scores were found among men who had experienced a nonconjugal loss, were widowed, and also did not belong to a church or temple.

A longitudinal study by Norris and Murrell (1990) further examined the role of social coping resources, comparing conjugal and nonconjugal bereavements. Data were available from three assessment waves at approximately 6-month intervals. Outcomes for three groups were compared (widowed persons, married persons who had lost a parent or child between Waves 1 and 3, and a matched sample of nonbereaved adults). Mean age for each of the groups was approximately 65 years. Dependent variables in the study were depressive symptoms (CES-D) and physical health. Independent variables included measures of social embeddedness in a helpful support network, global stress, and evidence of coping through pursuit of new life interests. Analyses showed the widowed group to have greater depression scores at Waves 2 and 3 compared with the other groups. Widowed persons also had more health problems at Wave 3 compared with those bereaved of a parent or child. Widowed persons reported greater global stress compared with the other groups. However, social embeddedness also increased among the widowed group (only) between Waves 1 and 2, and the widowed (only) were more likely to begin pursuit of new interests (and accompanying relational involvements). The independent variables also predicted depression and physical health most consistently among the widowed group compared with the other groups. Widowed participants' depressive symptoms at Wave 3 were associated with lower social embeddedness, fewer new interests, and global stress. Physical health problems were associated with fewer new interests and increased stress. In the other two groups, social embeddedness was unrelated to either depressive or physical health symptoms. Among those bereaved of a parent or child, new interests were associated with fewer health problems. Norris and Murrell drew a potentially important implication from the contrasts in these data. They noted that both bereavement groups can be viewed as experiencing an attachment loss. But the death of a spouse, especially when it occurs in late life, also signals a major life transition and demands for (restoration-oriented) adaptations far beyond those associated with their grief (adaptation to new social roles, a new identity, economic and physical security, etc.). Such a view is consistent with the widowed group's more intense symptomatology and with the greater likelihood that social embeddedness and involvement in new pursuits would be associated with better adjustment.

Both family and friends can be important sources of support in late life. Family members tend to provide tangible care, assistance, security, and a long-term sense of belonging. It is usually understood by members of the family, however, that such help is an obligation. It may therefore be taken for granted, becoming salient only in its absence.

Friendships, however, are voluntary, usually peer relationships. Thus, friends assume a larger role as companions and in shared activities that provide opportunities for pleasure (Antonucci & Akiyama, 1996; Connidis & Davies, 1990). In this context, then, it is consistent that psychological well-being in older persons generally has been found to be more closely associated with quality of friendships rather than family relationships (Crohan & Antonucci, 1989). This pattern emerges as well in studies of older widowed persons. For example, in a study of widowers over age 60, psychological well-being (a balance of positive to negative affect) at 1 year postloss was significantly related to degree of interaction with friends and neighbors but not to amount of contact and help available from children or siblings (Balaswamy & Richardson, 2001).

Talbott (1990) interviewed a sample of women (median age of 70 years, widowed between 2 and 5 years) to explore reasons why relationships with their children might not contribute to psychological well-being. About half of the women described some negative dynamic within the relationship. Some mothers simply felt neglected, dissatisfied with the amount of the child's attention or assistance they received. Some felt unappreciated as a person and member of the family, ignored, or only tolerated. An "adaptive" response to such feelings often involved trying not to burden the child or intrude in the child's life or becoming submissive to the children's needs. Some also felt uncomfortable in their emotional dependence on the child and the grand-children, given the loss of many of their own friends and an inability to get out on their own. A common theme also was an endeavor to exchange "services" (babysitting, cooking, money, housing, etc.) for involvement in the family's life and feeling their contributions were being taken for granted and underappreciated. Talbott cautioned, however, that despite such concerns regarding the relationship, most widows in the sample regarded their relationships with children with considerable pride and satisfaction, that most did receive important forms of support, and that most also enjoyed being able to contribute what they could to the family.

Subtle changes also appear to occur in the nonfamily support networks of older bereaved adults. In a longitudinal study, D. Morgan, Carder, and Neal (1997) analyzed the structure of the close-support networks of widows (mean age of 72 years) over a period of 1 year postloss. Over 1 year, the participants significantly increased the number of widowed friends in their networks and decreased the number of nonwidowed friends. During that time, these women also reported increased contact with their widowed friends and perceived greater emotional closeness in their friendships with other widows. However, such changes appeared mostly to serve needs for companionship, as married friends continued to make up the majority of persons in support networks and to account for a greater proportion of the variance in overall impact of support. The shifting emphasis to similar others in an older widow's network, then, may reflect the increasing likelihood with age that one's friends are also becoming widows, and that other widows can more easily relate to one's circumstances. It is unfortunate that this report did not include a comparison group of networks of still-married women of matched age, given that the demography of their networks is also aging.

Gender-Related Resources and Risks

In a review of the broader literature on risk factors, W. Stroebe and Schut (2001) found considerable evidence that gender (being male) is a risk factor for health outcomes of bereavement. In same-sex comparisons, for example, bereaved men (compared with married men) experience more depression in the short term and higher mortality rates.

Findings from research on older bereaved adults are generally consistent with the conclusions of W. Stroebe and Schut (2001), although patterns vary somewhat across studies. For example, Lee, Willetts, and Seccombe

(1998) found widow(er)hood to have a stronger association with depression among men in a sample of adults (mean age of 72 years). Lee, DeMaris, Bavin, and Sullivan (2001) found a similar pattern in a second sample with an average age in the early 70s. In a sample of men and women (age 55–85 years), van Grootheest et al. (1999) also found the association between widow(er)hood and depression to be stronger among men, notably in the longer term (over 4 years postloss). In contrast, Nieboer, Lindenberg, and Ormel (1998–1999) found that among people age 57 and older in the Netherlands, men reported greater depressive symptoms early in widow(er)hood, with gender differences in depression abating later in one's bereavement.

A variety of mechanisms (involving person and structural variables) have been suggested to account for the preponderance of findings that men are at greater risk. Lee et al. (2001), for example, noted that men are many times more likely than women to remarry but that there also may be a selection effect operating, such that healthier men remarry, thus leaving less healthy widowers to be included in studies of bereavement. Men also have a shorter life span, so those men included in bereavement studies are likely to be at an earlier point in their bereavement. Because the effects of bereavement abate over time, more intense effects found for men may then in part reflect a statistical artifact. Men also receive and benefit more from emotional support in a marriage, so may be more intensely affected by its loss. Widowed men appear at greater risk for health complications of bereavement, in part reflecting a decline in nutritional sufficiency and an increase in counterproductive health habits (drinking, smoking, etc.). Women tend to have had more kin and friendship involvements and are often able to develop new support relationships among other widows. Because in late life there are substantially fewer widowed men, there may simply be fewer opportunities for widowers to benefit from support from similar others.

In addition, it may be that women have and use a mix of coping skills that are better matched to the emotional challenges of bereavement and widow(er)hood. W. Stroebe and Schut (2001) noted, for example, a greater likelihood that women will use a more emotion-focused coping style, more effectively expressing their emotions and engaging those adaptive tasks considered important to adjustment.

Cultural Resources

The various cultures in which people live shape their experiences of grief. As we discussed in chapter 1, they provide the language for death, norms for expressions of grief, and norms for responding to those who are bereaved. They provide emotion scripts, produce norms for how to mourn and for how long, and help with rites of passage. From this viewpoint, then, grief is a social construction, and the particulars can vary considerably across societies (Klass, 2001; Rosenblatt, 1993, 2001; Walter, 1999). Our culture also shapes the emergence of many of the coping resources previously discussed (e.g., our informal and formal systems for economic security; the structure and responsibilities of family, interpersonal relations, and social support; our understandings of gender; and the religious beliefs that help in finding meaning in a death).

In a similar way, the culture in which people live influences considerably the experience and meaning of aging. All societies organize their social structure and the lives of their peoples by age, with implications for personal and public rights, interactions with gender, normative transitions with respect to status, freedom, obligation, demands for productivity, retirement, eventual dependency, bereavement, and death (C. L. Fry, 1996). Yet there is immense variability across cultures in each of these domains; aging too is in great part a social construction.

In recent decades, gerontological researchers have become aware of the need to gather data and to test assumptions not only across ethnic cultures within one country's boundaries but also internationally. Major programs of health, longevity, and epidemiologic research, for example, now routinely oversample previously underrepresented groups of older adults and conduct multisite replications or comparisons across diverse national cultures.

Lopata's (1996) comparative sociological studies across a variety of national cultures (beginning in the 1960s) provided important insights regarding the differing implications of widowhood for changes in a woman's social roles, status, personal identity, economic security, and integration into remaining family or friend networks. Since that time, the field has benefited from research on the peoples and cultures of many countries on several continents. However, there are to date few multisite, international studies on bereavement or widow(er)hood in old age.

A study by Antonucci et al. (2001), however, illustrates the potential value of such efforts. This study compared data from four countries (France, Germany, Japan, and the United States) in an investigation of the dynamics of the social relationships of older persons that have been shown to be important to health and coping. The research focused specifically on how culture might influence the dynamics of social networks in response to two resource deficits likely to occur in old age: widow(er)hood and illness. Participants in these studies ranged in age from 70 to 90 years. A number of within-country contrasts emerged, signaling potential cultural influences. For example, in France, Germany, and the United States, but not Japan, younger participants had larger networks. In France and Germany, only, participants with resource deficits had larger networks. In France and the United States, neither age, gender, nor resource deficits were related to the proportion of emotionally close persons in one's total network. Older participants and those with resource deficits in Germany, and women in Japan, had a larger proportion of emotionally close people in their network. In France and the United States, frequency of contact with network members was unrelated to age, gender, or resource deficits. In both Germany and Japan, however, men had more frequent contact (Antonucci et al., 2001).

These data raise important questions about the universality of some core assumptions regarding aging and support networks. Might size of network, for example, be less critical in a culture in which older widowed parents are included in the homes of their children or where there is a more comprehensive national scheme for income and health maintenance for the elderly? What features of family or community might diminish the importance of the generally found tendency in late life to begin to focus one's relational energies on those who are more emotionally close? What cultural norms or structural protections, in this case in France and the United States, might be expected to discourage or reduce the need for frequent contact with network members (Antonucci et al., 2001)?

LESSONS FROM THE RESEARCH REGARDING RISK FACTORS IN LATE-LIFE BEREAVEMENTS

Our review of the research in this chapter produced a number of insights that have implications for theory, future research, and intervention. We summarize these themes as follows:

- The unique mix of risks and resources that shape appraisal and coping among older bereaved adults can be usefully understood within the integrative framework and the dual process model, both introduced in chapter 3.
- The issue of the "timing" of the death may be less relevant in late life. Timing-related effects on adjustment will no longer reflect off-timeness (i.e., occurring early and unfairly in one's life) but rather suddenness and will be influenced more by subjective estimates of "preparedness."
- Our understanding of bereavement should pay greater attention to the changing contexts of death in later life. Death is more predictable, typically following the path of a chronic disease or condition. There is usually more time for communication and anticipatory adaptations. The burden of caregiving often shifts to nursing or institutional staff. The elevation of psychological and physical distress during caregiving implies that bereavement reactions should to an extent be viewed as a continuance of that distress.
- Emotional closeness and marital harmony, which can influence grief, will in old age reflect more the intimacy and commitment components of love rather than passionate attachment, suggesting a reduced pull for intensely emotional reactions and

a potential for increased perspective in coping and emotion regulation.

- The concept of a "good" or "bad" death will remain relevant but may reflect differing criteria in late life. Such criteria would include freedom from a patient's suffering and from caregiver burden or the unique implications from deaths from causes more characteristic of old age (e.g., cancer, dementia) rather than from causes of death characteristic of youth (e.g., unfair timing, homicide, suicide, accidents, AIDS).

- Bereavement theory in late life should more formally incorporate the dynamics of the transition from caregiving to bereavement (e.g., chronicity and emotional burden, potential for traumatic exposure in caregiving). It should also reflect the consequences of caregiving (e.g., social isolation, physical and psychological distress, financial burden, and threat of losing one's job) that can undermine one's coping reserves for dealing with subsequent bereavement.

- Caregivers for older patients with dementia may experience loss of the psychological relationship prior to the death and experience aspects of grief at this time.

- Comparisons of bereaved spouses and adult children suggest that spouses have more to lose (a life partner, their closest attachment, social roles, financial security, and independence) at a time of their own increased frailty.

- For women, especially, conjugal loss often signals potential economic insecurity; long-term adjustment problems for many may be more attributable to financial distress than to the emotional impact of the death (Blieszner, 1993).

- The availability and mix of coping resources take on particular meaning in late life and should figure more prominently in bereavement theory.

- Older bereaved persons are especially dependent on family for long-term support. Families usually rise to the occasion, but their resources are not unlimited, and the available mix of support resources (emotional, physical, financial) within a family may not be a good fit to the needs of the recipient.

- Social support in late life is associated with a variety of positive outcomes (health, feelings of inclusion, mastery, self-efficacy, and so on). However, it is not a stress-buffering effect—support appears useful to all older persons. Family support may be more important in the more tangible areas of assistance and security, whereas support from friends may contribute more to psychological well-being. Individual, gender, family differences, and age may influence access to support.

- The commonly found excess bereavement risk among men continues, and perhaps intensifies, during late life.

CONCLUSIONS

This chapter focused on those risk and resource factors likely to affect the nature and course of bereavement in older adults. Our review indicated the critical importance of contextual variables, the circumstances and predictability of the death, concurrent stress resulting from financial problems, caregiving, social isolation, available support, and so on. A number of person variables (e.g., gender, social roles) were also found to influence outcomes.

This research, however, has not, for the most part, addressed the implications of developmental processes that might also play a role in vulnerability, coping, or resilience. In the next two chapters we explore the kinds of variables from the aging and development literature that could provide further insights into the bereavement experience in late life, and the conditions under which it might be expected to resemble (or differ from) such experience at younger ages.

7

PROTECTIVE DEVELOPMENTAL PROCESSES

An array of protective developmental processes could reduce exposure to the consequences of bereavement or enhance coping resources. In this chapter, we broaden our focus to consider the *life span perspective* and a range of important age-related changes relevant to the experience of bereavement. These changes involve one's (a) emotional experience, (b) cognitive ability, (c) self-concept, and (d) strategies for coping and adaptation. Chapter 8, in turn, examines problematic developmental processes that could increase risk or undermine coping; these tend to reflect the pervasive impact of physiological decline and disablement, diminished personal capacity for coping and adaptation, and compromised social resources.

THE LIFE SPAN PERSPECTIVE

The age-related changes we describe in these chapters can be best understood within the context of the life span perspective (Baltes et al., 1999). This orientation stands in contrast to earlier stage theories of adult development and more easily accommodates the complexities of aging that reflect maturational, cohort, and individual-history factors.

A number of assumptions form the core of the life span perspective. For example, development is viewed to be a lifelong endeavor and to reflect complex interactions of person and external variables. Growth and positive change can occur at any point in the life span. However, individuals may take different developmental paths and progress at different rates, resulting in considerable within-age-group variation (at every age) in most areas of ability or performance. Developmental change will reflect a continuous mix of gains and losses, over time shifting in their balance toward loss. Occasional reverses will make demands on one's adaptive reserves (plasticity), and such reserves are not without their limits. Within an individual, some areas of competence may continue to improve as others are beginning to decline. The concept of life stages is not relevant, as no developmental peak (or "end state") is envisioned (Baltes, 1987; Baltes et al., 1999).

Developmental change is responsive to three kinds of influences: those that are normative age-graded for the species (e.g., physical maturation), those that are normative to one's cohort (e.g., having lived through a common historical event like the Great Depression), and those that reflect an individual's unique life history (e.g., one's experiences with family, illness, and education). Normative age-graded factors are proposed to be most influential in childhood and very old age. Cohort factors are considered most important in adolescence and young adulthood. Nonnormative (idiosyncratic) factors increase in importance throughout the life span (Baltes et al., 1999).

Genetic influences on development (advantages or disadvantages) are expected to decrease in importance across the life span, as any planful genetic programming is assumed to be linked to the first 40 to 50 years of life and to reproductive success of the species (Hayflick, 1994). In contrast, culture-based resources (e.g., language, the common knowledge base, acquired skills, social organization, technology, and support resources) are viewed to become increasingly important to development with age. However, a person's ability to benefit from such resources diminishes in late life with the onset of inevitable age-related decline and loss and diminishing adaptive reserves. Also, because people experience the culture in different ways and to different degrees, older people are expected to become a more heterogeneous population.

Baltes et al. (1999) made a related point about developmental influences in the context of their two-component model of intellectual development. The first component in their model involves the mechanics of cognition (e.g., perceptual speed, abstract reasoning, spatial ability), which reflect one's biological and genetic makeup. The second component involves the pragmatics of cognition (e.g., verbal knowledge and abilities), acquired and refined in the context of culture. Research on age-related change in intellectual function suggests that abilities linked to mechanics peak during one's 20s and then decline across a lifetime. Culture-based, pragmatics-related abilities peak in the 20s but do not begin to decline until much later in life.

Again, as individuals vary in their experience with and ability to benefit from culture-based influences, this process would be expected to result in considerable diversity in competence in late life. Baltes et al. (1999) proposed this model in connection with cognitive abilities, and we return to cognitive abilities later in this chapter. It would seem feasible, however, to generalize this model to apply as well to the development across the life span of one's emotional competence, self-concept, and ability to cope with life stressors such as bereavement.

EMOTIONAL PROCESSES

If the nature of emotional experience generally were to change in later life, reflecting either developmental or circumstantial factors, the emotional response to bereavement might be expected to reflect such change. In this connection, researchers have begun to explore age-related differences in sensitivity to emotional distress and in the processes of emotional maturation and emotion regulation. For example, a groundbreaking study by Lawton, Kleban, Rajagopal, and Dean (1992) compared reported emotional experience among three age groups (ages 18–29, 30–59, and 60+). Seven affective dimensions emerged in this research, reflecting not only characteristic emotional responsiveness to life events but also one's efforts to actively manage or regulate emotions (especially negative emotions). Significant age-related differences were observed on each of these dimensions, as follows:

- *Emotional control*: The oldest group reported trying and succeeding in staying calm, avoiding emotional situations, not betraying their emotions, and so on.
- *Surgency*: The oldest group reported that it was less likely they would get excited, joyful, or animated.
- *Emotional stability–moodiness*: The oldest group reported greater stability of good moods day to day, with any variations being short-lived and mild.
- *Emotional maturity through moderation*: The oldest group reported greater moderation of both positive and negative feelings as they have grown older, reflecting an effort to arrange one's life to include fewer highs or lows.
- *Leveling of positive affect*: Older participants were more likely than middle-aged participants to report that they experience fewer novel or exciting events these days.
- *Psychophysiological responsiveness*: Both middle-aged and older groups reported being less likely to experience physical sensations usually associated with more intense emotions (e.g., increased heart rate, hands shaking, perspiration).

- *Sensation seeking*: Older participants reported the least need to continuously seek variety, change, or excitement in their lives (Lawton et al., 1992).

Lawton (1996) suggested that such age-related patterns indicate a "dampening" of emotional experience, a general narrowing of the "intensity, frequency, duration, or quality" (p. 338) of one's emotional responsiveness. Such dampening was proposed to involve (a) increasing adaptation levels to both negative and positive stimulation, after a lifetime of experience with potentially arousing stimuli; (b) efforts on the part of older adults to actively regulate their emotional reactions and to control their exposure to emotionally demanding environments; and (c) age-related slowing or deterioration of the neurological response to emotional events. The emotional dampening process, then, might also be expected to constrain the intensity and duration of symptoms in a bereavement in late life, with potentially protective effects.

Considerable research has now addressed the issue of emotion regulation in later life. Of particular interest in this connection is research guided by the socioemotional selectivity theory (Carstensen, Gross, & Fung, 1998), which considers the role of emotion motivation across the life span. This theory holds that as older people become increasingly aware of their diminishing time left in life, they shift the focus of their goals and attention to ensuring an emotionally meaningful existence. Older people have been found, for example, to become more selective in their interpersonal involvements, increasing the proportion of emotionally close people in their networks, and to generally focus their coping resources and skills in the service of increasing positive emotional experience.

Research on emotion regulation is beginning to illustrate the adaptive potential of older adults. For example, Gross et al. (1997) conducted four studies involving culturally diverse samples of young and old adults. Assessments focused on reported frequency and intensity of positive and negative emotional experience and of perceived control over emotions (both internal and expressed). Across these studies, older people were generally found to report less negative emotion, increased positive emotion, and increased control over emotions (particularly their internal experience of emotions). Gross et al. concluded from these findings that older adults become increasingly effective at emotion control, leading to lower levels of negative and higher levels of positive emotional experience.

Two studies by Charles, Mather, and Carstensen (2003) examined age differences in memory for positive and negative images in an experimental setting. Participants (age 18–80 years) viewed a series of positive and negative images on a computer screen, and then after completing a distracting task were asked to recall all images viewed. Results indicated that with increasing age, there was a significant decrease in negative images recalled relative to positive images. A second study found a similar pattern when participants were shown the images again and were asked to identify those they recognized from the previous viewing. Charles and colleagues offered as an interpretation of these data that older adults, being more focused on emotion regulation, would have devoted fewer cognitive resources (attentional or encoding) to the negative images.

A study by Birditt and Fingerman (2003) asked participants from five age groups ranging from adolescence to very old age to describe their emotional (anger) responses to problematic experiences with members of their relational networks. Older adults reported experiencing less intense anger under such circumstances.

A study by Carstensen, Gottman, and Levenson (1995) illustrated the value of emotion regulation efforts in long-term marriage. Middle-age couples (mean age of 44 years) and older couples (mean age of 63 years) were videotaped as they discussed a problem in their marriage. Content analyses of their interactions revealed older couples to exhibit more affection; less interest or involvement in the problem; and less anger, disgust, belligerence, or whining. They were also less likely to follow up a spouse's neutral contribution with a negative contribution of their own. Consistent with the socioemotional selectivity theory, this pattern suggests a greater focus on positive emotion regulation in older couples' relationships, actively avoiding unnecessary negative interaction or any escalation of negative interaction, and embedding any negative feedback in a context of continued affection.

Older persons also appear to regulate their emotional experience with children, contributing not only to their own emotional well-being but also to that of the children. To examine this dynamic, Pasupathi, Henry, and Carstensen (2002) asked young adults (ages 25–35 years) and older adults (over age 60) to tell a story to a young child. A story picture book provided the story outline, but respondents were to formulate and tell the story in their own words. Stories were recorded to allow a systematic count of the "emotion" words used in the narrative. It was thus possible to assess the relative use of positive-emotion words (e.g., *happy, good, joy, love*) and negative-emotion words (e.g., *afraid, bitter, cry, hate*) used in each story. Results indicated a significant main effect for emotion words, with older storytellers using fewer negative words. Even in places where the story line prompted a description of negative reactions, older adults were less likely to mention angry or worried reactions and were more likely to emphasize feelings of relief on resolution of a problem. This pattern suggests that older people actively construe their environment so as to manage not only their own emotional exposure but also to ensure the stability and well-being of those around them.

Carstensen et al. (2000) examined emotional experience among adults age 18 to 94 years from a slightly different perspective. Participants rated their experience of 19 (positive and negative) emotions at five randomly selected times per day for 1 week. Age was unrelated to frequency and intensity of positive emotions experienced during the week and unrelated to intensity of negative emotions. However, between the ages of 18 and 60, the frequency of experienced negative emotions decreased, at which point it stabilized. Older persons also exhibited greater stability of emotion across time samples, for example, being more likely to maintain a high level of positive emotion (or low level of negative emotion) from one measurement to the next. Older persons also appeared to have a more differentiated emotional structure. The researchers factor-analyzed emotion ratings separately for each participant across all ratings, to identify the number of factors from each age group with an eigenvalue of 1.0. The average number of factors composing one's emotional structure increased with age. Greater differentiation, in turn, was associated with less frequent negative and positive affect (implying a stabilizing mechanism) and with less intense negative affect. Finally, older persons were more likely to report experiencing positive and negative emotions simultaneously, suggesting a potential for increasingly complex and integrative emotional responses in old age.

A study by Ong and Bergeman (2004) further examined the complexity of emotional experience in later life. Participants in this study (ranging in age from 60 to 85 years) rated (in a daily diary for 30 days) the frequency and intensity of a sampling of discrete positive and negative emotions experienced. Within this attenuated age sample, age was not a significant predictor. However, positive emotions were experienced more frequently and more intensely than were negative emotions. Two indices of emotional complexity were then computed: a *differentiation index* (reflecting the number of factors extracted for each participant from their combined emotion-intensity ratings) and a *co-occurrence index* (reflecting the average intraindividual correlation between positive and negative emotions over the study period). Higher scores on both the differentiation and co-occurrence indices were associated with greater psychological resilience and lower levels of perceived stress and neuroticism.

Generally consistent findings have emerged as well from studies that included physiological assessments of emotional response. For example, Labouvie-Vief, Lumley, Jain, and Heinze (2003) assessed heart reactivity as groups of younger and older participants (mean ages of 30 and 70 years, respectively) thought about past events from their own lives that had caused them to feel angry, scared, sad, or happy. During induction of each of these emotions, cardiac reactivity was lower in the older group. During induction of anger and fear only, there was also a main effect for gender, and a Gender × Age interaction, with younger women (but not older women) exhibiting greater cardiac reactivity compared with men. A study by Tsai, Levenson, and Carstensen (2000) produced similar findings, using a more standardized form of emotion induction. Older participants (mean age of 75 years) were found to experience smaller changes compared with younger participants (mean age of 28 years) in sympathetic cardiovascular response while viewing a sad film clip.

At this writing, there remain many unanswered questions about the relationship between aging and emotional experience. Not all studies have found the more positive emotion balance among older adults. It is a concern, also, that studies have varied in their assessment strategies and with regard to the range of ages compared. In addition, survey studies more broadly focused on happiness have sometimes found cohort effects, with higher scores evidenced among later cohorts. However, few studies have reported an increase in negative affect (Mroczek & Kolarz, 1998).

It is also an issue in this research whether age, per se, is a reliable proxy for those age-related variables that might more directly influence emotional experience. For example, a survey study by Mroczek and Kolarz (1998) on a large, national probability sample of people age 25 to 74 explored the relationships among age, positive affect, and negative affect. The overall relationship between age and positive affect was significant but nonlinear; lowest scores were exhibited by those at age 35, after which positive affect increased at an accelerating rate. The overall relationship between age and negative affect, in contrast, was negative and linear across the full age range. In subsequent regression analyses, age was entered as a predictor only after a group of demographic variables (gender, marital status, and education), personality dimensions (extraversion and neuroticism), and relevant contextual variables (e.g., stress, health status). Each of these variable groups was significantly related to affect, leading the researchers to conclude that future research needs to focus more specifically on "for whom does affect rise or fall with age. Age and affect do appear to be related, but only for certain groups" (p. 1345). For example, analyses suggested that the rate of increase in positive affect accelerates only among women; for men the increase is linear, although extraverts (whose positive affect was high at all ages) were outliers to this pattern. Analyses further suggested that the overall age-related decrease in negative affect was highly influenced by married men.

This issue seems even more pertinent among the very old (e.g., age 80 and older), among whom chronic health conditions, cognitive decline, and disability (commonly associated with depression) are more prevalent (Isaacowitz & Smith, 2003). In a sample of people age 70 to 100 years, Isaacowitz and Smith (2003) found no significant age effects on either positive or negative affect after statistically controlling for other variables (demographic, personality, health, and social support) that have elsewhere been linked to well-being. Hierarchical regression analyses found that in this sample, only extraversion and general intellectual function significantly predicted positive affect, whereas negative affect was predicted by neuroticism and level of intellectual functioning.

In summary, we believe that analyses of the emotional components of grief must reflect an appreciation of (a) the place of grief in the human emotion systems and (b) the immense complexity of emotions. The research previously described suggests that in response to stressful life events (like bereavement) older adults may experience a general dampening of both positive and negative emotions but that positive emotions appear dominant, even at a time of accumulating concerns about health and loss. Our models of the grief experience could thus benefit from the incorporation of a life span perspective and consideration of the issues we have discussed, including the following:

- a potential for age-related, physiological leveling of affect;
- increasing emotional maturity, differentiation, complexity, and control;
- growing expertise in emotion regulation;
- a shifting focus in one's personal and relationship goals, and a proactive focus on arranging one's social environment so as to ensure an emotionally meaningful and positive existence; and
- an understanding that such patterns are not universal, and that person and context variables that co-occur with age may play a role.

In the remaining sections of this chapter we focus on three other developmental influences on emotional experience that would also be expected to help shape the grief experience in late life. These involve cognitive processes, changing self-concepts, and coping processes.

COGNITIVE PROCESSES

We have seen that coping with bereavement involves dealing with a mix of emotional and practical problems (getting through the night, coming to understand one's emotions, rescuing one's finances, and so on). Solving such problems, however, requires a degree of intellectual competence and effort, raising the question of whether age-related changes in intellectual ability might help or hinder such coping.

Aging and Intelligence

The Seattle Longitudinal Study on aging and intelligence (Schaie, 1994), which assessed individuals every 7 years for 3 decades, provided some interesting insights into that process. The Seattle study found that overall intelligence scores do not begin to decline until people are in their mid-60s. Moreover, it is important to differentiate between the primary intellectual abilities classified as *fluid intelligence* or *crystallized intelligence* (Horn & Cattell, 1967). For example, scores on numeric ability and word fluency (measures of fluid intelligence) begin to decline earlier in life, in one's 50s. However, scores on verbal meaning and on inductive reasoning (measures of crystallized intelligence) remain stable until into the mid-70s. In a similar way, scores on practical, everyday problem solving appear to remain stable or improve into the late 60s. By the late-60s most people have begun to decline on at least one ability, but into the late 80s, in the absence of pathology very few show significant decline on all abilities. The good news from this discussion, then, may be that some important coping demands of late-life bereavement (making sense of the death, finding meaning and purpose associated with a new life, and so on) are a good match for one's crystallized abilities, which are stable later into the life span. However, coping with practical, restoration-oriented concerns (e.g., finances, security, nutrition) might be more related to fluid abilities, in which earlier declines would be expected.

The Seattle study also produced two additional findings of relevance to this volume. The first of these concerned generational (cohort) differences in abilities. Scores on verbal meaning and inductive reasoning increase in a linear fashion from the 1907 birth cohort to the 1966 birth cohort, a difference of approximately 1.5 standard deviations (Schaie, 1994). Schaie proposed as the most likely cause the continuously rising level of formal education across cohorts.

The second, perhaps more important finding was that patterns of change in intellectual function also vary considerably across individuals. Reduced risk for intellectual decline in these samples was significantly associated with a number of understandable variables (cardiovascular health and lack of chronic diseases, a complex and challenging environment, social involvement, a high degree of perceptual processing speed, and the presence of a high-cognitive-functioning spouse; Schaie, 1994). Of particular interest, Schaie (1990) speculated that individual differences may reflect a purposeful selection by individuals of certain of their abilities to optimize and maintain, a topic to be addressed in the next section of this chapter.

Aging and Cognitive Development

Life Experience

Although the psychometric literature on IQ finds age-related declines at some point for most abilities, the broader literature on adult cognitive development paints a more positive picture. For example, across a life span, older persons are viewed to accumulate life experience, expertise, and wisdom, each of which might constitute a generally protective coping resource in the face of stress. They will have experienced and had to cope with many of the life stressors that recur in late life and acquired a sense for how to prevent or manage the conditions likely to result in poor outcomes (Aldwin, 1991). In particular, older adults are more likely to have experienced the deaths of loved ones. In the process, they may also have acquired greater experience in assigning meanings to deaths and developed strategies for coping with the kinds of restoration-oriented challenges associated with a death in the family.

Postformal Thought

In earlier chapters, we explored the immense complexity that characterizes the bereavement reaction and associated demands for coping and adaptation. We saw that bereaved individuals often find themselves having to plan and solve real problems of living at the same time as they are coping with physical and emotional distress, disrupted support networks, and a disruption of their assumptive worlds. We noted also that they will likely feel the need to oscillate between efforts to process the loss itself and efforts to restore functioning in the practical areas of their life. Appraisals of the threatening aspects of the event and of their capacity to cope, and attempts to reconstruct meaning for their life and their future, will thus be conducted in an atmosphere of emotion and uncertainty. Their problem, then, is an ill-structured one, not likely to be served by logical coping styles and instead requiring concurrent processing of emotional and cognitive pressures, with high stakes for self and others.

Several of these themes are common also to notions of *postformal thought*, an extension of Piagetian stages of cognitive development that reflects adult maturation. Postformal thought is viewed to reflect an accumulation of life experiences that challenge the limits of formal logic structures and well-learned thinking and coping patterns, requiring accommodation of an emotional component or another person's point of view (Sinnott, 1996). Individuals at the postformal stage will be expected, therefore, to exhibit several characteristics. Their thinking will be more complex and relativistic. They will understand that many problems in life are ill defined and that a best solution will often depend on the context. They will understand that any problem can be viewed from multiple perspectives and that they may sometimes experience conflicting viewpoints and emotions. They will understand that what appears to be real or true may change as they acquire further experience with the problem and that the eventual solution may reflect a continuous process of formulating and integrating assumptions. They will increasingly focus on problem finding rather than problem solving, scanning the horizon for potential problems whose path might be influenced by taking immediate action. In addition, postformal thinkers would be better able to construe a problem such that it is possible to find a practical solution. Finally, such maturation of thinking process may not occur equally across all life domains, instead increasing in its emphasis on those areas of continued performance that remain critically important to the individual (e.g., family well-being; Berg & Klaczynski, 1996; Sinnott, 1996).

Wisdom

In recent years, gerontologists have begun to focus on wisdom as a psychological construct. The Berlin wisdom model (Baltes, Smith, & Staudinger, 1992), for example, proposes five components for wisdom. First, people who are wise should have a rich factual knowledge of life matters. Second, they should have a rich procedural knowledge, an expertise in situational contexts and the rules and constraints they impose on individuals, and knowledge regarding how best to negotiate their way through such contexts. Third, they should understand how life events are influenced by age and by generational factors. Fourth, they should appreciate how individual and cultural differences will (legitimately) influence a person's values and goals. Finally, they should understand and be comfortable with the fact that life and future events are sometimes unpredictable and that they must be prepared to respond to occasional surprises.

Wisdom, then, is viewed to reflect acquired expertise, perspective, and judgment regarding problems in life, with a potential to compensate for losses in one's more neurophysiologically based intellectual abilities across the life span. Older adults have been found to perform as well as younger people, for example, in solving problems that demand wise judgment (Baltes et al., 1992).

The Role of Purposeful Selectivity

A core theme has now emerged from several of the previous discussions. As they begin to feel challenged by age-related changes in their cognitive or emotional competence, older individuals may become purposefully selective with respect to those abilities they will continue to try to optimize and maintain. This is an assumption in theory on postformal thought. It is consistent with findings of the Seattle Longitudinal Study that the trajectories of age-related changes across primary intellectual abilities reflected substantial individual differences. It is consistent with research on the socioemotional selectivity theory that older people selectively reduce the size of their interpersonal networks, and in doing so increase the proportion of emotionally close people in those networks. Selection and a narrowing of focus on one's most critical areas of competence is also an important component of the model of selective optimization with compensation (Baltes & Baltes, 1990), to be described later. As we see in a later section, older adults may also become more selective with respect to the kinds of life stressors they attend to and prepare to cope with. It is instructive, for example, that in a life-stress inventory constructed especially for and with older persons, much of the focus in items shifted from one's own problems to the problems being experienced by their loved ones (children, spouse, siblings; Aldwin, 1990).

To the extent that a narrowing of focus permits increased practice and attention to one's most critical performance domains, older people would be expected to focus their adaptive resources and increase their expertise in retained domains. Being able to call on such expertise should help to compensate for declines in broader abilities to cope with or solve problems. However, those abilities or intellectual domains that are deselected might be expected to atrophy in later life. Cognitive research generally finds that competence and performance in later life can increase within one's selected areas of expertise but that learning and performance may suffer outside those domains (Hoyer & Roodin, 2003). We anticipate that this phenomenon could influence one's relative success in dealing with the wide range of *loss* and *restoration* coping demands (described in chap. 3, this volume) faced by bereaved persons in late life.

Implications of Cognitive Development

In summary, we believe that models of grief experience in late life could benefit from consideration of the issues previously discussed, including the following:

- the implications of a pattern of earlier declines in fluid intellectual abilities for success in restoration-oriented coping;
- the implications of declining crystallized abilities after the mid-70s for loss-oriented coping;
- the need for coping models to recognize generational patterns of change in cognitive (and presumably coping) abilities in late life, reflecting improved health and higher education levels with each succeeding generation;
- the multidetermined nature of cognitive change in late life (reflecting age-related physioneurological decline but also environmental variables);
- the implications of older adults' increasing selectivity (e.g., with respect to abilities to continue to optimize and maintain, and the composition of their relational networks) for breadth and effectiveness of their coping styles and resources, and formulation of goals for coping; and
- the implications of accumulated life experience and expertise and of postformal thinking for appraisals of risk and for engagement and efficacy in loss-oriented coping tasks.

SELF-CONCEPT

To this point, our consideration of variables that influence the experience of bereavement has focused on distinct entities (traits, strengths, coping resources, risk factors, and so on). But a person is more than simply an accumulation of traits, characteristics, and experiences. In this connection, theory on the self provides useful perspective. The self-concept is construed as an active and continuously developing (cognitive and affective) structure that integrates one's experiences, self-knowledge, self-evaluations, and spiritual and collective identities (J. D. Brown, 1998; Markus & Herzog, 1992). It provides a sense of continuity with respect to who one is, it structures one's self-efficacy beliefs, and it functions as a schema, framing one's perceptions of potentially threatening events and focusing one's attention, perceptions of others, and defensive energies.

It is a concern, however, that spousal bereavement in old age implies the loss of a number of one's social role identities that are core to sense of self (Lopata, 1996). Previously defining identities such as spouse, partner in parenting, and married friend in couple-companionate friendships are lost. It is thus not surprising that Lopata's research on older widows suggested the importance of developing substitute social roles and relationships through which to reestablish a sense of belonging and new sources of personal reward (Lopata, 1996).

From a social cognition perspective, Markus and Herzog (1992) proposed that as people become older, they continually add to, refine, and consolidate their self-schemas and understandings of previous experience. This process progressively broadens and deepens, and it renders more complex one's self-knowledge. The proposed result, then, is that "Stockpiling such self-understandings allows for feelings of mastery, competence, and control" (p. 115). In this context, successful adaptations to previous losses might lead to the development of a self-concept that could enhance adaptation to subsequent losses (including bereavement).

An important corollary in self-theory is that individuals are conscious of multiple current, past, and future-possible selves. Past selves may provide perspective and continuity. For old and young people alike, future selves incorporate a motivational element; one may devote greater energies to achieving realistic positive future selves, but one also may focus efforts on avoiding a feared (e.g., sick, poor, alone) future self (Markus & Herzog, 1992). Each person's current selves (identity as a parent, spouse, older adult, psychologist, etc.) are viewed to entail domain-specific beliefs and feelings with respect to competence, mastery, and life satisfaction. A rich mix of such identities, then, might be expected to buffer the consequences of the loss of any one identity, as might occur in the event of a spousal bereavement. There is some empirical support, for example, for the protective role of a more complex self-concept in response to stress (Linville, 1987). Finally, a study by J. Smith and Freund (2002) provides an important insight regarding the implications of future selves for coping among older adults. These investigators assessed future selves among older persons (age 70 and older) at two points in time, separated by 3 years. Positive future selves were operationalized to reflect respondents' reports of continuing hopes and wishes for who (and what kind of person) they wished to become someday. Feared selves reflected self-images, experiences, and feelings they hoped to avoid. The researchers anticipated that among people of this age, the focus of possible selves might shift more toward health issues and maintenance of status or deferring declines.

This expectation is consistent with Bearon's (1989) research, which suggested a shift in focus between middle-age and old age, from continued emphasis on hoped-for selves to simply achieving predictability and deferring health decline and dependency. In contrast to expectation, however, Smith and Freund found that their older respondents continued to experience a diversity of hoped-for selves. Health-related hopes were of course important to most, but so were hopes with respect to their relationships and other sources of identity and life satisfaction. Even at this age, a substantial portion of respondents' hopes involved a continuing potential for new experiences and growth rather than simply avoiding feared outcomes. Most respondents at the 3-year follow-up assessment reported new hopes (and fears) in different areas of their lives.

The self-concept, then, has proved a useful construct in thinking about adaptation to old age and to bereavement. We anticipate that future models of bereavement-related coping in older adults could benefit from the inclusion of a number of self-related themes, to include the following:

- the role of self-concept as a schema, in focusing appraisals and coping energies on threats perceived to be uniquely self-relevant;
- the implications of spousal bereavement (and lost roles and self-domains) for continuity of self;
- the effects of perceived multiple and future selves on motivation to cope and adapt; and
- the potentially buffering effects of complexity of self-concept on resilience in bereavement.

COPING, ADAPTATION, AND SUCCESSFUL AGING

We have seen that developmental changes in an older person's coping resources may have the potential to help compensate for increasing age-related vulnerabilities. Older adults appear to experience a leveling of affective experience, especially negative affect. They acquire considerable experience and skill in emotion regulation. They appear more likely to proactively focus on arranging their environments to minimize risk and to enhance positive relationships. Their coping and problem solving are likely to reflect postformal thought, the acquisition of expertise in life management, and wisdom. Their efforts may also reflect active specialization and more formalized coping. They are likely, as well, to develop across a lifetime a broader and more differentiated sense of self and an understanding of their unique domains of self-efficacy. We would expect each of these developmental changes to affect the processes of appraisal in times of stress and to broaden and render more flexible one's coping efforts.

Coping in Late Life

Older adults do appear to remain active in coping with stressful life events. Specific ways of coping, however, are often reported to change as older persons begin to have to deal with health and life events that appear increasingly uncontrollable, chronic, and progressive. The focus under such circumstances may begin to shift from problem-focused to emotion-focused coping, although this is a shift in balance, not an abandonment of problem-focused coping altogether. Older persons often find aspects of a problem or its context that can be addressed instrumentally (Aldwin, 1991).

This view is reinforced by the research of Brandtstadter and Renner (1990) on the related constructs of assimilative and accommodative coping. These investigators developed two complementary measures. The first of these, *tenacious goal pursuit* (TGP), focuses on one's disposition to tenaciously pursue a goal under difficult, high-risk circumstances. The second measure, *flexible goal adjustment* (FGA), assesses a willingness and tendency, where appropriate, to acknowledge one's own limitations, revise aspirations, turn to alternative pathways to satisfaction, and accommodate one's self to the situation. Both forms of coping are associated with well-being (e.g., lower depression, higher life satisfaction); cross-sectional analyses have found that endorsement of TGP items declines with age, whereas endorsement of FGA items increases with age (Brandstadter & Renner, 1990).

Rothermund and Brandtstadter (2003) further assessed the utility of an accommodating coping strategy among older persons (age 58–81 years) in a 4-year longitudinal study. Cross-sequential analyses showed that active efforts to compensate for age-related change in abilities and status tended to increase up to about age 70, after which they decreased in response to declining coping resources. However, degree of satisfaction with performance was unchanged across age groups. This reflected a conscious lowering of standards for continued performance, in response to diminished resources and perceived control. Rothermund and Brandtstadter concluded from this pattern that by the late 70s, there appears a "shift toward a predominantly accommodative mode of coping" (p. 903). Presumably, this would over time also lead to a revised self-concept, reflecting an understanding and acceptance of developmental realities at this point in the life span.

Finally, a study by Boerner (2004) illustrated the circumstances under which the utility of an accommodating coping style would generalize to younger adults. Boerner assessed TGP and FGA, degree of disability, and mental health among vision-disabled adults in two age groups (mean ages of 55 and 81 years). Both types of coping (but especially FGA) were associated with more positive mental outcomes (in terms of depressive symptoms, social dysfunction, and a global measure of mental problems). The most interesting finding in this study, however, was that among the older group only, higher scores on accommodative coping (FGA) were associated with fewer mental health problems *generally*. Among younger adults, however, accommodative coping was associated with fewer mental health problems only for those with high vision disability. Boerner concluded that accommodative coping, which appears adaptive in older persons, regardless of disability level, becomes adaptive for younger persons as well, when faced with a permanent disability. At this point, "disability rather than age became the critical variable" (Boerner, 2004, p. 40).

In this context, Lazarus (1996) also concluded that "most differences in the coping process in aging can be most simply explained by what younger and older adults have to cope with" (p. 302). Any developmental changes in coping might more accurately be attributed to how most people would react to the changing contexts, constraints, and coping demands that are characteristic of later life.

Successful Aging

We have seen that old age is a time of increasing heterogeneity. Some individuals appear to age more successfully than the norm in terms of objective indicators (e.g., cognitive and physical health status and longevity) but also in terms of more subjective criteria (e.g., maintenance of competence, personal control, and life satisfaction; Baltes & Baltes, 1990). Within the fields of gerontology and geriatrics, a comprehensive research effort is currently under way to identify those modifiable factors that predict successful aging, including avoidance of disease and disability, retention of high cognitive and physical function, and continued active engagement with life (Baltes & Baltes, 1990; Rowe & Kahn, 1997).

Strategies of Selection, Optimization, and Compensation

The symptoms of bereavement present an array of important adaptive challenges with respect to physical and psychological well-being and the ability to continue functioning. In late life, however, one's adaptive resources may be more limited and could constrain coping options. In this connection, Baltes and Baltes (1990) proposed three interrelated strategies for adapting to challenges of late life (and, we would argue, for adapting to bereavement-related challenges). The first of these strategies involves becoming more *selective* with respect to those goals, abilities, and domains of life satisfaction that can realistically be maintained (e.g., a new widow might decide to focus primarily on her health, putting off until later any efforts to reconstruct a social life or find employment). The second strategy involves devoting increasing efforts and resources to maintain performance or *optimize* adaptation with respect to selected goals and competencies (e.g., increased efforts could be put into recovering or maintaining health, watching nutritional needs, minimizing stress, getting exercise, etc.). The third strategy comes into play where developmental loss may be irreversible and it becomes necessary to find ways to *compensate* for lost abilities (finding alternative resources, asking others for help, using prosthetic devices, etc.).

There is now considerable evidence that older people who pursue these adaptive strategies in response to age-related loss and life stress benefit with respect to maintained areas of mastery and well-being (Freund & Baltes, 2002). Freund and Baltes found that the use of selection, optimization, and compensation (SOC) strategies for life management generally tended to increase into middle age, after which their usage tapered off. This trajectory may reflect a growing expertise in SOC strategies through young adulthood and middle age (Freund & Baltes, 2002). Declining use in later years, however, may reflect the fact that actively pursuing SOC strategies requires a high level of effort and resources at a time when older adults may be experiencing declines in personal resources. Consistent with this explanation, Lang, Rieckmann, and Baltes (2002) found older persons who were resource-poor (in terms of sensory–cognitive function and in terms of social integration and support) were less likely than resource-rich older persons to engage in SOC processes.

Finally, a program of research by Gignac, Cott, and Badley (2000, 2002) provided important insights into the use of SOC strategies by older persons as they attempt to cope with debilitating arthritis. Like bereavement in old age, this chronic illness raises issues of coping with painful symptoms over long periods of time, of increasing dependency, and a challenge to take some personal control and responsibility for adaptation. There are opportunities for problem-focused coping. But aspects of the condition are progressive and beyond one's control, thus raising demands for accommodative or emotion-focused coping as well. Respondents in this study reported engaging in a wide range of coping behaviors; these were coded to reflect SOC strategies. Analyses indicated that compensation responses were more frequent than optimization responses, and optimization was more frequent than selection. The percentages of respondents who had tried at least one SOC adaptation were 83%, 93%, and 96%, respectively (Gignac et al., 2002). There appeared to be less SOC-related coping among men, among respondents with fewer social coping resources, and among those whose level of physical capacity and disability had changed substantially.

CONCLUSIONS

We believe it is important to appreciate that most older persons remain active copers in the face of life stress. But they are likely to adopt (and benefit from) more emotion-focused and accommodating coping styles as they begin to face uncontrollable stressors at a time of diminishing coping resources. In the face of increasing developmental challenge, they appear to benefit from the strategies reflecting SOC. This latter finding, however, must be tempered by an understanding that usage of these strategies reflects a realistic consideration of what remains possible.

It is also important to emphasize a number of protective developmental processes in late life with implications for the bereavement experience. Older people appear to experience increasing emotional maturity and differentiation. They become more effective in emotion regulation. Until very late life, they retain considerable competence in terms of their crystallized cognitive abilities, which we have speculated should enhance loss-oriented coping. A pattern of improved health and education over succeeding generations suggests continuing improvement in cognitive coping ability into old age. Coping ability should also be enhanced by accumulated life experience and expertise, the development of postformal thought, and an increased willingness to become more selective and to adapt one's coping goals and style to changing circumstances.

In this chapter, we have focused on developmental (primarily psychological) processes with the potential to ease the experience of bereavement in late life—by minimizing exposure to or suffering from its consequences and by enhancing coping and adaptation. In chapter 8, we turn to consider problematic developmental processes with the potential to influence the course of late-life bereavements. These processes involve age-related physiological and health decline, constraints on coping, and diminished social resources.

8

PROBLEMATIC DEVELOPMENTAL PROCESSES

Physiological declines in late life mean that an older person will face stressful life events (like bereavement) from a more problematic health baseline. The implications of this situation need to be viewed from two opposing perspectives. First, diminished physiological status can threaten an older person's ability to cope with or adapt to stressful life events in general. The mechanisms are complex, reflecting not only a loss of adaptive reserves but also the interactions of physiologic change in late life with changes in cognitive abilities, emotion systems, styles of coping, and vulnerabilities to changing physical and social environments. Second, experiencing an especially stressful life event (such as bereavement) in one's later years would be expected to exacerbate normative age-related loss. Bereavement theorists have seldom addressed this level of complexity. Nor have they focused systematically on developmental dynamics as an influence on the nature and outcomes of bereavement. Theoretical assumptions, then, have not typically been formulated with an eye to their validity for older populations.

In this chapter, we describe briefly the nature of age-related change across a number of the most important physical and sensory abilities and protective systems. We also describe the changing nature of illness experience in late life, reflecting the accumulation and growing influence of progressive, chronic conditions that increase an older adult's vulnerability to disease processes, emotional distress, and dependency.

We then explore the implications of these phenomena as they relate to a number of more fundamental concerns among older adults. The first of these involves a diminished ability to cope with stressors—with *immediate* consequences for status, functioning, and well-being. Three issues are central to this reduced capacity to cope. First, older adults generally experience an age-related decline in their "adaptive reserves" and homeostatic capacity. Second, they often find that important, previously successful coping strategies are no longer feasible, usually because coping efforts require considerable energy and resources. Third, coping in late life does not occur in a vacuum. It reflects, instead, efforts to address the changing demands of a stressful situation, at a time when coping resources are becoming more limited. In this context, we review an important body of research from the aging literature (on the environmental docility hypothesis). This research generally finds an age-related reduction in adaptive competence when faced with stressful or nonsupportive physical and social environments. More important, it proposes and tests predictions regarding individual differences in adaptive competence among older persons.

A second general concern reflects a longer term focus on health processes in late life, identifying the implications of a health experience that has generally become more complex, progressive, and less controllable. In this context, we discuss four critical issues. First, progressive and chronic health conditions become more prevalent in old age, requiring an increased focus on managing symptoms and maintenance of status rather than rehabilitation. Second, a person's health experience in late life increasingly involves comorbidity (including co-occurrence of physical and psychological symptoms). We explore the implications of increasing interrelatedness of changes within one's physiological systems, which renders diagnosis and treatment more difficult, and also the growing connections among physical, emotional, and cognitive status (sometimes simply correlational relationships and sometimes reflecting several causal pathways). A third issue involves the increased likelihood with advancing age of an eventual health crisis. Finally, we describe the process of disablement at the end of life, a dynamic in which chronic and progressive disease eventually lead to impairment of physical or cognitive abilities, to loss of function, and to loss of one's capacity to perform routine activities of daily or social living.

Within the clinical literatures of gerontology and geriatrics, these topics are considered essential to understanding research, assessment, and intervention. But they have not typically been addressed in bereavement theory, even though older adults have been included in much of the research on bereavement (especially conjugal loss). In this chapter, therefore, we elaborate on the implications of problematic age-related processes for thinking about bereavement in late life. In concluding this discussion, we also propose how the late-life disablement process might be incorporated into the model for prediction of bereavement outcome (introduced in chap. 3, this volume) to improve our understanding of longer term outcomes.

PHYSICAL CHANGES IN LATE LIFE

Physical changes in late life reflect a mix of normal aging processes at the cellular and systems levels, disease processes, and potentially modifiable lifestyle factors such as nutritional and exercise history. These changes are complex and have an impact on all of the bodily systems. They have implications for continued physical function, adaptive resilience, and independence. To the extent that they are recognized and attributed to disease or modifiable factors, they may drive efforts to cope and adapt (Strecher, Champion, & Rosenstock, 1997). At some point, however, and this varies across one's physiological functions, they may signal to the individual the ways in which he or she is aging or becoming old (Whitbourne, 1999).

Physical and Sensory Changes

Some indicators of aging are quite visible, as they begin to affect appearance, function, and risk for disease. Skin wrinkles and changes in texture and color. Capacity for wound repair and the temperature control function of the skin diminish, and the incidence of skin cancer increases. Hair thins and loses color. Loss of bone mass and deterioration of joints affect posture, gait, and height and increase the likelihood of fractures. A 30% to 40% loss of muscle strength across adult life and deterioration of connective tissue reduce one's ability to perform work, constrain flexibility of movement, and increase the risk of falls. A 60% to 70% loss in aerobic capacity and a 50% loss of lung volume and breathing capacity across adulthood reduce stamina, endurance, and ability to engage in intense exercise or to perform heavy work (Hayflick, 1994; Whitbourne, 1999).

With aging there are also substantial declines in one's sensory abilities. Changes in vision, for example, include not only diminished sensitivity to light but also impaired depth perception, dark adaptation, color discrimination, and peripheral vision. Impaired vision is of course relevant to one's ability to see and negotiate the physical environment. But, in a context of musculoskeletal loss and reduced proprioceptive competence, it also contributes to problems with balance, body sway, and falls in older persons. Changes in hearing are reflected in heightened thresholds for sound recognition, poorer understanding of speech, and failure to discriminate differences among sounds, to hear alarms, or to discriminate relevant sounds from background noise (Fozard & Gordon-Salant, 2001; Simoneau & Leibowitz, 1996).

Protective and Regulatory Systems

An aging nervous system and the risk of age-related insults to the nervous system (e.g., from stroke) have implications for speed of neural transmission and reaction time, sensory and intellectual competence, and continued homeostatic functioning of the autonomic nervous system. Immune functioning appears to be affected by age-related change, although it also can be affected by nutrition, stress, exercise, and disease. For example, older persons are at higher risk for various kinds of infectious disease and certain cancers. Certain immune system diseases (e.g., chronic lymphatic leukemia) increase in incidence with age, and older people respond less effectively to vaccines (e.g., for influenza). There also appear to be increased risks to endocrine function in late life. Decreasing estrogen levels increase risk for cardiovascular disease and osteoporosis. Hypothyroidism is associated with speech and cognitive disorders, as well as problems with balance and fatigue. Diabetes generally exacerbates many of the processes associated with aging, to include damage to cardiovascular, circulatory, and cognitive functions, with direct implications for heart attack, retinopathy, neuropathy, failure to recover from wounds, gangrene, and so on. Finally, the respiratory system is at increased risk in old age for life-threatening conditions such pneumonia, bronchitis, and emphysema (Aldwin & Gilmer, 1999; Awad, Gagnon, & Messier, 2004; Whitbourne, 1999).

It is unfortunate that increased health risks in later life are not always matched with efforts to control modifiable risk factors. It is a concern, for example, that even among people age 51 to 61 years (in the United States), 64% report being overweight, 48% get little physical exercise, 27% smoke, and 24% have high cholesterol levels. In this age group, each of these risk factors is associated with the incidence of hypertension, heart disease, diabetes, and stroke, and all but cholesterol are associated with risk of cancer (National Academy on an Aging Society, 2000). Further, among adults age 65 and older, only 66% reported receiving a vaccination for influenza, and only 56% have ever been vaccinated for pneumonia. Only 19% had an adequate diet in relation to government nutrition guidelines (Federal Interagency Forum on Aging, 2004).

In this context, then, it is unsurprising that health becomes increasingly problematic in late life. As we noted in chapter 5, the incidence of chronic conditions and disease rises dramatically with advancing age, the most prominent of these involving hypertension; arthritis; heart disease; diabetes; cancer; and hearing, vision, and memory impairment. Older persons average about 13 physician visits or consultations per year. Over 30% have been hospitalized in the last year, with an average length of stay of about 6 days. Older persons with no chronic conditions fill 10 prescriptions on average per year, those with at least five conditions fill 57 prescriptions. An estimated 20% have a chronic disability, in which a chronic disease or injury interferes with their physical or cognitive performance, with implications for mobility, self-care, independence, and well-being (Federal Interagency Forum on Aging, 2004). Over 34% report that a chronic disability limits their activity (U.S. Department of Health and Human Services, 2003).

Psychological Ramifications

In chapter 5, we noted the prevalence of comorbidity issues among older adults. Older patients with chronic pain, heart disease, stroke, hip fracture, and diabetes, for example, experience a greater incidence of depressive symptoms. Comorbidity patterns, however, may vary across individuals. Depression among physically ill older adults may in part reflect a biological response associated with the illness or with medications. It may also reflect chronic psychological stress associated with illness and disability (Gatz, Kasl-Godley, & Karel, 1996). Depression is also understood to exacerbate the physical consequences of chronic disease or acute health events (Blazer, 2003).

Health concerns are also more complex among older persons. They are more likely to be experiencing multiple diseases or conditions simultaneously. A given illness may reflect an interaction between aging and disease processes. Different conditions may result in similar symptoms. A serious health event (e.g., heart attack) may present with different symptoms in older compared with younger people. The risk increases that a serious health event will have unpredictable effects on other health processes (e.g., a high fever can interfere with efforts to manage one's diabetes). A health incident can therefore be more difficult to accurately diagnose and quickly treat. It can test the limits of an older person's adaptive reserves, which may be sufficient to meet routine challenges but vulnerable to failure in the face of a more taxing demand (Aldwin & Gilmer, 1999; Rowe, 1985).

Coping with multiple chronic conditions or extraordinary health events in old age may present an enormous intellectual challenge, exceeding the competence or endurance of the older patient. Older persons are likely to have acquired worldly experience with respect to understanding their health and domain-specific expertise in managing a long-standing disease or chronic condition. However, they are likely to have fewer cognitive resources to devote to learning about and coping with new kinds of health problems (e.g., understanding new medication regimens, considering unfamiliar treatment options, deciding which medical claims to believe). There appear to be normative age-related declines in capacity for effortful intellectual processing (e.g., speed of processing, working memory, ability to focus on the most relevant features of a problem). Compounding the situation, the stress of dealing with serious medical conditions (e.g., cardiovascular disease, diabetes, and painful arthritis) is associated with diminished cognitive status in older persons (Awad et al., 2004; S. C. Brown & Park, 2003; Schaie, 1994).

Implications for Coping With Late-Life Bereavement

This brief analysis of the health experience of older people suggests a number of issues that might productively inform our understanding of coping with bereavement in late life. For example, age-related changes in outward appearance and body composition may encourage a shift in sense of self and self-efficacy beliefs. Diminished bone and muscle mass, deterioration of joints, and reduced cardiovascular and respiratory functioning can lead to self-imposed restriction of activity and mobility, avoidance of risk, reduced feelings of mastery, and a lowering of expectations or goals for interactions in the social and physical environment. Impaired vision and hearing can lead to frustration in trying to operate in an environment designed for those without such impairments, in reduced independence, greater risk of falls, and social isolation (Whitbourne, 1999).

From this summary of findings, we propose several assumptions that might usefully be incorporated into models of late-life bereavement experience:

1. Many of the symptoms of bereavement may be difficult to differentiate from those associated with disease or chronic conditions in old age.
2. Late life is a time of diminished adaptive reserves and homeostatic capacity. Physiological vulnerabilities in late life may thus (a) render one more vulnerable to the onset of health consequences of bereavement or (b) exacerbate symptoms resulting from the bereavement.
3. Age-related health crises may affect self-concept (I am now "old"), self-efficacy, and motivation to continue to meet rigorous goals for coping with bereavement.
4. Diminished capacity for "effortful" cognitive processing (reflecting declines in physiologic status) could interfere with restoration-oriented coping (as described in the dual process model introduced in chap. 3, this volume), for example, by inhibiting new learning, solving of new kinds of problems, and coping with the complex demands of new roles, life management, and independence. It could also undermine one's ability to reappraise the meaning of the death (an adaptive process proposed in connection with the loss-oriented component of the dual process model).

DIMINISHING UTILITY OF COPING STRATEGIES

Age-related changes in health and their implications for self-concept, self-efficacy, and functioning can also weaken an older person's ability to cope with stressful life events. In chapter 7 we described a number of coping strategies common to older adults. These included a shift in emphasis from problem-focused to emotion-focused coping (Aldwin, 1991), a shift from assimilative to accommodative coping (Brandtstadter & Renner, 1990), and an active focus on the coping strategies of selection, optimization, and compensation (SOC; Baltes & Baltes, 1990). The shifts from problem- to emotion-focused coping and from assimilative to accommodative coping are viewed in the literature as realistic responses to age-related declines in ability, coping resources, and controllability of events.

We noted also that a similar pattern emerges with respect to use of SOC coping strategies in old age. Freund and Baltes (2002) found, for example, that the use of SOC strategies increased into one's mid-60s as a way to cope with loss or changing abilities generally. These strategies, however, require considerable effort and personal resources, and their use lessened as respondents (in their late 60s to late 80s) began to experience declines in personal resources. We described, as well, how Gignac et al. (2000, 2002) found a similar relationship between age and use of SOC coping strategies among a sample of older adults with osteoarthritis. Most of these individuals reported using coping strategies related to selection (e.g., limiting or avoiding painful activities), optimization (e.g., focusing more effort or allowing more time for most important activities, finding ways to move without pain, planning activities so as to anticipate and avoid distress), or compensation (e.g., finding substitute activities, using prosthetic equipment or helpful gadgets). In this research, however, the old-old respondents reported a reduced use of SOC strategies, compared with the young-old. Again, this may reflect a realistic response to perceived uncontrollability as they begin to encounter significant changes in physical health status, disability, and available social resources. The researchers suggest an alternative explanation, however, reasoning that in very old age, arthritis and its implications for pain and diminished mobility may come to be viewed as normative and no longer a productive focus for active coping efforts (Gignac et al., 2002).

DIMINISHING CAPACITY OF SOCIAL COPING RESOURCES

Age-related health changes can also affect social coping resources in late life. As we noted in chapter 6, family support networks often decrease in size or competence as members themselves age and become more frail. Support networks may also be compromised by loss or transition. Family members may have little understanding of increasing care demands and become overwhelmed as support needs over time become more complex and more medical. At some point, as a result, a family support network may experience caregiver stress and burnout (Hansson & Carpenter, 1994).

It is unfortunate that the older care recipient may unintentionally compound such problems. For example, older people appear to purposefully reduce their networks in size and to increase their relational focus on emotionally close members (Carstensen et al., 1998). We characterized this phenomenon (and the socioemotional selectivity theory) in chapter 7 as an adaptive coping strategy in the service of emotion regulation.

These actions tend to intensify emotional closeness and support in the network, and in doing so should facilitate loss-oriented coping (from the perspective of the dual process model of coping described in chap. 3, this volume). However, they could also undermine an older person's efficacy with respect to the more practical, coping challenges characterized on the restoration-oriented side of the dual process model. In particular, systematically reducing a network violates a primary assumption of the ecological theory of stress (Hobfoll, 1988), which holds that an effective support network is one with a broad array of resources. A diverse network would be expected to have a wider range of instrumental support resources, increasing the availability of the kinds of support most appropriate to one's needs when dealing with increasingly complex and threatening life events. Reducing and narrowing the support network to emphasize only one support dimension (emotional closeness) may increase intimacy in the support relationship. However, shedding relationships with more peripheral members, whose support contributions might have been more instrumental, could reduce the probability that available resources will match needs.

DIMINISHING CAPACITY FOR ADAPTATION TO STRESSFUL OR NONSUPPORTIVE ENVIRONMENTS

In late life, changes in the characteristics or support capacity of one's environment can also lead to important coping challenges. We describe a number of these changes and the ways in which they interact with changing adaptive competence in late life next. We then explore the implications of this dynamic (a core precept of gerontological theory) for the experience of bereavement in old age.

Friendships and loved ones may have been lost to death or relocation. Important peer networks may have been lost through retirement. Older people are more likely to live in older housing or transitional or unsafe neighborhoods. Their support systems are becoming more formal (e.g., health care related), raising the need to deal with "gatekeepers," care staff, and professionals who do not really know the individual and may even view him or her through age-unfriendly stereotypes (Hansson & Carpenter, 1994). As we have seen, the likelihood of physical frailty and serious chronic conditions is increasing. The complexity of one's support needs is likely to be rising, straining the individual's personal coping resources and in many cases resulting in dependency on or intervention by adult children. Family networks usually rise to the occasion, providing important support. In some families, however, this increased responsibility, in a context of scarce resources, can result in caregiver stress, an increased risk for neglect or abuse, or an involuntary change of residence. Moving into the home of an adult child may create a strain not only for the child's family but also for the elder who usually has to renegotiate new understandings, roles, responsibilities, rights, and limits (Hansson et al., 1990). Moving to a more supportive senior housing or institutional setting can in turn raise challenges of finding new relationships that might provide companionship, inclusion, stimulation, and sense of belonging. Most older residents find little emotional solace in this arrangement and little success in developing meaningful personal relationships (Stephens & Bernstein, 1984).

Ecological Theory of Aging

The circumstance in which aging adults begin to experience environments that are either more stressed or less accommodating, at a time when they are becoming increasingly dependent, has been widely studied in the context of the *ecological theory of aging* (Lawton & Nahemow, 1973; Nahemow, 2000). This theory attempts to account for how older people respond to the challenges of a changing, increasingly complex or threatening environment. It assumes a capacity and motivation on the part of the individual to adapt to new levels of threat or demand. Within a reasonable range of such change, active attempts either to affect the threat source or to adapt to it may be successful. However, in the case of repeated exposures to the new level of challenge, a new adaptation level may also be reached (Helson, 1964) wherein the same level of threat would no longer be perceived or evoke a response. The ecological theory assumes that individuals can successfully adapt to most environments (physical or social) that do not cross a threshold for extraordinary threat (Lawton & Nahemow, 1973).

Environmental Docility Hypothesis

Given diminishing competence and resources in old age, however, older people would be expected to become less effective in reaching new adaptation levels. In this connection, Lawton and Simon (1968) proposed the *environmental docility* hypothesis. The essence of the hypothesis was that aging individuals who had become less competent (in terms of physical, psychological, or social competence) would experience a narrower range of adaptability to increasing environmental challenge (termed *environmental press* in the hypothesis). The hypothesis was quite inclusive, proposing its applicability to both physical and social environments.

Our discussion of adaptive competencies thus far has tended to focus on physical and social attributes, as well as on those psychological constructs associated with intellectual function, self-concept, and motivation. However, we would add to this list of psychological variables those dispositions, aspects of temperament, and social skills considered to reflect the construct of *relational competence* (Carpenter, 1993; Hansson & Carpenter, 1994; Hansson et al., 2004). Such dispositions and abilities are widely viewed to facilitate adaptation to changing, stressful social environments. Empirically, they tend to reflect two complementary domains of competence. The first of these domains, *initiation*, involves skills and dispositions likely to be useful in accessing or developing new relationships for purposes of support. Such skills would include, for example, assertiveness, extraversion, lack of shyness, and an ability to communicate one's needs. The second domain, *enhancement*, involves skills and dispositions likely to be useful in nurturing, maintaining, and enhancing existing relationships. Enhancement attributes include empathy, flexibility, and an ability to ensure that members of one's support network feel appreciated, are in turn rewarded, and so on (Hansson & Carpenter, 1994). Relational competence, thus construed, appears especially important in late life, as people become increasingly dependent on support networks who are themselves likely to be aging and becoming stressed.

The environmental docility hypothesis has received considerable empirical support over the years. A study by T. J. Morgan et al. (1984), for example, assessed the generalizability of the hypothesis in a sample of independently living persons 60 to 92 years of age. This study was particularly informative in that it focused broadly on the areas of personal competence identified as critical to adaptive success in the hypothesis. Measures of competence were included to represent health, access to social support, and protective psychological–dispositional dimensions. *Health measures* included a participant's age (age and health being strongly related), self-ratings of overall health, vision and hearing, and gender (with women assumed to be in better health). *Support measures* included marital status, frequency of contact with children and with other family, and size of one's community (a small community typically having fewer formal or specialized health resources). *Psychological–dispositional measures* included (and assumed to play a protective function) were self-esteem, assertiveness, internal locus of control, and nonaversion to dependency (reflecting a realistic willingness to accept help if needed).

A comprehensive index of environmental press was also developed that focused on potentially stressful characteristics of the participant's physical and social environment. In this measure, participants rated the safety of their home and neighborhood, their mobility in their home and neighborhood—their ability to get around and to get out to obtain needed services. In a social support component of the index, they rated the ease and effectiveness with which they were able to communicate with family, friends, and external services regarding their needs. Finally, they rated the predictability of their environment with respect to things in their home working as they should and the extent to which they could count on family, friends, shelter, and medical care being available should the need arise. Finally, a measure of *positive psychological adjustment* reflected participants' scores on widely used measures of geriatric morale, loneliness, anxiety, and depression, as well as ratings of the extent to which they had been able to adjust to experienced age-related problems.

The underlying premise of the study, drawn from the environmental docility hypothesis, was that "less competent" older adults (across dimensions of health, social support, and personality–disposition) would have a narrower range of adaptability to environmental press (or an environment that is a poor fit to their abilities). For purposes of analysis, then, participants were divided into a high-competent group and a low-competent group with respect to each of the competence variables. This classification was based on a median split for interval variables. For the gender and marital status variables, women and married persons were classified as the high-competent persons. Participants classified as low-competent persons would be expected to experience more positive psychological adjustment under low environmental press but poorer psychological adjustment under high environmental press. Among high-competent participants, however, who were assumed to have a greater range of adaptability, environmental press and positive psychological adjustment should not be substantially related. These predictions were supported. Among participants classified as high competent, environmental press was unrelated to psychological adjustment on all 13 variables measured. Among those classified as low competent, however, environmental press was significantly related (as predicted) to psychological adjustment on all 13 variables. In each case, for low-competent participants, a more supportive, less challenging environment was associated with significantly greater positive psychological adjustment.

Implications for Bereavement

We draw from the environmental docility research a sense that analyses of the bereavement experience in late life must take one's environment into account. We have seen (a) how both aging and bereavement might independently contribute to change in a person's environment, and, in turn, (b) how problematic environmental change may exacerbate the bereavement experience. Age-related declines in physical and sensory functioning can increase one's difficulty in routine interactions with the environment, leading to concerns for safety, mobility, isolation, psychological distress, and continued independence. In a similar way, we have seen normative, age-related implications for the size, stability, and efficacy of an older person's family and social support environment. The environmental docility research reviewed (T. J. Morgan et al., 1984) further illustrated how individuals of lower competence, in terms of physical, social, or psychological attributes, would likely experience lower thresholds at which environmental press would result in distress.

It follows from T. J. Morgan et al. (1984) that a late-life conjugal bereavement, especially, may contribute to distress, at least partially via its effects on one's experience of the physical or social environment. In very old age, particularly, the deceased partner may have been responsible for performing important instrumental functions in the relationship (e.g., cooking, monitoring health, or transportation). The loss of someone to perform such functions would make it more difficult for one to safely operate in the physical environment of home and community and could lead to pressures for institutionalization. In addition, older bereaved persons often suffer devastating disruptions to the structure and function of their social support networks, with the potential to weaken emotional supports.

Finally, we saw in the opening chapters of this volume that the symptoms of bereavement are not universally experienced, that physical and psychological consequences can vary widely in their nature, intensity, and duration. We suggest that these individual differences be viewed, within the context of the environmental docility hypothesis, in terms of competencies associated with one's range of adaptability to stressful environments. In this connection, it is also important to recognize the role of coping. We have seen that among older bereaved persons, successful coping can result in increased personal competence and areas of mastery. Such improvements should in turn contribute to an increased (regained) range of adaptability to environmental press.

In summary, five issues from the preceding sections might usefully be incorporated into models of coping with bereavement in late life:

1. Expect an age-related decline in problem-focused coping and in the use of SOC coping strategies, in part (a) because these forms of coping require considerable effort and resources and (b) because age-related decline and loss may come to be viewed as normative and an infeasible focus for effortful coping.

2. In late life, support networks tend to become smaller, more intimate, and more focused on emotional support. However, this phenomenon involves shedding the more peripheral members of one's network, who might have been able to provide a broader array of instrumental supports in time of need.

3. A bereavement can result in problematic changes in social and physical environments, and in counterpoint, a problematic environment can exacerbate the experience of bereavement.

4. Older people are generally less adaptable to the more threatening of these environmental changes.

5. Individual differences (a) in experienced bereavement symptoms and (b) in physical, social, and psychological competencies may substantially affect capacity to adapt to a problematic social or physical environment.

THE DYNAMICS OF DISABILITY IN LATE LIFE

In recent years, geriatric practitioners have begun to understand the need to broaden their focus, beyond simply diagnosing and treating a disease or condition, to include the implications of the condition for independent functioning (Kane & Kane, 2000). Hospital discharge planners and rehabilitation therapists, for example, need also to understand the impact of the disease on an older patient's ability to reenter and function in the home and his or her need for supportive housing or services. This analysis, then, implies a need for comprehensive and multidimensional assessments. Such assessment should focus not only on physical health and current and predicted level of function but also on emotional status, cognitive ability, ability to communicate, values, self-efficacy, and motivation to continue. It would also include an appreciation of the demands and challenges of the environment (physical and social) to which an older patient must return, and the availability and stability of instrumental and social support resources.

This broadening focus has also stimulated interest in the epidemiology of *disablement* among older adults (Jette, 1996; Nagi, 1991; Verbrugge & Jette, 1994). In the following sections, we briefly describe the disablement process. We then explore how models of disablement might provide a way to extend our thinking about the implications of bereavement in late life.

The process of disablement occurs in the context of chronic diseases and conditions, which tend to increase in incidence in late life. Even among people age 65 years and over, incidence increases with age, especially among the oldest old. Comorbidity is also a concern; some two thirds of people over 65 have at least two chronic conditions, and one third report having at least four conditions, placing a patient at risk for both additive and joint (interactive) consequences (Fried, Ferrucci, Darer, Williamson, & Anderson, 2004). There are also important gender differences in the incidence of chronic conditions in late life. Women are more likely to experience nonfatal conditions, such as arthritis, orthopedic impairment, migraines, and digestive disorders. So, they sustain more intense and more prolonged suffering but are unlikely to die from it. Men, however, are more likely to have life-threatening conditions such as heart and vascular disease, emphysema, and liver disease (Jette, 1996).

In late life, however, the more likely consequence of chronic conditions is disability rather than death (Jette, 1996). *Disability* is defined as involving loss of one's ability to perform daily tasks and activities central to independence and quality of life and to participate in important social or occupational roles. Such limitations imply an increased dependency on others and a growing need for medical, social, and institutional services. The incidence of disability also rises dramatically with age.

Chronic disease, however, does not always lead to disability. Some diseases, such as cardiovascular disease and arthritis, are more reliable predictors. Also, some conditions, in combination, increase the likelihood of disability. The co-occurrence of cardiovascular disease and osteoarthritis in the lower limbs would be an example (Fried et al., 2004). In addition, there are a number of important mediating variables. For example, many older people exhibit much plasticity; they enter the situation with greater adaptive reserves (physical, cognitive, or emotional) and are able to recover much of their functioning over time. Generational influences also play a role. Recent surveys conducted only 5 to 10 years apart find increasingly smaller percentages of people with chronic disease who then progress to become disabled over the next 5 years. Likely explanations include an older population with more education, more income (and access health care services), and increasingly effective medical and rehabilitative interventions (Jette, 1996). In a similar way, for those older persons who are already disabled, certain variables (e.g., higher education and being a male) are related to higher success in reestablishing functioning.

People who are poor are at greater risk of becoming disabled. Women in general are at greater risk of becoming disabled and appear less able to regain function (although this relationship may be confounded with a longer life span among women). However, married women appear at less risk of disablement and are more likely to eventually regain function. Older men are more likely to experience problems measured in terms of activities of daily living and tasks within the home, whereas women tend to be more at risk of losing physical mobility outside the home (Jette, 1996). Of particular interest, the two dynamics—onset of disability and subsequent improvement of function—are somewhat different and are predicted by different variables. The transition to disability (onset) appears to be associated with overall health status and with various demographic variables reflecting one's resources. Improvement of function, however, is associated with degree of lost ability and with amount of time since onset.

This sampling of findings suggests a need for more systematic research regarding why, among older persons with a chronic disease or condition, the condition does not always lead to disability. Specifically, there is a need for a more comprehensive understanding of protective factors, of moderator variables, and of the range of intervention strategies that might prevent chronic conditions from leading to significant loss of function (Jette, 1996). To this end, Verbrugge and Jette (1994) proposed a sequential (pathway) model of the disablement process. The first stage in the model is termed *impairment* and involves specific physical and mental abnormalities resulting from disease, injury, and aging. The second stage is termed *functional limitations*, an array of consequences of one's impairment for personal functioning (e.g., limits on ability to walk, think, read, or speak). The third stage in the model is termed *disability*, defined to include diminished ability to perform routine activities of daily living or to function in important family, social, or occupational roles and activities. Loss of such functioning is viewed to result in lost opportunities for interaction, inclusion, companionship, productive contributions, and independence.

Conceptualizing the third stage (disability) with respect to one's personal life contexts and lost opportunities for interaction, then, not only implies a need to understand the nature and degree of one's impairments and resulting loss of function. It also implies that the meaning of functional loss is in part determined by the opportunities and demands emanating from the situation—one's environment (Nagi, 1991). Further, any consideration of the situation or environment as a variable suggests an analysis of three dimensions of one's situation. The first of these dimensions, of course, involves the actual physical and cognitive attributes or challenges present in the situation. The second dimension, however, involves how the older person appraises and responds to the situation. The third involves how other people throughout one's support networks appraise and respond to the situation (Jette, 1996).

Research on the disablement process provides two final insights. First, it has been possible to identify many important risk factors that predict continued decline in functional status. These include depression, heavy use of alcohol or tobacco, substantial cognitive impairment, comorbidity, a previous history of functional limitations or falls, the use of multiple medications, poor nutrition, poor vision, and self-ratings indicating poor health. Social support variables are also indicated, to include low levels of instrumental and emotional support, felt isolation, and diminished social participation (Stuck et al., 1999). Second, there is growing empirical support for the sequential nature of the disablement process. Functional limitations (not the disease or condition, per se) appear to be the primary predictors of eventual disability. Presence of disease and physical impairment, age, gender, and counterproductive health behaviors all tend to influence eventual disability through their effects on functional limitations, suggesting that clinical prevention efforts also might most productively focus on the functional limitations stage (Lawrence & Jette, 1996).

IMPLICATIONS FOR THINKING ABOUT BEREAVEMENT IN LATE LIFE

We conceptualized this book, initially, as an effort to explore the implications of aging for the bereavement experience. Our discussions thus far have reinforced the importance of that approach, for both bereavement and gerontological research. However, we have also begun to ponder whether our basic research questions (when thinking about older adults) should change in emphasis to focus on the effects of bereavement on the aging experience rather than the reverse. The central questions then might focus on how and when bereavement and its consequences would come into play within the disablement process in late life.

Longitudinal studies of bereavement in late life have not typically adopted a process model, as is the case in the disability literature. This may reflect an underlying assumption that bereavement-related symptoms (physical, emotional, cognitive, and social) are just that—symptoms of bereavement rather than part of a larger dynamic characteristic of old age. Thus, the majority of studies simply track the trajectory of symptoms across time, with an eye to identifying patterns, trajectories, and interrelations among variables, prebereavement risk factors, and predictors of recovery or adaptation. Some of the longitudinal studies we reviewed in chapters 5 and 6 of this volume have progressed in design to identify consequences that occur early in a bereavement (e.g., depression or physical health problems) that subsequently predict depressive and physical outcomes at a later date (e.g., Murrell et al., 1988; Robinson-Whelen et al., 2001). Some researchers have also called for an extension of our thinking about bereavement to address the potential for positive outcomes (e.g., growth, mastery) among survivors (e.g., P. S. Fry, 1998; Lund et al., 1993). We agree, and in chapters 2, 3, and 5 (and in Figures 2.1 and 3.2) we discussed the role of positive outcomes in bereavement and the importance of positive emotions and reappraisals in coping. It must also be remembered that aging and late life involve much more than just the accumulation of losses and disablement (D. A. Lund, personal communication, November 21, 2005). Our focus in this chapter, and in the integrative risk factor framework, however, has concerned risks for poor outcomes, some of which are age related.

A major step, we believe, has been the introduction of integrative models for the prediction of bereavement outcome, such as the one introduced in chapter 3 of this volume. Such models propose a bereavement process, accounting for a wide range of loss- and restoration-oriented stressors arising out of the death, the role of mediator variables (interpersonal resources and risk factors, appraisal, coping, and intrapersonal resources and risk factors), and predicted bereavement outcomes (specified in terms of symptom intensities).

We believe, however, that it may be useful in thinking about *late-life* bereavements to consider a further integration of these bereavement models with models of the process of disablement. To accomplish this, it is necessary to differentiate in the integrative framework between short-term outcomes (which are the major focus of the model presented in chap. 3, Figure 3.3) and long-term outcomes. The endpoint of the integrative framework then would

EXHIBIT 8.1
Sequencing of Components Reflecting a Blending of the Integrative Risk
Factor Framework and the Disablement Model

---

1. Bereavement: loss- and restoration-oriented stressors
2. (a) Interpersonal resources and risks
   (b) Appraisal and coping
   (c) Intrapersonal resources and risks
3. Short-term outcomes
4. Long-term outcomes/*Impairments*
5. *Functional limitations*
6. *Disability*

Note. Components of the disablement model presented in italics.

focus on long-term outcomes (in terms of remaining grief intensity, continuing level of need for loss or restoration coping efforts, physical and mental health, and disrupted social engagement). The long-term outcomes component of the integrative framework would be understood to coincide with the impairments component of Verbrugge and Jette's (1994) disablement model. The long-term outcomes component of bereavement could then be conceptualized to lead to functional limitations, which (for some older bereaved persons) would in turn predict disability. This more comprehensive framework would reflect the sequence shown in Exhibit 8.1.

This extended framework for understanding bereavement process, specific to late life, suggests four final points. First, it realistically acknowledges the implications (in old age) of having to draw down one's increasingly limited adaptive reserves. Second, it deals directly with the process and implications of any failure by an older person to fully adapt to a loss. With few exceptions, bereavement researchers have not addressed these two issues. Longitudinal studies have shown the trajectory of symptoms over the period of a study, often differentiating among those bereaved who adapt more or less successfully. Theoretical developments regarding complicated grief reactions have, in turn, increased our understanding of such trajectories. Only studies that include mortality as an outcome, however, have actually followed the issue of failure to adapt to its logical outcome. But we have seen that bereavement–mortality studies (in late life) are problematic, with an increasing proportion of the variance in death outcomes reflecting normal aging process rather than any direct effects of bereavement.

Third, adopting an extended framework should also allow researchers and practitioners to identify risk factors relevant to each part of the process, and to propose prevention strategies (e.g., primary, secondary, tertiary) and where in the process they might most appropriately be targeted (Hansson & Stroebe, 2003). We noted earlier (in chap. 1, this volume) that at least two major reviews of the intervention literature (Jordan & Neimeyer, 2003; Schut et al., 2001) found therapy-based interventions to be beneficial among high-risk persons and among those already experiencing complications. Older bereaved persons whose status has progressed deep into the disablement process, even if their problems now reflect mostly an exacerbation of normal age-related decline, may thus be seen as viable candidates for treatment.

Finally, the last two components of the disablement process (functional limitations and disability) are defined with respect to the challenges they present in very practical areas of personal functioning. Functional limitations are those involving a person's most basic abilities, to walk, think, read, speak, and so on. The disability component then reflects the effect of diminished basic abilities for performance in those activities at the core of one's physical, psychological, and social well-being (e.g., performance of family or social role responsibilities). Diminishing competence in these important areas of personal and role performance suggests that the disablement process (when experienced by older bereaved persons) will affect primarily their efforts in the area of restoration-oriented coping (as conceptualized in the dual process model of coping with bereavement).

CONCLUSIONS

In this chapter, we examined how age-related changes in physiological functioning and health could (directly or indirectly) increase an older person's vulnerability for poor outcome of bereavement. The likelihood of entering a bereavement from a more problematic health baseline, the increased complexity and chronicity of health conditions in old age, and a diminishing capacity to adapt to nonsupportive environments all present important implications for cognitive and emotional coping.

However, we also explored ways in which bereavement might exacerbate normative age-related loss in late life. In this connection, it was useful to differentiate between short-term and long-term outcomes of bereavement. In late life, long-term physical outcomes are likely to reflect a depletion of one's adaptive reserves and a failure to fully adapt to the consequences of the loss. We proposed, therefore, that long-term outcomes of bereavement could be understood to coincide with the impairments component of Verbrugge and Jette's (1994) model of the disablement process.

Bereavement theory has not previously acknowledged the potential importance of these processes with respect to their influence on outcomes. We view this as a crucial oversight. As we have described in the earlier chapters, however, theory in the area of stress and coping, generally, has begun to consider issues of aging and provides leads that should be useful in now doing so with respect to bereavement experience. In the final chapter of this volume, we identify what appear to be the most important elements of interface and propose specific approaches to incorporating them into models of coping with bereavement.

9

INTEGRATING AGING AND BEREAVEMENT IN LATE LIFE

This volume evolved from our shared concern that a large population, the population most frequently represented among the bereaved, had been taken rather for granted and discounted in bereavement research and theory. Our sense was that this oversight reflected the earliest questions in the clinical literature (beginning in the 1940s) and the search for risk factors. Early studies that simply compared outcomes across age groups tended to find that younger bereaved persons experienced greater distress. A number of stereotypical explanations quickly emerged (e.g., "the death of an older spouse is less unexpected"), few researchers thought to consider the immense variability among older adults, and the field moved on to other questions.

In the intervening years, however, the knowledge base on human aging exploded. We have come to better understand the nature and course of physiological and cognitive aging. We have learned much about age-related changes in emotion, social motivation and relationships, self-concept, responses to stress, and experience of emotional distress and disorder. We have learned about age-related changes in the nature of health experience; comorbidity; causes of death; coping; and, of course, the compounding issues of disrupted support networks, poverty, and stereotypic thinking about older people. These new areas of knowledge have led to more integrative theory development in the field of aging and to a more coherent, late-life developmental perspective. Until the 1990s, however, the developmental perspective rarely found its way into bereavement research, even though much of that research included older adults as respondents.

As a result of our own collaborations across the years, one of us (Stroebe) a bereavement specialist and the other (Hansson) a gerontologist, we became increasingly interested in this gap in understanding the role of aging in bereavement experience. It matters that aging is a time of increasingly diminished physiological status and adaptive reserves. It matters that the numbers of older people are growing around the world, and that societies have had to struggle to adapt and provide for their changing needs. It matters that poor outcome of bereavement often results in greater dependency on family and community resources for basic needs and long-term care. It matters that many families and professional practitioners who may become involved in care are relatively unfamiliar with the complexities of human aging and the ways in which it can affect our capacity to adapt to stressful life events such as bereavement.

Throughout the book, we have examined the experience of bereavement among older people from a number of perspectives. We considered the extent to which their grief reflected our general understanding of the nature and course of grief, including patterns of normative and complicated reactions. We also considered the relevance to this population of contemporary theoretical analyses of adaptive coping, within the integrative risk factor framework and within the dual process model of coping (DPM). Finally, a comprehensive review of research on the impact and correlates of bereavement among older adults introduced a (previously neglected) life span developmental perspective.

In this concluding chapter, we consider the implications of infusing an aging perspective into the integrative framework and address a number of remaining questions. For example, how can the unique manifestations of bereavement among older people be understood within the integrative theoretical framework? How might the developmental changes and circumstances associated with late life influence core components of the integrative framework (i.e., the nature of loss- and restoration-oriented stressors, one's balance of intrapersonal and interpersonal risk factors and coping resources, appraisal and coping, need for oscillation, and the kinds of outcomes that should be assessed)? How might we address emerging practical issues to do with intervention and caring for older bereaved persons?

We propose possible extensions of the integrative framework, derived from this analysis, with implications for future research. We consider how the framework might be extended to accommodate other subgroups of bereaved persons (e.g., parents vs. spouses). Finally, we explore how other contemporary theories of bereavement experience described in chapter 1 (e.g., attachment theory, the psychosocial transition model, meaning-making theories, and social constructionist approaches) might benefit from consideration of late-life developmental issues.

BEREAVEMENT AMONG OLDER PERSONS WITHIN THE INTEGRATIVE FRAMEWORK

In chapter 3 we extended the DPM to provide a more integrative framework for understanding individual differences in adaptation to bereavement. We had originally described the DPM more specifically, as a taxonomy for understanding the ways that people come to terms with the death of a loved one (M. S. Stroebe & Schut, 1999). However, the extended structure of the integrative framework now allows an examination of cause–effect patterns in the relationship between the experience of a bereavement and short- and long-term adjustment. According to this perspective, adaptation (which is related to differences in outcome) occurs within the context of daily life and general activity. It involves two categories of stressors (loss- and restoration-oriented) and an assessment of intra- and interpersonal risk factors. It includes an analysis of coping in terms of strategies and appraisal and in terms of an emotion-regulation mechanism labeled *oscillation*. We examine each of these dimensions in the following section as they relate to bereavement among older people.

Context

The integrative framework assumes that adjustment (coping) takes place within the context of daily life. Thus, before examining stressors, resources, and coping-related parameters in relationship to older people's bereavements, it is useful to consider the life situation in which bereavement occurs. This is particularly important, because the variable, age, is in itself an imperfect predictor of differences in health status or adaptive potential among bereaved people.

We have seen that the circumstances of bereavement can vary substantially between older and younger persons, with implications for the nature of one's experience. Older bereaved spouses, for example, are less likely to remarry than are younger spouses, and they may lack the opportunity for developing new couple-companionate relationships on which Western culture is so firmly based. They are therefore more likely to have their lives disorganized in the long term by bereavement and to lose meaningful roles and opportunities for rewarding interactions. We have noted too the accumulation in numbers of deaths experienced by older persons, not only of family members but also of friends. Widowed persons may have turned to a sibling or a friend for support and companionship following the death of a spouse.

The subsequent death of the sibling or friend may leave a bereaved older person with few alternative sources for comfort and companionship. And yet, an older adult's grief on the death of a close person may be disenfranchised, their symptoms being attributed to old age or their grief assumed to be less intense than that of "primary" grievers (i.e., those with a more direct—parental or spousal—relationship to the deceased). Society is more likely to ignore the needs of an older bereaved person in this situation. Under these circumstances, the older person may not receive the acknowledgment and support that the bereavement situation really requires.

It is also useful to consider more closely the contrast between contextual factors in a younger and an older person's bereavement, for example, following conjugal loss. Among women, for example, a young widow has to start over. Having lost her partner, she may have to work out who she is and to explore possible new identities and life choices. She is likely to have responsibilities to young dependents who need care but who are also grieving. At the same time, she is herself likely to have the emotional needs of any young person, needs that will not be met because of her spouse's death. She may have to gradually build new social links that are not dependent on the spouse. Her economic future may be problematic, and she may need to access information sources in a variety of domains and to build alliance networks. Many young widows are troubled too by inappropriate expectations of those around them who set unrealistic recovery goals and schedules (e.g., "Grief takes a calendar year" or "You should be over it by now").

By contrast, an older widow may feel less pressure to work out her identity, because her identity and self-concept have become pretty well established by old age. One's identity is likely to involve some adjustment after bereavement, but not such active change as in the case of a younger widow. Caregiver or formal support networks may already be in place and be able to assist in adapting to increased instrumental demands. Older widows may also have begun to consolidate their emotional support resources, reducing support networks to include a greater proportion of emotionally close members. Compounding the difficulties of her bereavement, however, an older widow may increasingly need to deal with interactions between her emotional reactions and issues of physical health and economic status. As we indicate in the following section, such differences can influence an older person's selection of which stressors to confront and which to ignore in adapting to bereavement.

Such contrasts in experience illustrate why the age-related contexts of bereavement must be considered when comparing the impact of loss on younger versus older persons. As we noted in our discussion in chapter 8 of the environmental docility research, many features of bereavement could have their effect on health and well-being through their effects on contextual variables.

Loss-Oriented and Restoration-Oriented Stressors

For most people, young or old, the loss of a loved one is an upsetting, often harrowing experience associated with a range of life changes requiring adjustment. Indeed, early researchers widely considered the death of a spouse to be the life event requiring the most intense readjustment (Holmes & Rahe, 1967). Subsequent research has focused on identifying more precisely the components of this stressor, and in that connection we have proposed a classification system that differentiates between loss- and restoration-oriented stressors.

On closer examination, however, the stressors associated with bereavement among older people appear to be somewhat different from those experienced by younger people. We look first at loss-oriented stressors: We have already noted (in chaps. 1 and 2) that older people are less likely to experience bereavements from traumatic types of deaths or, in general, to have to endure deaths that occur suddenly, without any time for preparation or in an untimely manner. We noted also (in chap. 7) the phenomenon of "emotional dampening" among older adults, reflecting increased emotional control, moderation, stability, and a leveling of affect—even in stressful situations. It follows that there would be less emotional disintegration on the death of a loved one.

Although such factors would tend to reduce an older person's vulnerability to extreme grief reactions, other loss-related factors could be associated with an opposite effect. For example, loss of a partner in old age is likely to follow a relationship of longer duration. A longer relationship that has survived into old age (particularly in contemporary Western society where divorce has become easier) is likely to entail emotional interdependency, long-lasting attachment and emotional closeness, and, following bereavement, greater isolation. There is much to be missed in terms of joint history and memories.

The experience of bereavement in late life, however, can extend well beyond the loss of a spouse. The longer one lives, the greater the likelihood of experiencing the death of children, even grandchildren, and these types of loss are associated with especially intense grief reactions. Also, the number of deaths experienced will increase as one ages; there may be multiple, concurrent losses and an accumulation of grief from losses that have occurred across the lifetime. Although the latter occurrence may bring with it some resilience (through greater experience with bereavement), it could also cause a "bereavement overload," whereby the bereaved person becomes overwhelmed because of the number of losses (Kastenbaum, 1969).

The empirical studies that we reviewed in chapters 5 and 6 also suggested a number of restoration-oriented stressors that could become more problematic for older bereaved persons. For example, work and legal problems that arise as a consequence of the death would likely be more taxing as one gets older, becomes less robust, and is less used to dealing with change (e.g., relating to increasing technology in society). Loss of the deceased person's skills, abilities, and resources could cause additional aggravation. In general, we have noted that concurrent, seemingly minor hassles or more major life events may interact with the transition to bereavement among older people, causing extreme suffering and distress. Furthermore, caring for a chronically ill spouse over a period of months or years (which occurs more frequently in late life) may affect an older bereaved person's own health and result in withdrawal from a more social life. Returning to optimal health and becoming reintegrated may be more difficult to achieve when one is older, more frail, and alone.

Loss of income following the death can also become more problematic for older adults. Younger bereaved persons may need to (re)enter the workforce to increase earnings, but for an older person this may not be an option. Financial loss may mean relocation, another potential secondary stressor. Relocation may also result from the death of a partner who had been the caregiver, necessitating a move to a nursing home, again producing discontinuity in daily routine (which can be especially important to older people).

Contrasting the stressors associated with loss and restoration illustrates the range of concerns that bereaved persons have to deal with while they are grieving. In particular, it facilitates a classification of the types of issues with which—according to the growing body of empirical research reviewed earlier—older bereaved persons are frequently confronted. It has become evident that a wide variety of factors can easily be represented within the loss and restoration categories. It is hoped that this will be useful for researchers and caregivers in understanding the situation of older bereaved persons.

We turn next to a consideration of how patterns of resources fit within the integrative framework. Some of these have more to do with the loss-oriented types of stressors previously described, others with restoration-oriented stressors. Still others may serve as less specific resources.

Interpersonal and Nonpersonal Resources

How an older person manages to cope with the stressors identified earlier will depend partly on available interpersonal and nonpersonal resources (e.g., money or services). In the preceding chapters, we discussed many resources and a variety of protective factors that have been shown to affect bereavement outcomes among older persons. However, any resource may also be considered a potential risk factor in that insufficient amounts of a critical resource create a vulnerability.

Paradoxically, in late-life bereavement the deceased spouse would likely have been the person turned to for emotional support. Experience of the loss is thus compounded by a realization that the death has also devastated one's emotional base. Such a phenomenon is not, of course, unique to the experience of older persons. But older persons are likely to have more limited networks, and in the case of spousal bereavement, they are likely to have a much longer history of relying on their spouse for support in times of difficulty. Fortunately for some, however, such vulnerability may be tempered by greater experience with grief across the life span, and a greater likelihood that the death was expected, prepared for, and more timely.

A lack of interpersonal resources is also reflected in the restoration-oriented stressors discussed in the previous section, including high levels of isolation, lack of integration, or lack of support available from others. This in part reflects dwindling family and friendship circles in late life, but it also reflects emerging role constraints (e.g., limited remarriage possibilities). We noted earlier that there is little evidence of a stress-buffering effect of social support. Support from others during bereavement has not been shown to foster recovery from symptoms specific to grief (although people in general clearly benefit from being supported). However, we have seen that among older adults support from others may make a critical difference with respect to restoration-oriented tasks. Our review of empirical studies suggested that the older bereaved person will have many more such tasks to face.

With respect to social support on a more formal level, bereavement support groups, counseling, and therapy have become increasingly available in Western cultures in recent decades. However, older adults are less likely than younger ones to use mental health services, and when they do, are more likely than younger adults to contact their physician rather than a mental health provider. A variety of reasons have been advanced to explain this pattern. These include the cost of treatment, generational sensitivity to stigma associated with mental health treatment, transportation problems, and so on. It is understandable, under such conditions, that among older adults there is a tendency to try to manage psychological distress with medications (Gatz & Smyer, 2001). We have seen, however, that whether or not they seek them, older bereaved persons are likely to need such services. Researchers and clinicians are actively exploring improved strategies for the delivery of mental health services in general to older persons (see Appendix A for a brief summary). We believe such efforts should extend as well to the provision of formal interventions to older bereaved persons who may benefit.

Nonpersonal resources include the availability of supportive housing and care arrangements for bereaved persons (but in many communities, such provision is inadequate). For example, we noted in chapter 5 that older persons who became widowed experienced twice the risk of being moved to a nursing home over the first 2 years of bereavement, compared with nonwidowed persons. It is clear that, because of their greater frailty, older persons will be much more in need of such services than younger bereaved persons. Issues of financial security raise similar concerns. Older widowed persons are less likely to be able to compensate for lost income (e.g., by finding employment). Poverty is not uncommon among older bereaved persons (especially women, at least in Western societies). It may preclude participation in social activities or access to health care (and possibly grief counseling).

A further resource for coping with bereavement may be provided through one's cultural setting. However, we noted in chapter 6 a paucity of multisite, international studies of bereavement or widow(er)hood in old age. Available research suggests that differences in cultural patterns can influence adjustment among older bereaved persons in critical ways. Factors that merit additional investigation include cultural norms regarding the inclusion of a bereaved parent in the homes of their children, varying national schemes for income and health maintenance, and normative size, composition, and involvement of social-care networks.

Intrapersonal Resources

What coping skills and resources does the older bereaved person bring to the situation? What personal characteristics might provide strength or adaptive potential? The studies reviewed in chapter 5 confirmed that a majority of older bereaved persons bring remarkable personal resources to their bereavement situation. Most appear to be highly resilient. They manage to adapt to their new circumstances across the course of time, difficult though the experience may be for them. Many say that they have learned needed skills. Many report that they have experienced a new sense of personal potential and self-discovery. Feelings of increased personal control and autonomy and growing self-confidence have also frequently been reported. Older persons may also benefit from having developed a well-established identity over their longer life span, with a clearer life narrative and sense of spiritual meaning (e.g., being more involved in a traditional religious system, they may receive more comfort from religious beliefs and rituals). They are likely to have fewer stressful responsibilities to younger dependents, yet gain strength from their roles as parent and grandparent.

However, deficits affect some, and inequalities occur between subgroups of older bereaved persons. For example, we noted that older persons of ethnic minority and lower socioeconomic status have less access to certain opportunities for social participation, which may exacerbate loneliness and grieving. We also noted evidence that widowers experience more depression in the short term and higher mortality rates than do widows (compared with same-sex controls), a pattern which pertains for older spouses, with the possibility that it may even intensify. Here, again, more studies are needed.

Prebereavement health status is also a critical variable. Physical and mental health deficits prior to the death can (at any age) exacerbate the psychological, physical, and practical consequences of bereavement, but health becomes an increasing source of difficulties in older bereaved persons. Prebereavement health may have been compromised by age-related changes in physical and sensory abilities, the accumulation of chronic conditions, and consequent vulnerability to disease or emotional distress. We saw in earlier chapters the kinds of difficulties experienced by those who had suffered poor health status—sometimes combined with greater dependency—prior to their bereavement. Older bereaved persons, particularly those who are grieving intensely, tend not to eat well or to enjoy food. Many lose weight. They sleep poorly, which has been shown to lead to greater difficulties in bereavement-related adjustment. Although older bereaved persons are in general quite resilient, many would appear to be placed at increased risk by these circumstances.

We also discussed (in chap. 7) patterns of age-related changes in intellectual ability, some of which might help and others hinder adjustment to bereavement in later life. For example, fluid intellectual abilities (including numeric ability and word fluency, which more closely reflect physiological status) begin to decline in early-old age. We would expect such change to have serious implications for dealing with restoration-oriented stressors (e.g., finances). By contrast, crystallized abilities (e.g., verbal meaning and intuitive reasoning) remain stable until one is in the mid-70s. We would expect these kinds of retained ability to help a bereaved person in understanding the meaning and emotional impact of the loss itself. It is also noteworthy that improved health and higher education levels across succeeding generations are associated with improved cognitive abilities in late life; this should improve the ability of older people in general to cope with bereavement.

Finally, individual differences related to personality or disposition would seem relevant in the context of coping with bereavement (viewed as a life stressor). Of particular interest, we have seen how one's evolving self-concept could be particularly relevant to adaptation among older adults. But this dynamic can be complex. For example, old age implies the loss of a number of competencies and social role identities central to one's sense of self. Yet, it has been suggested that as people age, they continually add to and refine the self-concept, and that ongoing consolidation of self-schemas and understanding of previous experience can lead to gains in feelings of mastery, competence, and control. Successful adaptations to previous losses should contribute to the development of a robust self-concept that could enhance adaptation to subsequent bereavements. However, it is a concern that bereavement can disrupt the continuity of self among older adults (e.g., a lost marital role that is more difficult to "replace"). Then again, the complexity of the self-concept among older people may have a buffering effect, fostering resilience to bereavement. We view these issues to be worthy of direct investigation in future research.

Coping

In earlier chapters we explored the implications of developmental change for appraisal and coping among older adults. The work of Lawton (1996;

Lawton et al., 1992), for example, provided valuable insights into the nature of emotional experience and ways of coping with emotions that are more typical for older than for younger people. These suggest unique patterns among older adults in dealing with a life event such as bereavement. For example, compared with younger people, older adults reported having greater emotional control (e.g., trying and managing to stay calm in times of stress), less excitement, more stable good moods, and fewer psychophysiological sensations associated with intense emotions.

All these aspects would suggest increased maturity, flexibility, and control in dealing with life events. They also suggest an emotional dampening among older persons, especially with respect to negative emotions. Indeed, the larger body of research reviewed suggested that positive emotions appear dominant and that older persons exhibit considerable skill and effort in the service of emotion regulation. We would expect these emotional patterns to protect older adults from excessive bereavement-related trauma and to facilitate adjustment. To our knowledge, however, empirical studies have not yet put this directly to the test. In our view, such life span perspectives could usefully be applied in future bereavement research.

A further characteristic of older persons' coping, proposed by Baltes and Baltes (1990), is selectivity. Older people appear to become purposefully selective in focusing on those abilities and activities that they want to optimize and maintain. They do something similar with respect to their interpersonal networks, reducing the size of their network and, at the same time, increasing the proportion of emotionally close persons in those networks. They also become more selective with respect to the types of life stressors they attend to and prepare to cope with. We saw in the research by Gignac and colleagues (Gignac et al., 2000, 2002), for example, how older people with osteoarthritis try to limit or avoid painful activities, anticipate stressful situations, and then find ways to optimize their daily functioning and where necessary compensate for lost abilities and activities.

We believe that it could be immensely useful to conduct research on how older adults use coping strategies, reflecting selection, optimization, and compensation to adapt to the consequences of bereavement. Much of the conceptual groundwork for such research has been laid. For example, in the integrative framework we have classified a spectrum of loss- and restoration-oriented stressors likely to require coping efforts. Relatedly, the literature specifies a diversity of tasks of adaptation (e.g., achieving cognitive and emotional acceptance; meaning making; identity change; reestablishing relationships; reestablishing independence, competence, assumption of responsibility; and so on). We understand, however, that older individuals will vary in their vulnerability to each of these kinds of stressors and in their appraisals of which stressors appear most threatening. Will they become more selective in which coping tasks to engage or in establishing standards for coping success? How will they make those choices? Will they become more selective in one domain (e.g., in restoration-oriented coping rather than loss-oriented coping)? Will they choose to forgo some of the common tasks of grieving that are "socially prescribed" and necessary only to the extent that one feels compelled to rise to the occasion to cope, succeed, or regain all former levels of function (Hansson, 1986)? Some normative tasks of grieving involve responsibilities to other people; will older bereaved persons discriminate in these responsibilities on the basis of emotional closeness of the other? Some areas of coping also allow others to help, but some do not. Will age-related reductions of one's support network result in a reduced access to coping resources (e.g., in more instrumental-restoration tasks) and constrain options with respect to exercising selectivity? Will selections reflect components of one's self-concept, resulting in more aggressive coping on tasks for which a failure has implications for their sense of identity as an independent person, sense of personal control, or self-esteem? If so, would we predict greater attention to either loss- or restoration-oriented tasks (and for whom)?

We reported too that older adults remain active in coping with life events such as bereavement. But as they get older and have to deal with increasingly uncontrollable, chronic, and progressive health and life events, they are likely to shift from problem-focused to more emotion-focused coping, and from assimilative to accommodative strategies. It is important to note that these differences in their coping, compared with younger adults, reflect a difference with respect to what has to be coped with. Under circumstances that cannot be controlled, emotion-focused coping is likely (and adaptive), regardless of age.

Age-related changes in coping, then, appear in general to be positive and adaptive. They enable a breadth and flexibility of coping styles. They encourage the formulation of realistic goals. They allow an older adult to draw on accumulated life experience and expertise, as well as on perspectives associated with postformal thought. They should enable a more effective appraisal of risk and, in particular, facilitate engagement in loss-oriented coping tasks.

But age-related change can also complicate coping. We noted, for example, the likelihood of diminished capacity for "effortful" cognitive processing as one gets older, making it potentially more difficult for bereaved persons to cope with restoration-oriented matters such as learning new tasks, solving unfamiliar kinds of problems, and coping with new roles. A further complicating factor reflects age-related changes in access to social coping resources. Reductions in one's social network would, for example, tend to decrease the range of available instrumental support resources, making it difficult to cope with restoration-oriented tasks.

A final topic to be discussed in this section on coping involves the regulation of the emotions associated with loss- and restoration-oriented stressors. Emotion regulation is fundamental to the DPM (and thereby, to the integrative framework). We have postulated the dynamic, regulatory process of oscillation: Healthy grieving entails dealing with both types of stressors, intermingled with periods of respite from coping (which are recuperative), thus involving confrontation and avoidance of the stressors. However, a number of questions seem pertinent. For example, on what dimensions of oscillation might age-related differences appear? How might such differences affect our understanding of oscillation itself? The aging research reviewed in this book suggests a number of possibilities regarding age differences and some insights regarding how the construct of oscillation itself might be strengthened by further refinement and specification.

It is conceivable that older persons may oscillate between loss- and restoration-oriented stressors less frequently and less intensely than younger persons, assuming reduced emotional vulnerability. Emotional dampening, for example, may make it easier—perhaps less painful—to regulate one's emotions. Older people's greater emotional control, maturity, and skills at emotional regulation should play a protective role in this (indeed, older bereaved persons might be expected to spend less time in general in coping with stressors). We have noted that older persons may have a greater need to address tasks associated with restoration and a lesser need to focus on tasks associated with loss. If older persons are more selective in the stressors they choose to attend to, and if they have a greater need to attend to restoration stressors, they would be expected to engage less frequently in upsetting confrontations with loss stressors.

Contextual factors should also play a role. For example, older bereaved people will typically have had a longer relationship with the deceased. Also, they will likely have had more time to prepare for bereavement (e.g., more time with their spouse to leaf through photos and other memories). They might therefore take more comfort in bereavement from reminiscing about shared experiences, and any confrontation with memories involving the deceased, when they occur, would be likely to be less intensely emotional. These hypotheses need further empirical investigation.

Turning to the implications for theory building: A focus on oscillation among older bereaved persons raises a number of interesting considerations. To take just two features that emerged from our literature review: Older bereaved persons are likely to have (a) diminished capacity for effortful cognitive processing and (b) more limited access to social resources. It would seem reasonable to expect such deficits to impair adaptive coping efforts involving oscillation. Yet little is known about oscillation. To what extent is it a conscious, assertive, active dynamic that requires personal or social resources or coping styles? Again, there is scope for further investigation.

The many and varied practical challenges that older bereaved persons face (declines in physical health, the need to learn new skills, dwindling social resources, etc.) also raise an interesting theoretical issue. That is, they raise the possibility that with older bereaved persons, we should increasingly focus our attention on oscillation between tasks within one domain—

restoration. Among older bereaved persons, some restoration tasks may be more easily attended to than others, for example, those that require less rigorous learning or problem-solving efforts. Thus, older bereaved persons may try to avoid confrontation with more difficult problems, such as financial crises. Yet dealing with financial difficulties would be a necessary part of adaptation too. The notion that flexibility is needed not just across the loss and restoration domains, but also within them, needs to be emphasized within the integrative framework.

Finally, research on bereavement among older people underscores the need to differentiate short- and long-term oscillations and to stipulate predictions more precisely. On the one hand, the DPM specifies that there will be daily fluctuation, on the other hand, that there will be longer term changes in patterns of alternation between attention to loss- and restoration-oriented stressors (with gradual reduction in the overall time spent on coping). We suggested earlier that older persons may not oscillate so frequently or so intensely between loss- and restoration-oriented stressors. However, it has become evident that coping among older bereaved persons can be prolonged, because of the persistence of restoration-oriented stressors. The original formulation of the DPM simply assumed a shift in relative attention from loss- to restoration-oriented stressors across the duration of bereavement, and a gradual decline in the amount of time investment spent on coping as the months and years pass. Research suggests that this prediction may not be applicable to older bereaved persons, whose restoration-oriented coping efforts may continue for a much longer time. This will become clearer in the next section as we turn to a consideration of the outcomes of bereavement.

Outcomes

Age-related issues can also complicate the kinds of outcomes associated with bereavement. In particular, we need to consider both short- and long-term outcomes. We have already described (in chap. 8, this volume) the ways in which previously successful, short-term coping strategies can sometimes become infeasible with age, with implications for recovery of status and return of function. But a failure to cope also has much to do with longer term health dynamics in late life, and as we have seen, the distinction between short-term and longer term outcomes of bereavement in older people has received little systematic attention. In this section, we revisit the integrative framework for predicting outcomes of bereavement and the implications of the two time perspectives.

Our review of the research in chapter 5 found the bereavement experience of older adults to reflect a mix of affective, physical, cognitive, behavioral, and social consequences, just as it does among young adults. There are also similarities in the temporal course of bereavement across age groups, with intense symptoms typically more characteristic of the first few months.

Within these symptom patterns, however, there are considerable individual differences in outcome among older people (as with younger people), reflecting a variety of dispositional and contextual factors.

Our review of the empirical literature also revealed that bereavement research has largely neglected the influence of developmental factors on bereavement. In this volume, we have therefore tried to focus on the experience of bereavement in terms of late-life developmental theory, probing potential links with our own integrative framework. Conversely, the influence of bereavement on late-life development has also been neglected. In this connection, our distinction between short-term and longer term outcomes allowed us to draw connections to the late-life disablement sequence.

In chapter 8 we described age-related changes in our physical and sensory abilities and in our protective systems that could affect bereavement reactions among older adults. These include the changing nature of illness experience in late life generally, reflecting the impact of chronic, worsening conditions and increasing comorbidity (across both psychological and physical conditions). We also saw how many of the symptoms of bereavement may be difficult to differentiate from those associated with disease and chronic conditions of old age in general.

The increasing experience in late life of chronic, progressive, and complex health conditions suggested to us the connection between long-term (residual) bereavement outcomes and disablement, with its sequential progression from impairment, through functional limitations, to disability (Verbrugge & Jette, 1994). The concept of disablement has been the subject of much attention among gerontologists and geriatricians, because it is understood to involve the loss of one's ability to perform daily tasks and activities central to independence and quality of life and to participate in important social or occupational roles. From this perspective, we might usefully explore the implications of aging for the bereavement experience, but also the ways in which bereavement and its outcomes might affect disablement. We have attempted, therefore, to incorporate the features of the disablement into our integrative bereavement model. A great advantage in doing so is that it allows a finer grained understanding not only of short-term outcomes, on which bereavement researchers have frequently focused (this being the time of most acute distress), but also of longer term outcomes. This extension of the integrative framework (shown in abbreviated form in Figure 9.1) enhances its utility in understanding late-life bereavement in particular. Specifically, longer term outcomes relating to impairments, functional limitations, and disability have been added, extending the end point of the integrative bereavement model. This extension takes into account the implications of residual grief symptoms, continuing need for loss and restoration coping efforts, declining physical and mental health, and disrupted social engagement (all of which are associated with increasing disablement). Bereaved older persons who move along this trajectory of increasing disability

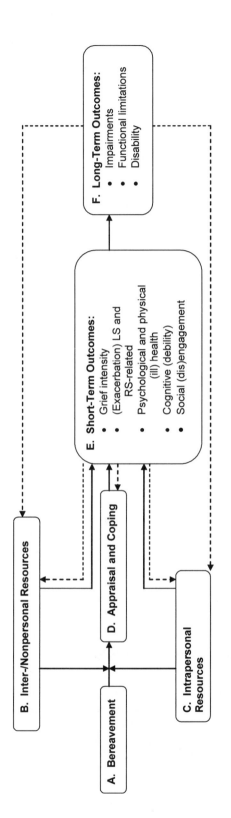

Figure 9.1. Revised integrative framework: Prediction of bereavement outcome in late life. LS = loss-oriented stressors; RS = restoration-oriented stressors.

would be expected to experience increasing difficulty in their efforts to deal with restoration-oriented stressors, especially, because their competence in dealing with such aspects as personal and role performance will be severely affected.

THE INTEGRATIVE FRAMEWORK IN BROADER PERSPECTIVE

A number of more general conclusions from our review of the aging and bereavement literatures deserve further emphasis. The integrative framework for predicting bereavement outcome has been useful in thinking about the experience of bereavement among older people specifically. It was possible to identify both loss- and restoration-oriented stressors particularly characteristic of the experience of bereavement among older people. In turn, the distinction between loss- and restoration-oriented stressors helped in advancing our understanding of aging issues. A range of (a) intrapersonal, nonpersonal, and interpersonal resources and (b) appraisal–coping processes available to older bereaved persons are clearly associated with development and the circumstances of old age. The original framework (presented in chap. 3, this volume), however, required extension with respect to long-term outcomes among older bereaved persons. Adding the life span and disablement perspectives enabled us to suggest additional predictors of outcome and finer grained analysis across a much longer duration of bereavement. This extension of the framework, however, is specific to the bereavement experience of older people.

The extended theoretical perspective has also suggested some important new leads with respect to continued model-building. For example, it illustrated the potential value of trying to apply the integrative framework to other specific subgroups as well (e.g., bereaved parents vs. spouses; those with preexisting psychological disorders), to explore the relevance and comprehensiveness of its parameters for other types of loss. Such examination of different bereavement experiences should help in refining our theoretical propositions.

RELATED THEORETICAL APPROACHES

In examining the implications of aging for bereavement in this volume, we have been guided primarily by a cognitive stress perspective and by our own models for coping with bereavement. However, the more rigorous test of these connections would involve thinking about late-life development from a number of theoretical perspectives. A number of contemporary theories (described in the first few chapters of this book) might also provide insights into bereavement in late life.

We noted, for example, that attachment theory provides a conceptual analysis of an intrapersonal resource: People who are secure in their pattern of attachment with others are more likely to cope with their grief and adjust to loss than those who are insecure. Our exploration of bereavement among older adults suggested that attachment theory propositions are relevant. Specific attachment patterns in older adults may be different than for younger adults, for example, with respect to the need for and expression of continuing bonds (issues of attachment and security needs may be less relevant to older adults); indeed the bonds themselves may be different (e.g., less likely to involve death of a parent; bonds with siblings and friends may be closer).

Attachment theorists (e.g., Weiss, 1973, 1988) have further distinguished between social loneliness (e.g., feeling a lack of integration in a network) and emotional loneliness (e.g., feeling alone even when among people). It is possible, given the patterns that researchers have described, that older bereaved persons, compared with younger bereaved, would feel social loneliness more intensely than emotional loneliness. This is surprising given previous findings (W. Stroebe et al., 1996) that emotional loneliness, rather than social loneliness, mediated between bereavement and the intensity of grief among younger widowed persons. Perhaps the mediator might be different (social rather than emotional loneliness) for older persons. This deserves further investigation.

Other theories with attachment theory underpinnings, such as Parkes's (1993, 1996) psychosocial transition model, specify a need for changes in assumptions about the world, processes similar to those of reappraisal, as we have described in our integrative perspective. A central question here concerns whether older adults would experience as great a need to review and change such assumptions.

Meaning-making theories (e.g., Neimeyer, 2001) also have much to offer in the context of late-life bereavement. If old age is characterized by a more mature, more differentiated, established sense of self and by more life experience, expertise, and postformal thinking, older bereaved persons should feel fewer pressures to engage in meaning making. They may have fewer life questions to be answered for the first time and a deeper understanding of the reality that people's lives change. Similar predictions could be derived from Nadeau's (1998, 2001) family interaction approach to meaning making. The family of an older bereaved person might themselves be older, allowing them to bring more combined life experience with death and other stressors to bear on their bereavement situation. A greater pool of understandings and coping skills should therefore be available within the family and could ease efforts at meaning making. However, we can imagine certain limitations on family meaning making. Some older bereaved persons, for example, may not be comforted by (or willing to put up with) the philosophical or cognitive-restructuring efforts of their children, given generational differences in values or experiences.

Social constructionists such as Rosenblatt (2001) have offered additional challenges with respect to age-related predictions. For example, how might age play into the definition of normative guidelines and rules for social behavior, rights, and responsibilities in the context of bereavement? Might the influence of normative "cultural constructions" of death and bereavement develop across a lifetime (reflecting increasing experience in the culture, diminishing social control efforts by the culture with respect to the beliefs and behavior of older persons, or simply evolving attitudes and behaviors with each new generation)? Other culture-related factors could play a part as well. For example, we noted that in late life, increased comfort may be provided by religion (which is usually a product of the culture). In addition, there may be a diminished need or demand for public performances associated with mourning, or age-related differences in felt need to continue grieving for long periods of time. We would expect a reduction, with increasing age, in society's efforts to "control and instruct the bereaved how to think, feel, and behave" (Walter, 1999, p. 119). Such predictions about older persons' grieving, deriving from meaning-making and constructionist theories, are clearly compatible with our own approach and could usefully be put to the test.

This discussion of related theories has been illustrative rather than exhaustive. But it is clear that late-life developmental issues could be addressed productively from many theoretical perspectives. It will be interesting to examine how certain of these perspectives might suggest important additional variables to be incorporated into the integrative framework to improve prediction of bereavement outcome.

IMPLICATIONS FOR SUPPORT AND INTERVENTION

It is beyond the scope of this volume to address support and intervention issues for older bereaved persons in detail (although, in Appendix A, we provide a brief summary of assessment and treatment issues associated with older adults generally). Nevertheless, in this final section, we would like to briefly illustrate the main implications deriving from our review of empirical studies and theoretical perspectives. Again, we can follow the parameters of the integrative framework (see Figure 9.1) to identify key elements for support and intervention. Such efforts, however, should be careful to consider the demands of the situation in which bereavement takes place, with an eye to potential age-related confounds in assessment and understanding of symptoms.

Distinguishing loss-oriented versus restoration-oriented stressors enables the identification of two different types of assistance that older bereaved persons may need. The empirical studies reviewed in earlier chapters found that problems exist in both domains. For example, following their examination of coping in older bereaved adults, Bonanno et al. (2004) concluded, interventions with individuals who were not depressed prior to the loss but exhibit relatively acute and enduring grief reactions should focus on fostering the processing and the construction of new meanings around the loss . . . among respondents with enduring depression, interventions should perhaps focus on bolstering these individuals' self-esteem and assisting them in dealing with the day-to-day strains associated with widowhood. (p. 269)

In cases of acute grief, then, intervention should probably focus more on loss orientation (processing the loss itself), whereas for persistent depression, intervention would, in addition, need to address the tasks of restoration (assistance in learning to cope with the strains of meeting life's daily demands). It is important to note that in the latter case, chronically depressed older bereaved persons scored higher than all other groups on a scale measuring perceived difficulties resulting from the loss (e.g., cleaning, paying bills).

In our earlier discussions of coping, we noted an increased tendency to selectivity in coping among older persons. They appear to become purposely more selective in their choices of abilities to optimize and maintain, as well as in their decisions regarding stressors that require coping attention. In supporting older bereaved persons, it would be necessary to understand this phenomenon and to build on its use and functions in adaptation to bereavement. More research is also needed to focus directly on the implications of emotional dampening for coping with bereavement and for the development of intervention strategies. For example, interventions might more productively concentrate on helping older bereaved persons to manage the ongoing difficulties in their daily lives rather than focusing on providing encouragement to confront and dwell on their loss.

Finally, we identified both short-term and longer term consequences among older bereaved persons. This distinction suggests implications as well for the provision of support and intervention. Younger bereaved persons are more likely to need help early on during bereavement, when their grief is acute. For older bereaved persons, however, support may need to continue. The issues are likely to shift from loss-oriented to restoration-oriented ones as time goes on, and as bereavement-related symptoms, in some cases, become increasingly embedded in a progression to disablement. At some point in this progression, it may be more useful to emphasize protecting existing strengths and resources, managing symptoms, and maintaining function rather than recovery or rehabilitation. Given the interrelation of physical and psychological problems among older adults, providers may consider physical therapy, pain control, or environmental modifications as a part of intervention.

Although most older bereaved persons will adapt well, some will likely experience complicated grief. This is cause for concern. Will these cases be recognized (e.g., if emotional dampening works in such a way as to camouflage symptoms)? Might caregivers be slower in diagnosing (and so in treating) older persons? Might it be harder to diagnose complicated grief in older persons, given the issues of comorbidity, assessment confounds, or fear of stigmatization associated with mental health settings? These issues require further investigation.

A FINAL THOUGHT

We have in these last chapters delved deeply into health and clinical issues associated with bereavement. But we want to leave the reader with a final thought. It is important to remember that bereavement is a normal, emotional reaction to the loss of a loved person, not a psychiatric disorder, even though in some cases it is associated with higher risks of intense symptomatology. It may be, as attachment theorists have suggested, that grief is the price we humans pay for our ability to form nurturing and rewarding attachment relationships. Our capacity to feel and understand loss, and to adapt across a lifetime, reflects a mix of developmental and contextual influences that result in considerable cultural and individual variability of outcome. It is worth voicing our questions with an appreciation for this complexity.

APPENDIX A:
ASSESSMENT AND INTERVENTION
ISSUES WITH OLDER ADULTS

In chapter 8, we proposed an extended model for predicting bereavement outcomes in late life. We argued that such a model would allow researchers and practitioners to identify risk factors relevant to each part of the process and to consider prevention strategies (e.g., primary, secondary, tertiary) and where in the process they might most appropriately be targeted. We noted also that critical reviews of the bereavement-intervention literature (Jordan & Neimeyer, 2003; Schut et al., 2001) had found therapy-based interventions to be beneficial among high-risk persons and among those already experiencing complications. We thus proposed that older bereaved persons whose status has progressed deep into the disablement process, even if their problems now reflect mostly an exacerbation of normal age-related decline, may be seen as viable candidates for treatment.

That said, it remains a concern that many bereavement researchers and clinical practitioners may not be familiar with the assessment and treatment issues likely to arise when dealing with older adults. Our goal for Appendix A, therefore, is to briefly summarize these issues and to provide an entry point into the relevant literatures for readers who may not specialize in aging. Appendix B provides authoritative bibliographic detail on those topics and Web site addresses for the major professional organizations concerned with psychological and psychiatric issues among older persons.

ASSESSMENT ISSUES

In 1998, the American Psychological Association (APA) Working Group on the Older Adult published an authoritative report titled "What Practitioners Should Know About Working With Older Adults." This report discusses general assessment issues, diagnostic guidelines, issues of when cognitive and neuropsychological testing may be appropriate, recommendations regarding brief assessments, and so on. Some of the most important issues noted in the APA Working Group report may be summarized as follows:

1. We must recognize the possibility that age-related changes in physical, sensory, or cognitive ability may affect test performance in unexpected ways. To accommodate these changes, it may be useful to speak more slowly and in a louder voice, increase lighting and the size of print on test materials, pro-

vide a quiet space free of distractions, allow for wheelchairs, be sure the client has required eyeglasses or hearing aid devices, and adapt protocols to allow materials to be read to an older client.

2. Issues of understanding also arise. Test materials may not be in the client's first language. More generally, older adults may not understand the purpose of the assessment, potentially undermining interpretation of results and giving of informed consent for the assessment. In addition, adults from an older generation may be unfamiliar with the content of tests, which may have been developed and normed using younger persons.

3. Current health problems can also become an issue. The older client may be experiencing pain or taking medications at the time of testing, with the potential to affect performance (where possible, assessment and research protocols sometimes use a "medication holiday" prior to testing to minimize drug effects). More generally, older people are likely to fatigue more quickly during testing. In response, the practitioner may wish to take fatigue into account when interpreting results or adopt more flexible protocols that allow more time for each test component, allow for rest breaks, and so on. It may also be useful to investigate time-of-day differences in performance through repeat testing.

4. A number of unique issues also arise in preparing for a diagnostic interview with older adults. For example, it may be necessary to test for understanding in the informed consent process or to involve the participation of a legal guardian. Current medical or psychiatric status also may become a factor in testing. Preparations will therefore require access to medical records, including information pertaining to any concurrent stressors, all prescribed and over-the-counter medications, prior treatment for conditions that might influence the intensity or course of bereavement, and so on. Here, too, it may be relevant to investigate the status of the older client's living conditions, family support, recent history of loss, and so on.

5. Cognitive impairment is more frequent in older persons, especially hospitalized older persons. In the case of cognitive impairment, accounts of family members are often used to supplement and verify client's reporting of symptoms. It may also be useful to conduct cognitive or neuropsychological assessments to refine estimates of competence or to differentiate dementia from depression.

6. In response to health and fatigue issues, a number of brief measures have been developed or adapted for use with older adults. In practice, scores may also be interpreted in terms of performance relative to one's own age group rather than established diagnostic cutoffs, as subclinical symptom patterns can be important in older populations. Qualitative measures may also be more feasible than their quantitative counterparts.

7. Test reports should take into account the developmental and contextual factors of old age described in earlier chapters of this volume, and include guidance with respect to goals for maintenance of functioning in addition to rehabilitation or therapeutic intervention.

ASSESSMENT TOOLS FOR USE WITH OLDER ADULTS

The authoritative source on available measures for use with older adults is *Assessing Older Persons: Measures, Meaning, and Practical Applications*, edited by Robert Kane and Rosalie Kane (2000). For a comprehensive guide to grief-specific measures, we refer the reader to the excellent review of these measures by Neimeyer and Hogan (2001). Kane and Kane (2000) provided critical reviews of available instruments for 11 domains of assessment. Each review surveys the broad array of instruments currently in use for purposes of research or intervention and provides comparisons in terms of reliability, validity, and feasibility of use with older adults. Recommended instruments are presented in full within each review, along with scoring information and normative data. Researchers and clinicians are encouraged to find instruments that are a best-fit to their client population with respect to sensitivity, specificity, and predictive utility and to develop multidimensional assessment strategies to match the complexity of problems facing an older client. The 11 assessment domains reviewed in this volume are as follows:

1. *Assessment of function.* Measures focus on abilities to perform activities of daily living (e.g., feeding, continence, dressing, bathing, mobility, meal preparation, shopping, and household tasks), identification of impairments, and inability to function in social roles.

2. *Physiological well-being and health.* Measures address general health indicators, pain, mobility, nutritional risk, risk for falls, incontinence, sleep problems, substance use, and problems characteristic of nursing settings, to include ulcers, skin lesions, foot problems, and deterioration of muscle and bone.

3. *Cognitive assessment.* Measures range from brief screening instruments that focus on orientation, immediate memory, language, and visual-spatial ability (all factors related to competence for self-care); to indices of recent cognitive decline; to brief neuropsychological batteries; to measures of dementia, severe impairment, and global deterioration. A subsequent chapter goes on to consider methods for assessing older persons who because of physical, sensory, or cognitive decline are unable to communicate.

4. *Assessment of emotions.* This review considers a diversity of measures, some developed specifically within the context of aging, and many developed on broader populations but adapted or normed for older adults. Instruments focus on depressive symptoms and diagnosis, anxiety, life satisfaction, positive and negative affect, morale, and hopelessness.

5. *Social functioning.* Instruments are included that measure perceived social support, characteristics and sufficiency of support networks, personal social resources, preferences for social interaction, social integration and activities, functioning in social roles, and social dysfunction (emotional withdrawal, overdependency, loneliness, etc.).

6. *Quality of life.* This section, reflecting its broadly construed title, includes measures of health, activities, support, role and sexual functioning, life satisfaction, and psychological and physiological functioning.

7. *Values and preferences.* Measures focus on preferences for support or services in late life; desires for autonomy, choice, and control; attitudes toward important others, health care providers, and caregivers; and attitudes toward life, dying, and religion.

8. *Satisfaction.* Instruments focus on assessing satisfaction with access to and treatment by a diversity of likely entities (e.g., patient or client satisfaction with interpersonal and professional services from physicians, nursing staff, hospitals, nursing home facilities, laboratories, and so on).

9. *Spiritual.* Measures address nature of religious preference and history; degrees of felt religious support, church commitment, intrinsic religious motivation, spiritual coping, private daily involvements in ritual, prayer, or service; and perceived spiritual well-being.

10. *Assessment of family caregivers.* Instruments focus on positive and negative impacts of caregiving, components of caregiver burden (e.g., time, isolation, physical and emotional costs), caregiver appraisals of burden versus satisfactions, and indi-

ces of the caregiver stress process as mediated through role overload, loss of freedom, family conflict, work, and financial strain.

11. *Assessment of physical environments.* General measurement criteria for these instruments include supportiveness, accessibility, adaptability, and safety. Instruments have been developed to assess the attributes, supports, barriers, and problems characteristic of a diversity of settings (nursing homes, hospitals, elderly housing units).

TREATMENT ISSUES

The APA Working Group on Older Adults (1998) found that many psychological interventions developed for use with younger populations are also effective with the elderly. They noted, however, that intervention techniques and settings (like assessment strategies) may need to be adapted to accommodate age-related changes in physical, sensory, or cognitive ability. They cautioned, in particular, a need to test the older persons' understanding of the goals and methods of treatment, given an increased likelihood that others (family, physicians) may have been involved in the referral. In addition, there may be a need to discuss with the older client any fears or elements of embarrassment associated with mental health settings, as these are more likely to be encountered in older cohorts. Also, because physical, cognitive, and emotional health are more interrelated in late life, it can be important to conceptualize treatment goals as part of a multidisciplinary team.

The APA Working Group (1998) concluded from their review that psychological interventions for older persons should be guided by assessments of the problem (e.g., depressive symptoms) rather than by following any age-specific rationale. Individual, group, cognitive–behavioral, behavior modification, brief psychodynamic, and interpersonal approaches may be appropriate, given the circumstances and assessed need. Educational interventions with family caregivers and environment modifications also appear beneficial with respect to improved client function and well-being.

APPENDIX B:
GERONTOLOGICAL RESOURCES FOR BEREAVEMENT RESEARCHERS AND PRACTITIONERS

ORGANIZATIONS

American Geriatrics Society
    http://www.americangeriatrics.org
American Psychological Association, Division 20: Adult Development and
    Aging
    http://apadiv20.phhp.ufl.edu/
American Society on Aging
    http://www.asaging.org
British Society of Gerontology
    http://www.britishgerontology.org
Gerontological Society of America (informal interest group on Death, Dy-
    ing, and Bereavement)
    http://www.geron.org
International Association of Gerontology
    http://www.sfu.ca/iag
National Council on Aging
    http://www.ncoa.org
National Institute on Aging
    http://www.nia.nih.gov

PUBLICATIONS

Periodicals

American Journal of Geriatric Psychiatry. A journal of the American Associa-
    tion for Geriatric Psychiatry.
Annual Review of Gerontology and Geriatrics. Springer Publishing Company.
The Gerontologist. A journal of the Gerontological Society of America.
The International Journal of Aging and Human Development. Baywood Publishing.
Journal of the American Geriatrics Society. A journal of the American Geriat-
    rics Society.
The Journals of Gerontology (Biological Sciences; Medical Sciences; Psycho-
    logical Sciences; Social Sciences). Journals of the Gerontological Society
    of America.
Psychology and Aging. A journal of the American Psychological Association.

Books

Binstock, R. H., & George, L. K. (Eds.). (2005). *Handbook of aging and the social sciences* (6th ed.). San Diego, CA: Academic Press.

Birren, J. E., & Schaie, K. W. (Eds.). (2005). *Handbook of the psychology of aging* (6th ed.). San Diego, CA: Academic Press.

Kane, R. L., & Kane, R. A. (Eds.). (2000). *Assessing older persons: Measures, meaning, and practical applications.* Oxford, England: Oxford University Press.

Knight, B. G. (1996). *Psychotherapy with older adults* (2nd ed.). Thousand Oaks, CA: Sage.

Nordhus, I. H., VandenBos, G. R., Berg, S., & Fromholt, P. (1998). *Clinical gerontology.* Washington, DC: American Psychological Association.

Qualls, S. H., & Ables, N. (Eds.). (2000). *Psychology and the aging revolution.* Washington, DC: American Psychological Association.

Zarit, S. H., & Knight, B. G. (Eds.). (1996). *A guide to psychotherapy and aging: Effective clinical interventions in a life-stage context.* Washington, DC: American Psychological Association.

Zarit, S. H., & Zarit, J. M. (1998). *Mental disorders in older adults: Fundamentals of assessment and treatment.* New York: Guilford Press.

Specific Readings

American Psychological Association. (2004). Guidelines for psychological practice with older adults. *American Psychologist, 59*, 236–260.

American Psychological Association Working Group on the Older Adult. (1998). What practitioners should know about working with older adults. *Professional Psychology: Research and Practice, 29*, 413–427.

Arean, P. A., Cook, B. L., Gallagher-Thompson, D., Hegel, M. T., Schulberg, H. C., & Schulz, R. (2003). Guidelines for conducting geropsychotherapy research. *American Journal of Geriatric Psychiatry, 11*, 9–16.

Molinari, V., Karel, M., Jones, S., Zeiss, A., Cooley, S. G., Wray, L., et al. (2003). Recommendations about the knowledge and skills required of psychologists working with older adults. *Professional Psychology: Research and Practice, 34*, 435–443.

Schulz, R., & Martire, L. M. (1998). Intervention research with older adults: Introduction, overview, and future directions. *Annual Review of Gerontology and Geriatrics, 18*, 1–16.

REFERENCES

Aldwin, C. M. (1990). The Elders' Life Stress Inventory: Egocentric and nonegocentric stress. In M. A. P. Stephens, S. E. Hobfoll, J. H. Crowther, & D. L. Tennenbaum (Eds.), *Stress and coping in late life families* (pp. 49–69). New York: Hemisphere.

Aldwin, C. M. (1991). Does age affect the stress and coping process? Implications of age differences in perceived control. *Journal of Gerontology: Psychological Sciences, 46,* P174–P180.

Aldwin, C. M., & Gilmer, D. F. (1999). Immunity, disease processes, and optimal aging. In J. C. Cavanaugh & S. K. Whitbourne (Eds.), *Gerontology: An interdisciplinary perspective* (pp. 123–154). New York: Oxford University Press.

American Psychiatric Association. (1987). *Diagnostic and statistical manual of disorders* (3rd ed., rev). Washington, DC: Author.

American Psychiatric Association. (1994). *Diagnostic and statistical manual of disorders* (4th ed.). Washington, DC: Author.

American Psychological Association. (2004). Guidelines for psychological practice with older adults. *American Psychologist, 59,* 236–260.

American Psychological Association Working Group on the Older Adult. (1998). What practitioners should know about working with older adults. *Professional Psychology: Research and Practice, 29,* 413–427.

Antonucci, T. C., & Akiyama, H. (1996). Convoys of social relations: Family and friendships within a life span context. In R. Blieszner & V. H. Bedford (Eds.), *Aging and the family: Theory and research* (pp. 355–371). Westport, CT: Praeger.

Antonucci, T. C., Langfahl, E. S., & Akiyama, H. (2004). Relationships as outcomes and contexts. In F. R. Lang & K. L. Fingerman (Eds.), *Growing together: Personal relationships across the lifespan* (pp. 24–44). Cambridge, England: Cambridge University Press.

Antonucci, T. C., Lansford, J. E., Schaberg, L., Smith, J., Baltes, M., Akiyama, H., et al. (2001). Widowhood and illness: A comparison of social network characteristics in France, Germany, Japan, and the United States. *Psychology and Aging, 16,* 655–665.

Archer, J. (1999). *The nature of grief: The evolution and psychology of reactions to loss.* London: Routledge.

Arean, P. A., Cook, B. L., Gallagher-Thompson, D., Hegel, M. T., Schulberg, H. C., & Schulz, R. (2003). Guidelines for conducting geropsychotherapy research. *American Journal of Geriatric Psychiatry, 11,* 9–16.

Averill, J. (1968). Grief: Its nature and significance. *Psychological Bulletin, 70,* 721–748.

Averill, J., & Nunley, E. (1993). Grief as an emotion and as a disease: A social–constructionist perspective. In M. S. Stroebe, W. Stroebe, & R. O. Hansson (Eds.), *Handbook of bereavement: Theory, research, and intervention* (pp. 77–90). New York: Cambridge University Press.

Awad, N., Gagnon, M., & Messier, C. (2004). The relationship between impaired glucose tolerance, Type 2 diabetes, and cognitive function. *Journal of Clinical and Experimental Neuropsychology, 26,* 1044–1080.

Balaswamy, S., & Richardson, V. E. (2001). The cumulative effects of life event, personal and social resources on subjective well-being of elderly widowers. *International Journal of Aging and Human Development, 53,* 311–327.

Ball, J. (1976–1977). Widow's grief: The impact of age and mode of death. *Omega, 7,* 307–333.

Baltes, P. B. (1987). Theoretical propositions of life-span developmental psychology: On the dynamics between growth and decline. *Developmental Psychology, 23,* 611–626.

Baltes, P. B., & Baltes, M. (1990). Psychological perspectives on successful aging: The model of selective optimization with compensation. In P. B. Baltes & M. Baltes (Eds.), *Successful aging: Perspectives from the behavioral sciences* (pp. 1–34). Cambridge, England: Cambridge University Press.

Baltes, P. B., Smith, J., & Staudinger, U. M. (1992). Wisdom and successful aging. In T. B. Sonderegger (Ed.), *Nebraska symposium on motivation* (pp. 123–167). Lincoln: University of Nebraska Press.

Baltes, P. B., Staudinger, U. M., & Lindenberger, U. (1999). Lifespan psychology: Theory and application to intellectual functioning. *Annual Review of Psychology, 50,* 471–507.

Barry, L. C., Kasl, S. V., & Prigerson, H. G. (2002). Psychiatric disorders among bereaved persons: The role of perceived circumstances of death and preparedness for death. *American Journal of Geriatric Psychiatry, 10,* 447–457.

Baumeister, R., & Vohs, K. (Eds.). (2004). *Handbook of self-regulation: Research, theory, and applications.* New York: Guilford Press.

Bearon, L. B. (1989). No great expectations: The underpinnings of life satisfaction for older women. *The Gerontologist, 29,* 772–778.

Beck, A. T., Ward, C. H., Mendelson, M., Mock, J. E., & Erbaugh, J. (1961). An inventory for measuring depression. *Archives of General Psychiatry, 4,* 561–571.

Beery, L. C., Prigerson, H. G., Bierhals, A. J., Santucci, L. M., Newsom, J. T., Maciejewski, P. K., et al. (1997). Traumatic grief, depression and caregiving in elderly spouses of the terminally ill. *Omega, 35,* 261–279.

Bennett, K. M. (1997a). A longitudinal study of well-being in widowed women. *International Journal of Geriatric Psychiatry, 12,* 61–66.

Bennett, K. M. (1997b). Widowhood in elderly women: The medium- and long-term effects on mental and physical health. *Mortality, 2,* 137–148.

Berg, C. A., & Klaczynski, P. A. (1996). Practical intelligence and problem solving: Searching for perspectives. In F. Blanchard-Fields & T. M. Hess (Eds.), *Perspectives on cognitive change in adulthood and aging* (pp. 323–357). New York: McGraw-Hill.

Bernard, L. L., & Guarnaccia, C. A. (2002). Husband and adult-daughter caregivers' bereavement. *Omega, 45,* 153–165.

Bernard, L. L., & Guarnaccia, C. A. (2003). Two models of caregiver strain and bereavement adjustment: A comparison of husband and daughter caregivers of breast cancer hospice patients. *The Gerontologist, 43*, 801–816.

Billings, A. G., & Moos, R. H. (1981). The role of coping responses and social resources in attenuating the stress of life events. *Journal of Behavioral Medicine, 4*, 139–157.

Binstock, R. H., & George, L. K. (Eds.). (2005). *Handbook of aging and the social sciences* (6th ed.). San Diego, CA: Academic Press.

Birditt, K. S., & Fingerman, K. L. (2003). Age and gender differences in adults' descriptions of emotional reactions to interpersonal problems. *Journal of Gerontology: Psychological Sciences, 58B*, P237–P245.

Birren, J. E., & Schaie, K. W. (Eds.). (2005). *Handbook of the psychology of aging* (6th ed.). San Diego, CA: Academic Press.

Blazer, D. G. (2003). Depression in late life: Review and commentary. *Journal of Gerontology: Medical Sciences, 58A*, 249–265.

Blieszner, R. (1993). A socialist–feminist perspective on widowhood. *Journal of Aging Studies, 7*, 171–182.

Blieszner, R., & Roberto, K. A. (2004). Friendship across the life span: Reciprocity in individual and relationship development. In F. R. Lang & K. L. Fingerman (Eds.), *Growing together: Personal relationships across the lifespan* (pp. 159–182). Cambridge, England: Cambridge University Press.

Boelen, P., van den Bout, J., & de Keijser, J. (2003). Traumatic grief as a disorder distinct from bereavement-related depression and anxiety: A replication study with bereaved mental health care patients. *American Journal of Psychiatry, 160*, 1339–1341.

Boerner, K. (2004). Adaptation to disability among middle-aged and older adults: The role of assimilative and accommodative coping. *Journal of Gerontology: Psychological Sciences, 59B*, P35–P42.

Boerner, K., Wortman, C. B., & Bonanno, G. A. (2005). Resilient or at risk: A 4-year study of older adults who initially showed high or low distress following conjugal loss. *Journal of Gerontology: Psychological Sciences, 60B*, P67–P73.

Bonanno, G. (2001a). Grief and emotion: A social–functional perspective. In M. S. Stroebe, R. O. Hansson, W. Stroebe, & H. Schut (Eds.), *Handbook of bereavement research: Consequences, coping, and care* (pp. 493–515). Washington, DC: American Psychological Association.

Bonanno, G. A. (2001b). Introduction: New directions in bereavement research and theory. *American Behavioral Scientist, 44*, 718–725.

Bonanno, G. A., & Kaltman, S. (1999). Toward an integrative perspective on bereavement. *Psychological Bulletin, 125*, 760–776.

Bonanno, G. A., & Keltner, D. (1997). Facial expressions of emotion and the course of conjugal bereavement. *Journal of Abnormal Psychology, 106*, 126–137.

Bonanno, G. A., Keltner, D., Holen, A., & Horowitz, M. J. (1995). When avoiding unpleasant emotions may not be such a bad thing: Verbal-autonomic response dissociation and midlife conjugal bereavement. *Journal of Personality and Social Psychology, 69,* 975–989.

Bonanno, G. A., Wortman, C. B., Lehman, D. R., Tweed, R. G., Haring, M., Sonnega, J., et al. (2002). Resilience to loss and chronic grief: A prospective study from preloss to 18-months postloss. *Journal of Personality and Social Psychology, 83,* 1150–1164.

Bonanno, G. A., Wortman, C. B., & Nesse, R. M. (2004). Prospective patterns of resilience and maladjustment during widowhood. *Psychology and Aging, 19,* 260–271.

Bornstein, P., Clayton, P. J., Halikas, J. A., Maurice, W. L., & Robbins, E. (1973). The depression of widowhood after 13 months. *British Journal of Psychiatry, 122,* 561–566.

Bound, J., Duncan, G. J., Laren, D. S., & Olenick, L. (1991). Poverty dynamics in widowhood. *Journal of Gerontology: Social Sciences, 46,* S115–S124.

Bowlby, J. (1969). *Attachment and loss: Vol. 1. Attachment.* London: Hogarth Press.

Bowlby, J. (1973). *Attachment and loss: Vol. 2. Separation.* London: Hogarth Press.

Bowlby, J. (1980). *Attachment and loss: Vol. 3. Loss: Sadness and depression.* London: Hogarth Press.

Bowling, A. (1988). Who dies after widow(er)hood? A discriminant analysis. *Omega, 19,* 135–153.

Bowling, A. (1994). Mortality after bereavement: An analysis of mortality rates and associations with mortality 13 years after bereavement. *International Journal of Geriatric Psychiatry, 9,* 445–459.

Bowling, A., & Charlton, J. (1987). Risk factors for mortality after bereavement: A logistic regression analysis. *Journal of the Royal College of General Practitioners, 37,* 551–554.

Bradbeer, M., Helme, R. D., Yong, H. H., Kendig, H. L., & Gibson, S. J. (2003). Widowhood and other demographic associations of pain in independent older people. *Clinical Journal of Pain, 19,* 247–254.

Bradley, M. J., & Cafferty, T. P. (2001). Attachment among older adults: Current issues and directions for future research. *Attachment & Human Development, 3,* 200–221.

Bradsher, J. E., Longino, C. F., Jr., Jackson, D. J., & Zimmerman, R. S. (1992). Health and geographic mobility among the recently widowed. *Journal of Gerontology: Social Sciences, 47,* S261–S268.

Brandstadter, J., & Renner, G. (1990). Tenacious goal pursuit and flexible goal adjustment: Explication and age-related analysis of assimilative and accommodative strategies of coping. *Psychology and Aging, 5,* 58–67.

Breckenridge, J., Gallagher, D., Thompson, L., & Peterson, J. (1986). Characteristic depressive symptoms of bereaved elders. *Journal of Gerontology, 41,* 163–168.

Brown, J. D. (1998). *The self.* New York: McGraw-Hill.

Brown, L. F., Reynolds, C. F., III, Monk, T. H., Prigerson, H. G., Dew, M. A., Houck, P. R., et al. (1996). Social rhythm stability following late-life spousal bereavement: Associations with depression and sleep impairment. *Psychiatry Research, 62,* 161–169.

Brown, S. C., & Park, D. C. (2003). Theoretical models of cognitive aging and implications for translational research in medicine. *The Gerontologist, 43,* 57–67.

Buda, M., & Tsuang, M. (1990). The epidemiology of suicide: Implications for clinical practice. In S. Blumenthal & D. Kupfer (Eds.), *Suicide over the life cycle: Risk factors, assessments, and treatments of suicidal patients* (pp. 17–38). Washington, DC: American Psychiatric Press.

Byrne, G. J. A., & Raphael, B. (1994). A longitudinal study of bereavement phenomena in recently widowed elderly men. *Psychological Medicine, 24,* 411–421.

Byrne, G. J. A., & Raphael, B. (1997). The psychological symptoms of conjugal bereavement in elderly men over the first 13 months. *International Journal of Geriatric Psychiatry, 12,* 241–251.

Byrne, G. J. A., & Raphael, B. (1999). Depressive symptoms and depressive episodes in recently widowed older men. *International Psychogeriatrics, 11,* 67–74.

Cafferata, G. L. (1987). Marital status, living arrangements, and the use of health services by elderly Americans. *Journal of Gerontology, 43,* 613–619.

Campbell, J., Swank, P., & Vincent, K. (1991). The role of hardiness in the resolution of grief. *Omega, 23,* 53–65.

Carnelley, K. B., Wortman, C. B., & Kessler, R. C. (1999). The impact of widowhood on depression: Findings from a prospective survey. *Psychological Medicine, 29,* 1111–1123.

Carpenter, B. N. (1993). Relational competence. In D. Perlman & W. H. Jones (Eds.), *Advances in personal relationships* (Vol. 4, pp. 1–28). New York: Jessica Kingsley.

Carr, D. (2003). A "good death" for whom? Quality of spouse's death and psychological distress among older widowed persons. *Journal of Health and Social Behavior, 44,* 215–232.

Carr, D., House, J. S., Kessler, R. C., Nesse, R. M., Sonnega, J., & Wortman, C. (2000). Marital quality and psychological adjustment to widowhood among older adults: A longitudinal analysis. *Journal of Gerontology: Social Sciences, 55B,* S197–S207.

Carr, D., House, J. S., Wortman, C., Nesse, R., & Kessler, R. C. (2001). Psychological adjustment to sudden and anticipated spousal loss among older widowed persons. *Journal of Gerontology: Social Sciences, 56B,* S238–S248.

Carr, D., Nesse, R. M., & Wortman, C. B. (2005). *Late life widowhood in the United States.* New York: Springer Publishing Company.

Carstensen, L. L., Gottman, J. M., & Levenson, R. W. (1995). Emotional behavior in long-term marriage. *Psychology and Aging, 10,* 140–149.

Carstensen, L. L., Gross, J. J., & Fung, H. H. (1998). The social context of emotional experience. *Annual Review of Gerontology and Geriatrics, 17,* 325–352.

Carstensen, L. L., Pasupathi, M., Mayr, U., & Nesselroade, J. R. (2000). Emotional experience in everyday life across the adult life span. *Journal of Personality and Social Psychology, 79,* 644–655.

Charles, S. T., Mather, M., & Carstensen, L. L. (2003). Aging and emotional memory: The forgettable nature of negative images for older adults. *Journal of Experimental Psychology: General, 132,* 310–324.

Charles, S. T., & Mavandadi, S. (2004). Social support and physical health across the life span: Socioemotional influences. In F. R. Lang & K. L. Fingerman (Eds.), *Growing together: Personal relationships across the lifespan* (pp. 240–267). Cambridge, England: Cambridge University Press.

Chentsova-Dutton, Y., Shuchter, S., Hutchin, S., Strause, L., Burns, K., Dunn, L., et al. (2002). Depression and grief reactions in hospice caregivers: From pre-death to 1 year afterwards. *Journal of Affective Disorders, 69,* 53–60.

Connidis, I. G., & Davies, L. (1990). Confidants and companions in later life: The place of friends and family. *Journal of Gerontology: Social Sciences, 45,* S141–S149.

Cook, A., & Oltjenbruns, K. (1998). *Dying and grieving: Lifespan and family perspectives.* Ft. Worth, TX: Harcourt Brace.

Crohan, S. E., & Antonucci, T. C. (1989). Friends as a source of social support in old age. In R. Adams & R. Blieszner (Eds.), *Older adult friendship: Structure and process* (pp. 129–146). Beverly Hills, CA: Sage.

Davis, C., Nolen-Hoeksema, S., & Larson, J. (1998). Making sense of loss and benefiting from the experience: Two construals of meaning. *Journal of Personality and Social Psychology, 75,* 561–574.

de Ridder, D. (1997). What is wrong with coping assessment? A review of conceptual and methodological issues. *Psychology and Health, 12,* 417–431.

de Vries, B., Davis, C. G., Wortman, C. B., & Lehman, D. (1997). Long-term psychological and somatic consequences of later life parental bereavement. *Omega, 35,* 97–117.

de Vries, B., Lana, R., & Falck, V. (1994). Parental bereavement over the life course: A theoretical intersection and empirical review. *Omega, 29,* 47–69.

de Vries, B., & Roberts, P. (2004). Expressions of grief on the World Wide Web [Special issue]. *Omega, 49*(1).

Dijkstra, I., & Stroebe, M. (1998). The impact of a child's death on parents: A myth (not yet) disproved. *Journal of Family Studies, 4,* 159–185.

Dijkstra, I., van den Bout, J., Schut, H., Stroebe, M., & Stroebe, W. (1999). Coping with the death of a child. A longitudinal study of discordance in couples. *Gedrag & Gezondheid, 27,* 103–108.

Elklit, A., & O'Connor, M. (2005). Post-traumatic stress disorder in a Danish population of elderly bereaved. *Scandinavian Journal of Psychology, 46,* 439–445.

Farberow, N. L., Gallagher-Thompson, D., Gilweski, M., & Thompson, L. (1992). Changes in grief and mental health of bereaved spouses of older suicides. *Journal of Gerontology: Psychological Sciences, 47,* P357–P366.

Federal Interagency Forum on Aging-Related Statistics. (2004). *Older Americans 2004: Key indicators of well-being.* Washington, DC: U.S. Government Printing Office.

Ferrario, S. R., Cardillo, V., Vicario, F., Balzarini, E., & Zotti, A. M. (2004). Advanced cancer at home: Caregiving and bereavement. *Palliative Medicine, 18*, 129–136.

Folkman, S. (1997). Positive psychological states and coping with severe stress. *Social Science & Medicine, 45*, 1207–1221.

Folkman, S. (2001). Revised coping theory and the process of bereavement. In M. S. Stroebe, R. O. Hansson, W. Stroebe, & H. Schut (Eds.), *Handbook of bereavement research: Consequences, coping, and care* (pp. 563–584). Washington, DC: American Psychological Association.

Folkman, S., Chesney, M., McKusick, L., Ironson, G., Johnson, D., & Coates, T. (1991). Translating coping theory into an intervention. In J. Eckenrode (Ed.), *The social context of coping* (pp. 239–260). New York: Plenum Press.

Folkman, S., & Lazarus, R. S. (1988). *Ways of Coping Questionnaire*. Palo Alto, CA: Consulting Psychologists Press.

Folkman, S., Lazarus, R. S., Gruen, R. J., & De Longis, A. (1986). Appraisal, coping, health status, and psychological symptoms. *Journal of Personality and Social Psychology, 50*, 571–579.

Folkman, S., & Moskowitz, J. (2000). Positive affect and the other side of coping. *American Psychologist, 55*, 647–654.

Folkman, S., & Moskowitz, J. (2004). Coping: Pitfalls and promise. *Annual Review of Psychology, 55*, 745–774.

Fozard, J. L., & Gordon-Salant, S. (2001). Changes in vision and hearing with aging. In J. E. Birren & K. W. Schaie (Eds.), *Handbook of the psychology of aging* (5th ed., pp. 241–266). San Diego, CA: Academic Press.

Francis, M., & Pennebaker, J. W. (1993). *LIWC: Linguistic Inquiry and Word Count* (Technical manual). Dallas, TX: Southern Methodist University.

Freud, S. (1957). Mourning and melancholia. In J. Strachey (Ed. & Trans.), *Standard edition of the complete psychological works of Sigmund Freud* (Vol. 2, pp. 251–268). London: Hogarth. (Original work published 1917)

Freund, A. M., & Baltes, P. B. (2002). Life-management strategies of selection, optimization, and compensation: Measurement by self-report and construct validity. *Journal of Personality and Social Psychology, 82*, 642–662.

Fried, L. P., Ferrucci, L., Darer, J., Williamson, J. D., & Anderson, G. (2004). Untangling the concepts of disability, frailty, and comorbidity: Implications for improved targeting and care. *Journal of Gerontology: Medical Sciences, 59*, 255–263.

Fry, C. L. (1996). Age, aging, and culture. In R. H. Binstock & L. K. George (Eds.), *Handbook of aging and the social sciences* (4th ed., pp. 117–136). San Diego, CA: Academic Press.

Fry, P. S. (1997). Grandparents' reactions to the death of a grandchild: An exploratory factor analytic study. *Omega, 35*, 119–140.

Fry, P. S. (1998). Spousal loss in late life: A 1-year follow-up of perceived changes in life meaning and psychosocial functioning following bereavement. *Journal of Personal and Interpersonal Loss, 3*, 369–391.

Fry, P. S. (2001). Predictors of health-related quality of life perspectives, self-esteem, and life satisfactions of older adults following spousal loss: An 18-month follow-up study of widows and widowers. *The Gerontologist, 41*, 787–798.

Gallagher-Thompson, D., Futterman, A., Farberow, N., Thompson, L. W., & Peterson, J. (1993). The impact of spousal bereavement on older widows and widowers. In M. S. Stroebe, W. Stroebe, & R. O. Hansson (Eds.), *Handbook of bereavement: Theory, research, and intervention* (pp. 227–239). Cambridge, England: Cambridge University Press.

Gass, K. A. (1987). The health of conjugally bereaved older widows: The role of appraisal, coping and resources. *Research in Nursing & Health, 10*, 39–47.

Gatz, M., & Fiske, A. (2003). Aging women and depression. *Professional Psychology: Research and Practice, 34*, 3–9.

Gatz, M., Kasl-Godley, J. E., & Karel, M. J. (1996). Aging and mental disorders. In J. E. Birren & K. W. Schaie (Eds.), *Handbook of the psychology of aging* (4th ed., pp. 365–382). San Diego, CA: Academic Press.

Gatz, M., & Smyer, M. A. (2001). Mental health and aging at the outset of the twenty-first century. In J. E. Birren & K. W. Schaie (Eds.), *Handbook of the psychology of aging* (5th ed., pp. 523–544). San Diego, CA: Academic Press.

Gentry, J., Kennedy, P., Paul, C., & Hill, R. (1995). Family transitions during grief: Discontinuities in household consumption patterns. *Journal of Business Research, 34*, 67–79.

Gignac, M. A. M., Cott, C., & Badley, E. M. (2000). Adaptation to chronic illness and disability and its relationship to perceptions of independence and dependence. *Journal of Gerontology: Psychological Sciences, 55B*, P362–P372.

Gignac, M. A. M., Cott, C., & Badley, E. M. (2002). Adaptation to disability: Applying selective optimization with compensation to the behaviors of older adults with osteoarthritis. *Psychology and Aging, 17*, 520–524.

Gilbert, K., & Smart, L. (1992). *Coping with infant or fetal loss.* New York: Brunner/Mazel.

Goodman, M., Rubinstein, R. L., Alexander, B. B., & Luborsky, M. (1991). Cultural differences among elderly women in coping with the death of an adult child. *Journal of Gerontology: Social Sciences, 46*, S321–S329.

Gross, J. (1998). The emerging field of emotion regulation: An integrative review. *Review of General Psychology, 2*, 271–299.

Gross, J. J., Carstensen, L. L., Pasupathi, M., Tsai, J., Skorpen, C. G., & Hsu, A. Y. C. (1997). Emotion and aging: Experience, expression, and control. *Psychology and Aging, 12*, 590–599.

Hansson, R. O. (1986). Relational competence, relationships, and adjustment in old age. *Journal of Personality and Social Psychology, 50*, 1050–1058.

Hansson, R. O., & Carpenter, B. N. (1994). *Relationships in old age: Coping with the challenge of transition.* New York: Guilford Press.

Hansson, R. O., Daleiden, E. L., & Hayslip, B., Jr. (2004). Relational competence across the life span. In F. R. Lang & K. L. Fingerman (Eds.), *Growing together:*

Personal relationships across the lifespan (pp. 317–340). Cambridge, England: Cambridge University Press.

Hansson, R. O., Nelson, R. E., Carver, M. D., NeeSmith, D. H., Dowling, E. M., Fletcher, W. L., & Suhr, P. (1990). Adult children with frail elderly parents: When to intervene? *Family Relations, 39*, 153–158.

Hansson, R. O., Remondet, J. H., & Galusha, M. (1993). Old age and widowhood: Issues of personal control and independence. In M. S. Stroebe, W. Stroebe, & R. O. Hansson (Eds.), *Handbook of bereavement: Theory, research, and intervention* (pp. 367–380). Cambridge, England: Cambridge University Press.

Hansson, R. O., & Stroebe, M. S. (2003). Grief, older adulthood. In T. P. Gullotta & M. Bloom (Eds.), *Encyclopedia of primary prevention and health promotion* (pp. 515–521). New York: Kluwer Academic/Plenum.

Harwood, D. (2001). Grief in old age. *Reviews in Clinical Gerontology, 11*, 167–175.

Hayflick, L. M. (1994). *How and why we age.* New York: Ballantine Books.

Hays, J. C., Gold, D. T., & Pieper, C. F. (1997). Sibling bereavement in late life. *Omega, 35*, 25–42.

Helsing, K., Comstock, G., & Szklo, M. (1982). Causes of death in a widowed population. *American Journal of Epidemiology, 116*, 524–532.

Helsing, K., & Szklo, M. (1981). Mortality after bereavement. *American Journal of Epidemiology, 114*, 41–52.

Helsing, K., Szklo, M., & Comstock, G. (1981). Factors associated with mortality after widowhood. *American Journal of Public Health, 71*, 802–809.

Helson, H. (1964). *Adaptation-level theory.* New York: Harper & Row.

Hillyard, D., & Dombrink, J. (2001). *Dying right: The death with dignity movement.* New York: Routledge.

Hobfoll, S. E. (1988). *The ecology of stress.* New York: Hemisphere.

Hogan, N. S., & Schmidt, L. A. (2002). Testing the grief to personal growth model using structural equation modeling. *Death Studies, 26*, 615–634.

Holmes, T. H., & Rahe, R. H. (1967). The Social Readjustment Rating Scale. *Journal of Psychosomatic Research, 11*, 213–218.

Horowitz, M. (1986). *Stress response syndromes* (2nd ed.). Northvale, NJ: Jason Aronson.

Horowitz, M., Segal, B., Holen, A., Bonanno, G., Milbrath, C., & Stinson, C. (1997). Diagnostic criteria for complicated grief disorder. *American Journal of Psychiatry, 137*, 1157–1160.

Horowitz, M., Wilner, N., & Alvarez, W. (1979). Impact of Event Scale: A measure of subjective stress. *Psychosomatic Medicine, 41*, 209–218.

Horn, J. L., & Cattell, R. B. (1967). Age differences in fluid and crystallized intelligence. *Acta Psychologica, 26*, 107–129.

Hoyer, W. J., & Roodin, P. A. (2003). *Adult development and aging.* New York: McGraw-Hill.

Hungerford, T. L. (2001). The economic consequences of widowhood on elderly women in the United States and Germany. *The Gerontologist, 41*, 103–110.

Isaacowitz, D. M., & Smith, J. (2003). Positive and negative affect in very old age. *Journal of Gerontology: Psychological Sciences, 58B*, P143–P152.

Jacobs, S. (1993). *Pathologic grief: Maladaptation to loss.* Washington, DC: American Psychiatric Press.

Jacobs, S. C., Kosten, T. R., Kasl, S. V., Ostfeld, A. M., Berkman, L., & Charpentier, P. (1987–1988). Attachment theory and multiple dimensions of grief. *Omega, 18*, 41–52.

Janoff-Bulman, R. (1992). *Shattered assumptions: Toward a new psychology of trauma.* New York: Free Press.

Janoff-Bulman, R., & Berg, M. (1998). Disillusionment and the creation of value: From traumatic losses to existential gains. In J. Harvey (Ed.), *Perspectives on loss: A sourcebook* (pp. 35–47). Philadelphia: Taylor & Francis.

Jette, A. M. (1996). Disability trends and transitions. In R. H. Binstock, & L. K. George (Eds.), *Handbook of aging and the social sciences* (pp. 94–116). San Diego, CA: Academic Press.

Jones, D., & Goldblatt, P. (1987). Cause of death in widow(er)s and spouses. *Journal of Biosocial Sciences, 19*, 107–121.

Jordan, J. R., & Neimeyer, R. A. (2003). Does grief counseling work? *Death Studies, 27*, 765–786.

Kagan, H. (2001, March–April). *The normalcy of parental bereavement: Re-thinking complicated mourning.* Paper presented at the Annual Conference of the Association for Death Education and Counseling, Toronto, Ontario, Canada.

Kaminer, H., & Lavie, P. (1993). Sleep and dreams in well-adjusted and less adjusted Holocaust survivors. In M. S. Stroebe, W. Stroebe, & R. O. Hansson (Eds.), *Handbook of bereavement: Theory, research and intervention* (pp. 331–345). New York: Cambridge University Press.

Kane, R. L., & Kane, R. A. (Eds.). (2000). *Assessing older persons: Measures, meaning, and practical applications.* Oxford, England: Oxford University Press.

Kaprio, J., Koskenvuo, M., & Rita, H. (1987). Mortality after bereavement: A prospective study of 95,647 widowed persons. *American Journal of Public Health, 77*, 283–287.

Kastenbaum, R. (1969). Death and bereavement in later life. In A. H. Kutscher (Ed.), *Death and bereavement* (pp. 28–54). Springfield, IL: Charles C Thomas.

Kelly, A. E., & McKillop, K. J. (1996). Consequences of revealing personal secrets. *Psychological Bulletin, 120*, 450–465.

Keltner, D., & Bonanno, G. (1997). A study of laughter and dissociation: Distinct correlates of laughter and smiling during bereavement. *Journal of Personality and Social Psychology, 73*, 687–702.

Klass, D. (2001). Continuing bonds in the resolution of grief in Japan and North America. *American Behavioral Scientist, 44*, 742–763.

Kleber, R., & Brom, D. (1992). *Coping with trauma: Theory, prevention, and treatment.* Amsterdam: Swets & Zeitlinger.

Knight, B. G. (1996). *Psychotherapy with older adults* (2nd ed.). Thousand Oaks, CA: Sage.

Kraus, A. S., & Lilienfeld, A. M. (1959). Some epidemiological aspects of the high mortality rate in the young widowed group. *Journal of Chronic Diseases, 10,* 207–217.

Kreitman, N. (1988). Suicide, age, and marital status. *Psychological Medicine, 18,* 121–128.

Labouvie-Vief, G., Lumley, M. A., Jain, E., & Heinze, H. (2003). Age and gender differences in cardiac reactivity and subjective emotion responses to emotional autobiographical memories. *Emotion, 3,* 115–126.

Lang, F. R., Rieckmann, N., & Baltes, M. M. (2002). Adapting to aging losses: Do resources facilitate strategies of selection, compensation, and optimization in everyday functioning? *Journal of Gerontology: Psychological Sciences, 57B,* P501–P509.

Last, J. M. (Ed.). (1995). *A dictionary of epidemiology* (3rd ed.). New York: Oxford University Press.

Lawrence, R. H., & Jette, A. M. (1996). Disentangling the disablement process. *Journal of Gerontology: Social Sciences, 51B,* S173–S182.

Lawton, M. P. (1996). Quality of life and affect in later life. In C. Magai & S. H. McFadden (Eds.), *Handbook of emotion, adult development, and aging* (pp. 327–348). San Diego, CA: Academic Press.

Lawton, M. P., Kleban, M. H., Rajagopal, D., & Dean, J. (1992). Dimensions of affective experience in three age groups. *Psychology and Aging, 7,* 171–184.

Lawton, M. P., & Nahemow, L. (1973). Ecology and the aging process. In C. Eisdorfer & M. P. Lawton (Eds.), *The psychology of adult development and aging* (pp. 619–674). Washington, DC: American Psychological Association.

Lawton, M. P., & Simon, B. (1968). The ecology of solid relationships in housing for the elderly. *Gerontologist, 8,* 108–115.

Lazarus, R. S. (1996). The role of coping in the emotions and how coping changes over the life course. In C. Magai & S. H. McFadden (Eds.), *Handbook of emotion, adult development, and aging* (pp. 289–306). San Diego, CA: Academic Press.

Lazarus, R. S., & Folkman, S. (1984). *Stress, appraisal, and coping.* New York: Springer Publishing Company.

Leahy, J. (1992). A comparison of depression in women bereaved of a spouse, child, or parent. *Omega, 26,* 207–217.

Lee, G. R., DeMaris, A., Bavin, S., & Sullivan, R. (2001). Gender differences in the depressive effect of widowhood in later life. *Journal of Gerontology: Social Sciences, 56B,* S56–S61.

Lee, G. R., Willetts, M. C., & Seccombe, K. (1998). Widowhood and depression. *Research on Aging, 20,* 611–630.

Leon, I. (1990). *When a baby dies.* New Haven, CT: Yale University Press.

Lepore, S. J., Silver, R., Wortman, C., & Wayment, H. A. (1996). Social constraints, intrusive thoughts, and depressive symptoms among bereaved mothers. *Journal of Personality and Social Psychology, 70,* 271–282.

Levy, L., Martinkowski, K., & Derby, J. (1994). Differences in patterns of adaptation in conjugal bereavement: Their sources and potential significance. *Omega: Journal of Death and Dying, 29*, 71–87.

Li, G. (1995). The interaction effect of bereavement and sex on the risk of suicide in the elderly: An historical cohort study. *Social Science & Medicine, 40*, 825–828.

Li, J., Precht, D., Mortensen, P., & Olsen, J. (2003). Mortality in parents after death of a child in Denmark: A nationwide follow-up study. *Lancet, 361*, 363–367.

Lindemann, E. (1979). *Beyond grief: Studies in crisis intervention.* New York: Jason Aronson.

Linville, P. W. (1987). Self-complexity as a cognitive buffer against stress-related illness and depression. *Journal of Personality and Social Psychology, 52*, 663–676.

Lopata, H. Z. (1993). The support systems of American urban widows. In M. S. Stroebe, W. Stroebe, & R. O. Hansson (Eds.), *Handbook of bereavement: Theory, research, and intervention* (pp. 381–396). Cambridge, England: Cambridge University Press.

Lopata, H. Z. (1996). *Current widowhood: Myths and realities.* Thousand Oaks, CA: Sage.

Lund, D. (Ed.). (2001). *Men coping with grief.* Amityville, NY: Baywood Publishing.

Lund, D. A., & Caserta, M. S. (2001). When the unexpected happens: Husbands coping with the deaths of their wives. In D. A. Lund (Ed.), *Men coping with grief* (pp. 147–167). Amityville, NY: Baywood Publishing.

Lund, D. A., Caserta, M. S., de Vries, B., & Wright, S. (2004). Restoration after bereavement. *Generations Review: British Society of Gerontology, 14*, 9–15.

Lund, D. A., Caserta, M. S., & Dimond, M. F. (1989). Impact of spousal bereavement on the subjective well-being of older adults. In D. A. Lund (Ed.), *Older bereaved spouses: Research with practical implications* (pp. 3–15). New York: Taylor & Francis/Hemisphere.

Lund, D. A., Caserta, M. S., & Dimond, M. F. (1993). The course of spousal bereavement in later life. In M. S. Stroebe, W. Stroebe, & R. O. Hansson (Eds.), *Handbook of bereavement: Theory, research, and intervention* (pp. 240–254). Cambridge, England: Cambridge University Press.

Lundin, T. (1984). Morbidity following sudden and unexpected bereavement. *British Journal of Psychiatry, 144*, 84–88.

Luoma, J. B., & Pearson, J. L. (2002). Suicide and marital status in the United States, 1991–1996: Is widowhood a risk factor? *American Journal of Public Health, 92*, 1518–1522.

Machin, L. (2001). *Measuring attitudes to grief.* Unpublished doctoral dissertation, University of Keele, Keele, England.

Maddison, D. C., & Walker, W. L. (1967). Factors affecting the outcome of conjugal bereavement. *British Journal of Psychiatry, 113*, 1057–1067.

Malkinson, R. (1996). Cognitive behavioural grief therapy. *Journal of Rational Emotive and Cognitive Behavior Therapy, 14*, 155–171.

Manor, O., & Eisenbach, Z. (2003). Mortality after spousal loss: Are there sociodemographic differences? *Social Science & Medicine, 56*, 405–413.

Markus, H. R., & Herzog, A. R. (1992). The role of the self-concept in aging. *Annual Review of Gerontology and Geriatrics, 11*, 110–143.

Marris, P. (1974). *Loss and change.* New York: Pantheon Books.

Martikainen, P., & Valkonen, T. (1996). Mortality after death of a spouse in relation to duration of bereavement in Finland. *Journal of Epidemiology and Community Health, 50*, 264–268.

Marwit, S. J., & Meuser, T. M. (2002). Development and initial validation of an inventory to assess grief in caregivers of persons with Alzheimer's disease. *The Gerontologist, 42*, 751–765.

McCrae, R. R., & Costa, P. T. (1993). Psychological resilience among widowed men and women: A 10-year follow-up of a national sample. In M. S. Stroebe, W. Stroebe, & R. O. Hansson (Eds.), *Handbook of bereavement: Theory, research, and intervention* (pp. 196–207). New York: Cambridge University Press.

Meinow, B., Kareholt, I., Parker, M. G., & Thorslund, M. (2004). The effect of the duration of follow-up in mortality analysis: The temporal pattern of different predictors. *Journal of Gerontology: Social Sciences, 59B*, S181–S189.

Mellström, D., Nilsson, A., Oden, A., Rundgren, A., & Svanborg, A. (1982). Mortality among the widowed in Sweden. *Scandinavian Journal of Social Medicine, 10*, 33–41.

Mendes de Leon, C. F., Kasl, S. V., & Jacobs, S. (1994). A prospective study of widowhood and changes in symptoms of depression in a community sample of the elderly. *Psychological Medicine, 24*, 613–624.

Mesquita, B., & Frijda, N. (1992). Cultural variations in emotions: A review. *Psychological Bulletin, 112*, 1179–1204.

Molinari, V., Karel, M., Jones, S., Zeiss, A., Cooley, S. G., Wray, L., et al. (2003). Recommendations about the knowledge and skills required of psychologists working with older adults. *Professional Psychology: Research and Practice, 34*, 435–443.

Morgan, D., Carder, P., & Neal, M. (1997). Are some relationships more useful than others? The value of similar others in the networks of recent widows. *Journal of Social and Personal Relationships, 14*, 745–759.

Morgan, T. J., Hansson, R. O., Indart, M. J., Austin, D. M., Crutcher, M. M., Hampton, P. W., et al. (1984). Old age and environmental docility: The roles of health, support and personality. *Journal of Gerontology, 39*, 240–242.

Moss, M. S., & Moss, S. Z. (1989). Death of the very old. In K. J. Doka (Ed.), *Disenfranchised grief: Recognizing hidden sorrow* (pp. 213–227). New York: Lexington Books.

Moss, M. S., & Moss, S. Z. (1994). Death and bereavement. In R. Blieszner & V. H. Bedford (Eds.), *Aging and the family: Theory and research* (pp. 422–439). Westport, CT: Praeger.

Moss, M. S., Moss, S. Z., & Hansson, R. O. (2001). Bereavement and old age. In M. S. Stroebe, R. O. Hansson, W. Stroebe, & H. Schut (Eds.), *Handbook of bereavement research: Consequences, coping, and care* (pp. 241–260). Washington, DC: American Psychological Association.

Mroczek, D. K., & Kolarz, C. M. (1998). The effect of age on positive and negative affect: A developmental perspective on happiness. *Journal of Personality and Social Psychology, 75*, 1333–1349.

Murdock, M. E., Guarnaccia, C. A., Hayslip, B., Jr., & McKibbin, C. L. (1998). The contribution of small life events to the psychological distress of married and widowed older women. *Journal of Women & Aging, 10*, 3–22.

Murrell, S. A., Himmelfarb, S., & Phifer, J. F. (1988). Effects of bereavement/loss and pre-event status on subsequent physical health in older adults. *International Journal of Aging and Human Development, 27*, 89–107.

Nadeau, J. W. (1998). *Families making sense of death.* Thousand Oaks, CA: Sage.

Nadeau, J. W. (2001). Meaning making in family bereavement: A family systems approach. In M. S. Stroebe, R. O. Hansson, W. Stroebe, & H. Schut (Eds.), *Handbook of bereavement research: Consequences, coping, and care* (pp. 329–347). Washington, DC: American Psychological Association.

Nagi, S. Z. (1991). Disability concepts revisited. Implications for prevention. In A. Pope & A. Tarlov (Eds.), *Disability in America: Toward a national agenda for prevention* (pp. 309–327). Washington, DC: National Academy Press.

Nahemow, L. (2000). The ecological theory of aging: Powell Lawton's legacy. In R. L. Rubinstein, M. Moss, & M. H. Kleban (Eds.), *The many dimensions of aging* (pp. 22–40). New York: Springer Publishing Company.

National Academy on an Aging Society. (2000, February). *At risk: Developing chronic conditions later in life* (Publication No. 4). Washington, DC: Author.

National Institute of Mental Health. (2003). *Older adults: Depression and suicide facts* (NIH Publication No. 03-4593). Retrieved April 7, 2006, from http://www.nimh.nih.gov/publicat/elderlydepsuicide.cfm

Neimeyer, R. (1996). Process interventions for the constructivist psychotherapist. In K. Kuehlwein & H. Rosen (Eds.), *Constructing realities: Meaning-making perspectives for psychotherapists* (pp. 371–411). San Francisco: Jossey-Bass.

Neimeyer, R. (2000). *Lessons of loss: A guide to coping.* Keystone Heights, FL: PsychoEducational Resources.

Neimeyer, R. (Ed.). (2001). *Meaning reconstruction and the experience of loss.* Washington, DC: American Psychological Association.

Neimeyer, R. A., & Hogan, N. S. (2001). Quantitative or qualitative: Measurement issues in the study of grief. In M. S. Stroebe, R. O. Hansson, W. Stroebe, & H. Schut (Eds.), *Handbook of bereavement research: Consequences, coping, and care* (pp. 89–118). Washington, DC: American Psychological Association.

Neimeyer, R., Keesee, N., & Fortner, B. (1998). Loss and meaning reconstruction: Propositions and procedures. In S. Rubin, R. Malkinson, & E. Witztum (Eds.), *Traumatic and non-traumatic bereavement* (pp. 197–230). Madison, CT: International Universities Press.

Nieboer, A. P., Lindenberg, S. M., & Ormel, J. (1998–1999). Conjugal bereavement and well-being of elderly men and women: A preliminary study. *Omega, 38,* 113–141.

Nolen-Hoeksema, S. (2001). Ruminative coping and adjustment to bereavement. In M. S. Stroebe, R. O. Hansson, W. Stroebe, & H. Schut (Eds.), *Handbook of bereavement research: Consequences, coping, and care* (pp. 545–562). Washington, DC: American Psychological Association.

Nolen-Hoeksema, S., & Larson, J. (1999). *Coping with loss.* Mahwah, NJ: Erlbaum.

Nolen-Hoeksema, S., Parker, L. E., & Larson, J. (1994). Ruminative coping with depressed mood following loss. *Journal of Personality and Social Psychology, 67,* 92–104.

Nordhus, I. H., VandenBos, G. R., Berg, S., & Fromholt, P. (1998). *Clinical gerontology.* Washington, DC: American Psychological Association.

Norris, F. (1985). Characteristics of older nonrespondents over five waves of a panel study. *Journal of Gerontology, 40,* 627–636.

Norris, F. H., & Murrell, S. A. (1990). Social support, life events, and stress as modifiers of adjustment to bereavement by older adults. *Psychology and Aging, 5,* 429–436.

O'Bryant, S. L., & Hansson, R. O. (1994). Widowhood. In R. Blieszner & V. H. Bedford (Eds.), *Aging and the family: Theory and research* (pp. 440–458). Wesport, CT: Praeger.

Ong, A. D., & Bergeman, C. S. (2004). The complexity of emotions in later life. *Journal of Gerontology: Psychological Sciences, 59B,* P117–P122.

Parkes, C. M. (1964). Effects of bereavement on physical and mental health: A study of the medical records of widows. *British Medical Journal, 2,* 274–279.

Parkes, C. M. (1993). Bereavement as a psychosocial transition: Processes of adaptation to change. In M. S. Stroebe, R. O. Hansson, W. Stroebe, & H. Schut (Eds.), *Handbook of bereavement: Theory, research, and intervention* (pp. 91–101). New York: Cambridge University Press.

Parkes, C. M. (1996). *Bereavement: Studies of grief in adult life* (3rd ed.). New York: International Universities Press. (Original work published 1972)

Parkes, C. M. (1997). Bereavement and mental health in the elderly. *Reviews in Clinical Gerontology, 7,* 47–53.

Parkes, C. M. (1998). Editorial comments. *Bereavement Care, 17,* 18.

Parkes, C. M. (2001a). *Bereavement: Studies of grief in adult life* (3rd ed.). New York: Routledge/Taylor & Francis.

Parkes, C. M. (2001b). A historical overview of the scientific study of bereavement. In M. S. Stroebe, R. O. Hansson, W. Stroebe, & H. Schut (Eds.), *Handbook of bereavement research: Consequences, coping, and care* (pp. 25–45). Washington, DC: American Psychological Association.

Parkes, C., Benjamin, B., & Fitzgerald, R. (1969) Broken heart: A statistical study of the increased mortality among widowers. *British Medical Journal, 1,* 740–743.

Parkes, C. M., Laungani, P., & Young, B. (1997). *Death and bereavement across cultures*. London: Routledge.

Parkes, C. M., & Weiss, R. S. (1983). *Recovery from bereavement*. New York: Basic Books.

Pasupathi, M., Henry, R. M., & Carstensen, L. L. (2002). Age and ethnicity differences in storytelling to young children: Emotionality, relationality, and socialization. *Psychology and Aging, 17*, 610–621.

Pennebaker, J. W. (1997). *Opening up: The healing power of expressing emotions* (Rev. ed.). New York: Guilford Press.

Pennebaker, J. W., Francis, M., & Booth, R. (2001). *Linguistic inquiry and word count: LIWC 2001*. Mahwah, NJ: Erlbaum.

Pennebaker, J. W., Mayne, T., & Francis, M. (1997). Linguistic predictors of adaptive bereavement. *Journal of Personality and Social Psychology, 72*, 863–871.

Pennebaker, J., Zech, E., & Rimé, B. (2001). Disclosing and sharing emotion: Psychological, social, and health consequences. In M. S. Stroebe, R. O. Hansson, W. Stroebe, & H. Schut (Eds.), *Handbook of bereavement research: Consequences, coping, and care* (pp. 517–543). Washington, DC: American Psychological Association.

Perkins, H. W., & Harris, L. (1990). Familial bereavement and health in adult life course perspective. *Journal of Marriage and the Family, 52*, 233–241.

Prigerson, H. G., Cherlin, E., Chen, J. H., Kasl, S. V., Hurzeler, R., & Bradley, E. H. (2003). The Stressful Caregiving Adult Reactions to Experiences of Dying (SCARED) Scale. *American Journal of Geriatric Psychiatry, 11*, 309–319.

Prigerson, H. G., Frank, E., Kasl, S. V., Reynolds, C. F., III, Anderson, B., Zubenko, G. S., et al. (1995). Complicated grief and bereavement-related depression as distinct disorders: Preliminary empirical validation in elderly bereaved spouses. *American Journal of Psychiatry, 152*, 22–30.

Prigerson, H., & Jacobs, S. (2001). Traumatic grief as a distinct disorder: A rationale, consensus criteria, and a preliminary empirical test. In M. S. Stroebe, R. O. Hansson, W. Stroebe, & H. Schut (Eds.), *Handbook of bereavement research: Consequences, coping, and care* (pp. 613–645). Washington, DC: American Psychological Association.

Prigerson, H. G., Maciejewski, P. K., & Rosenheck, R. A. (2000). Preliminary explorations of the harmful interactive effects of widowhood and marital harmony on health, health service use, and health care costs. *The Gerontologist, 40*, 349–357.

Qualls, S. H., & Ables, N. (Eds.). (2000). *Psychology and the aging revolution*. Washington. DC: American Psychological Association.

Raphael, B., Minkov, C., & Dobson, M. (2001). Psychotherapeutic and pharmacological intervention for bereaved persons. In M. S. Stroebe, R. O. Hansson, W. Stroebe, & H. Schut (Eds.), *Handbook of bereavement research: Consequences, coping, and care* (pp. 587–612). Washington, DC: American Psychological Association.

Remondet, J. H., & Hansson, R. O. (1987). Assessing a widow's grief: A short index. *Journal of Gerontological Nursing, 13,* 31–34.

Richardson, S. J., Lund, D. A., Caserta, M. S., Dudley, W. N., & Obray, S. J. (2003). Sleep patterns in older bereaved spouses. *Omega, 47,* 361–383.

Richardson, V. (in press). A dual process model of grief counseling: Findings from the Changing Lives of Older Couples (CLOC) study. *Journal of Gerontological Social Work.*

Richardson, V. E., & Balaswamy, S. (2001). Coping with bereavement among elderly widowers. *Omega, 43,* 129–144.

Robinson-Whelen, S., Tata, Y., MacCallum, R. C., McGuire, L., & Kiecolt-Glaser, J. K. (2001). Long-term caregiving: What happens when it ends? *Journal of Abnormal Psychology, 110,* 573–584.

Rosenblatt, P. C. (1993). Grief: The social context of private feelings. In M. S. Stroebe, W. Stroebe, & R. O. Hansson (Eds.), *Handbook of bereavement: Theory, research, and intervention* (pp. 102–111). Cambridge, England: Cambridge University Press.

Rosenblatt, P. C. (2001). A social constructionist perspective on cultural differences in grief. In M. S. Stroebe, R. O. Hansson, W. Stroebe, & H. Schut (Eds.), *Handbook of bereavement research: Consequences, coping, and care* (pp. 285–300). Washington, DC: American Psychological Association.

Rosenbloom, C. A., & Whittington, F. J. (1993). The effects of bereavement on eating behaviors and nutrient intakes in elderly widowed persons. *Journal of Gerontology: Social Sciences, 48,* S223–S229.

Rosenzweig, A., Prigerson, H., Miller, M. D., & Reynolds, C. F., III. (1997). Bereavement and late-life depression: Grief and its complications in the elderly. *Annual Review of Medicine, 48,* 421–428.

Rothermund, K., & Brandtstadter, J. (2003). Coping with deficits and losses in later life: From compensatory action to accommodation. *Psychology and Aging, 18,* 896–905.

Rowe, J. W. (1985). Health care of the elderly. *New England Journal of Medicine, 312,* 827–835.

Rowe, J. W., & Kahn, R. L. (1987, July 3). Human aging: Usual and successful. *Science, 237,* 143–149.

Rowe, J. W., & Kahn, R. L. (1997). Successful aging. *The Gerontologist, 37,* 433–440.

Rubin, S. (1981). A two-track model of bereavement: Theory and application in research. *American Journal of Orthopsychiatry, 51,* 101–109.

Rubin, S. (1993). The death of a child is forever: The life course impact of child loss. In M. S. Stroebe, W. Stroebe, & R. O. Hansson (Eds.), *Handbook of bereavement: Theory, research, and intervention* (pp. 285–299). New York: Cambridge University Press.

Rubin, S. (1999). The two-track model of bereavement: Overview, retrospect, and prospect. *Death Studies, 23,* 681–714.

Sable, P. (1989). Attachment, anxiety, and loss of a husband. *American Journal of Orthopsychiatry, 59,* 550–556.

Sable, P. (1991). Attachment, loss of spouse, and grief in elderly adults. *Omega, 23,* 129–142.

Sanders, C. (1983). Effects of sudden versus chronic illness death on bereavement outcome. *Omega, 11,* 227–241.

Sanders, C. (1989). *Grief: The mourning after.* New York: Wiley.

Schaefer, C., Quesenberry, C., & Wi, S. (1995). Mortality following conjugal bereavement and the effects of a shared environment. *American Journal of Epidemiology, 141,* 1142–1152.

Schaie, K. W. (1990). Intellectual development in adulthood. In J. E. Birren & K. W. Schaie (Eds.), *Handbook of the psychology of aging* (3rd ed., pp. 291–309). San Diego, CA: Academic Press.

Schaie, K. W. (1994). The course of adult intellectual development. *American Psychologist, 49,* 304–313.

Schulz, R., Beach, S. R., Lind, B., Martire, L. M., Zdaniuk, B., Hirsch, C., et al. (2001, June 27). Involvement in caregiving and adjustment to death of a spouse. *Journal of the American Medical Association, 285,* 3123–3129.

Schulz, R., & Martire, L. M. (1998). Intervention research with older adults: Introduction, overview, and future directions. *Annual Review of Gerontology and Geriatrics, 18,* 1–16.

Schulz, R., Mendelsohn, A. B., Haley, W., Mahoney, D., Allen, R. S., Zhang, S., et al. (2003). End-of-life care and the effects of bereavement on family caregivers of persons with dementia. *New England Journal of Medicine, 349,* 1936–1942.

Schut, H. (1992). *Omgaan met de dood van de partner: Effecten op gezondheid en effecten van rouwbegeleiding* [Coping with the death of the partner: Effects on health and effects of grief counseling] (Doctoral dissertation, Utrecht University, 1992). Amsterdam: Thesis Publications.

Schut, H. A. W., Stroebe, M. S., van den Bout, J., & de Keijser, J. (1997). Intervention for the bereaved: Gender differences in the efficacy of grief counseling. *British Journal of Clinical Psychology, 36,* 63–72.

Schut, H., Stroebe, M., van den Bout, J., & Terheggen, M. (2001). The efficacy of bereavement interventions: Who benefits? In M. S. Stroebe, R. O. Hansson, W. Stroebe, & H. Schut (Eds.), *Handbook of bereavement research: Consequences, coping, and care* (pp. 705–737). Washington, DC: American Psychological Association.

Seltzer, M. M., & Li, L. W. (2000). The dynamics of caregiving: Transitions during a three-year prospective study. *The Gerontologist, 40,* 165–178.

Shapiro, E. (2001). Grief in interpersonal perspective: Theories and their implications. In M. S. Stroebe, R. O. Hansson, W. Stroebe, & H. Schut (Eds.), *Handbook of bereavement research: Consequences, coping, and care* (pp. 301–327). Washington, DC: American Psychological Association.

Shaver, P. R., & Tancredy, C. M. (2001). Emotion, attachment, and bereavement: A conceptual commentary. In M. S. Stroebe, R. O. Hansson, W. Stroebe, & H. A. W. Schut (Eds.), *Handbook of bereavement research: Consequences, coping, and care* (pp. 63–88). Washington, DC: American Psychological Association.

Shear, K., Frank, E., Houck, P., & Reynolds, C. (2005, June 1). Treatment of complicated grief: A randomized controlled trial. *Journal of the American Medical Association, 293*, 2601–2608.

Sheik, J. I., & Yesavage, J. A. (1986). Geriatric Depression Scale (GDS): Recent evidence and development of a shorter version. In T. L. Brink (Ed.), *Clinical gerontology: A guide to assessment and intervention* (pp. 165–173). New York: Haworth Press.

Shuchter, S., & Zisook, S. (1993). The course of normal grief. In M. S. Stroebe, W. Stroebe, & R. O. Hansson (Eds.). *Handbook of bereavement: Consequences, coping, and care* (pp. 23–43). New York: Cambridge University Press.

Shurtleff, D. (1955). Mortality and marital status. *Public Health Reports, 70*, 248–252.

Siegel, J. M., & Kuykendall, D. H. (1990). Loss, widowhood, and psychological distress among the elderly. *Journal of Consulting and Clinical Psychology, 58*, 519–524.

Simoneau, G. G., & Leibowitz, H. W. (1996). Posture, gait, and falls. In J. E. Birren & K. W. Schaie (Eds.), *Handbook of the psychology of aging* (4th ed., pp. 204–217). San Diego, CA: Academic Press.

Sinnott, J. (1996). The developmental approach: Post formal thought as adaptive intelligence. In F. Blanchard-Fields & T. M. Hess (Eds.), *Perspectives on cognitive change in adulthood and aging* (pp. 358–383). New York: McGraw-Hill.

Skinner, E., Edge, K., Altman, J., & Sherwood, H. (2003). Searching for the structure of coping: A review and critique of category systems for classifying ways of coping. *Psychological Bulletin, 129*, 216–269.

Smith, J., & Freund, A. M. (2002). The dynamics of possible selves in old age. *Journal of Gerontology: Psychological Sciences, 57B*, P492–P500.

Smith, J., Mercy, J., & Conn, J. (1988). Marital status and the risk of suicide. *American Journal of Public Health, 78*, 78–80.

Smith, K., Zick, K., & Duncan, G. (1991). Remarriage patterns among recent widows and widowers. *Demography, 28*, 361–374.

Stephens, M. A. P., & Bernstein, M. D. (1984). Social support and well-being among residents of planned housing. *The Gerontologist, 24*, 144–148.

Strecher, V. J., Champion, V. L., & Rosenstock, I. M. (1997). The health belief model and health behavior. In D. S. Gochman (Ed.), *Handbook of health behavior research: Vol. 1. Personal and social determinants* (pp. 71–91). New York: Plenum Press.

Stroebe, M. S. (1992). Coping with bereavement: A review of the grief work hypothesis. *Omega, 26*, 19–42.

Stroebe, M. S., Folkman, S., Hansson, R. O., & Schut, H. (2006). *The prediction of bereavement outcome: Development of an integrative risk factor framework.* Manuscript submitted for publication.

Stroebe, M. S., Hansson, R. O., Stroebe, W., & Schut, H. (Eds.). (2001). *Handbook of bereavement research: Consequences, coping, and care.* Washington, DC: American Psychological Association.

Stroebe, M. S., & Schut, H. A. W. (1999). The dual process model of coping with bereavement: Rationale and description. *Death Studies, 23,* 197–224.

Stroebe, M. S., & Schut, H. (2001). Meaning making in the dual process model. In R. Neimeyer (Ed.), *Meaning reconstruction and the experience of loss* (pp. 55–73). Washington, DC: American Psychological Association.

Stroebe, M., Schut, H., & Finkenauer, C. (2001). The traumatization of grief: A conceptual framework for understanding the trauma–bereavement interface. *Israeli Journal of Psychiatry, 38,* 185–201.

Stroebe, M. S., & Stroebe, W. (1991). Does "grief work" work? *Journal of Consulting and Clinical Psychology, 59,* 479–482.

Stroebe, M. S., & Stroebe, W. (1993). The mortality of bereavement: A review. In M. S. Stroebe, W. Stroebe, & R. O. Hansson (Eds.), *Handbook of bereavement: Theory, research, and intervention* (pp. 175–195). Cambridge, England: Cambridge University Press.

Stroebe, M. S., Stroebe, W., & Hansson, R. O. (1993). *Handbook of bereavement: Theory, research, and intervention.* Cambridge, England: Cambridge University Press.

Stroebe, M. S., Stroebe, W., & Schut, H. (2001). Gender differences in adjustment to bereavement: An empirical and theoretical review. *Review of General Psychology, 5,* 62–83.

Stroebe, M. S., Stroebe, W., & Schut, H. (2005a). Attachment in coping with bereavement: A theoretical integration. *Review of General Psychology, 9,* 48–66.

Stroebe, M. S., Stroebe, W., & Schut, H. (2005b). Who benefits from disclosure? Exploration of attachment style differences in the effects of expressing emotions. *Clinical Psychology Review, 9,* 48–60.

Stroebe, W. (2000). *Social psychology and health.* Milton Keynes, England: Open University Press.

Stroebe, W., & Schut, H. A. W. (2001). Risk factors in bereavement outcome: A methodological and empirical review. In M. S. Stroebe, R. O. Hansson, W. Stroebe, & H. Schut (Eds.), *Handbook of bereavement research: Consequences, coping, and care* (pp. 349–371). Washington, DC: American Psychological Association.

Stroebe, W., Schut, H., & Stroebe, M. (2005). Grief work, disclosure and counseling: Do they help the bereaved? *Clinical Psychology Review, 25,* 395–414.

Stroebe, W., & Stroebe, M. S. (1987). *Bereavement and health: The psychological and physical consequences of partner loss.* Cambridge, England: Cambridge University Press.

Stroebe, W., Stroebe, M., Abakoumkin, G., & Schut, H. (1996). Social and emotional loneliness: A comparison of attachment and stress theory explanations. *Journal of Personality and Social Psychology, 70,* 1241–1249.

Stroebe, W., Zech, E., Stroebe, M., & Abakoumkin, G. (2005). Does social support help in bereavement? *Journal of Social and Clinical Psychology, 24,* 1030–1050.

Stuck, A. E., Walthert, J. M., Nikolaus, T., Bula, C. J., Hohmann, C., & Beck, J. C. (1999). Risk factors for functional status decline in community-living elderly people: A systematic literature review. *Social Science & Medicine, 48,* 445–469.

Stylianos, S. K., & Vachon, M. L. S. (1993). The role of social support in bereavement. In M. S. Stroebe, W. Stroebe, & R. O. Hansson (Eds.), *Handbook of bereavement: Theory, research, and intervention* (pp. 397–410). Cambridge, England: Cambridge University Press.

Szanto, K., Gildengers, A., Mulsant, B. H., Brown, G., Alexopoulos, G. S., & Reynolds, C. F., III. (2002). Identification of suicidal ideation and prevention of suicidal behavior in the elderly. *Drugs Aging, 19,* 11–24.

Szanto, K., Prigerson, H., Houck, P., Ehrenpreis, L., & Reynolds, C. F., III. (1997). Suicidal ideation in elderly bereaved: The role of complicated grief. *Suicide and Life-Threatening Behavior, 27,* 194–207.

Talbott, M. M. (1990). The negative side of the relationship between older widows and their adult children: The mothers' perspective. *The Gerontologist, 30,* 595–603.

Tedeschi, R., Park, C., & Calhoun, L. (Eds.). (1998). *Posttraumatic growth: Positive changes in the aftermath of crisis.* Mahwah, NJ: Erlbaum.

Telonidis, J. S., Lund, D. A., Caserta, M. S., Guralnik, J. M., & Pennington, J. L., Jr. (2004–2005). The effects of widowhood on disabled older women (the Women's Health and Aging Study). *Omega, 50,* 217–235.

Thompson, L. W., Gallagher-Thompson, D., Futterman, A., Gilewski, M. J., & Peterson, J. (1991). The effects of late-life spousal bereavement over a 30-month interval. *Psychology and Aging, 6,* 434–441.

Tsai, J. L., Levenson, R. W., & Carstensen, L. L. (2000). Autonomic, subjective, and expressive responses to emotional films in older and younger Chinese Americans and European Americans. *Psychology and Aging, 15,* 684–693.

Turvey, C. L., Carney, C., Arndt, S., Wallace, R. B., & Herzog, R. (1999). Conjugal loss and syndromal depression in a sample of elders aged 70 years or older. *American Journal of Psychiatry, 156,* 1596–1601.

U.S. Department of Health and Human Services. (2002, September 16). *National vital statistics report* (Vol. 50, No. 16). Hyattsville, MD: Centers for Disease Control and Prevention, National Center for Health Statistics. Retrieved September 1, 2005, from http://www.cdc.gov/nchs/fastats/pdf/hvsr_16t1.pdf

U.S. Department of Health and Human Services. (2003). *Health, United States, 2003—Special excerpt: Trend tables on 65 and older population.* Hyattsville, MD: Centers for Disease Control and Prevention, National Center for Health Statistics.

Utz, R. L., Carr, D., Nesse, R., & Wortman, C. B. (2002). The effect of widowhood on older adults' social participation: An evaluation of activity, disengagement, and continuity theories. *The Gerontologist, 42,* 522–533.

Vachon, M., Rogers, J., Lyall, W., Lancee, W., Sheldon, A., & Freeman, S. (1982). Predictors and correlates of adaptation to bereavement. *American Journal of Psychiatry, 139,* 998–1002.

van Baarsen, B., van Duijn, M. A. J., Smit, J. H., Snijders, T. A. B., & Knipshcheer, K. P. M. (2001–2002). Patterns of adjustment to partner loss in old age: The widowhood adaptation longitudinal study. *Omega, 44,* 5–36.

van Grootheest, D. S., Beekman, A. T. F., van Groenou, M. I. B., & Deeg, D. J. H. (1999). Sex differences in depression after widowhood. Do men suffer more? *Social Psychiatry Psychiatric Epidemiology, 34,* 391–398.

van Heck, G., & de Ridder, D. (2001). Assessment of coping with loss: Dimensions and measurement. In M. Stroebe, R. O. Hansson, W. Stroebe, & H. Schut (Eds.), *Handbook of bereavement research: Consequences, coping, and care* (pp. 449–469). Washington, DC: American Psychological Association.

Verbrugge, L., & Jette, A. (1994). The disablement process. *Social Science & Medicine, 38,* 1–14.

Walter, T. (1996). A new model of grief: Bereavement and biography. *Mortality, 2,* 263–266.

Walter, T. (1999). *On bereavement: The culture of grief.* Buckingham, England: Open University Press.

Wayment, H. A., & Vierthaler, J. (2002). Attachment style and bereavement reactions. *Journal of Loss and Trauma, 7,* 129–149.

Weiss, D., & Marmar, C. (1997). The Impact of Event Scale—Revised. In J. Wilson & T. Keane (Eds.), *Assessing psychological trauma and PTSD* (pp. 339–411). New York: Guilford Press.

Weiss, R. S. (1973). *Loneliness: The experience of emotional and social isolation.* Cambridge, MA: MIT Press.

Weiss, R. S. (1988). Loss and recovery. *Journal of Social Issues, 44,* 37–52.

Wells, Y. D., & Kendig, H. L. (1997). Health and well-being of spouse caregivers and the widowed. *The Gerontologist, 37,* 666–674.

Whitbourne, S. K. (1999). Physical changes. In J. C. Cavanaugh & S. K. Whitbourne (Eds.), *Gerontology: An interdisciplinary perspective* (pp. 91–122). New York: Oxford University Press.

Wijngaards-de Meij, L., Stroebe, M., Schut, H., Stroebe, W., van den Bout, J., Heijmans, P., & Dijkstra, I. (2005). Couples at risk following the death of their child: Predictors of grief versus depression. *Journal of Consulting and Clinical Psychology, 73,* 617–623.

Wikan, U. (1988). Bereavement and loss in two Muslim communities: Egypt and Bali compared. *Social Science & Medicine, 27,* 451–460.

Winchester-Nadeau, J. (1998). *Families making sense of death.* Thousand Oaks, CA: Sage.

Winchester-Nadeau, J. (2001). Meaning making in family bereavement: A family systems approach. In M. S. Stroebe, R. O. Hansson, W. Stroebe, & H. Schut (Eds.), *Handbook of bereavement research: Consequences, coping, and care* (pp. 329–347). Washington, DC: American Psychological Association.

Wolinsky, F. D., & Johnson, R. J. (1992). Widowhood, health status, and the use of health services by older adults: A cross-sectional and prospective approach. *Journal of Gerontology: Social Sciences, 47,* S8–S16.

Worden, J. W. (1982). *Grief counseling and grief therapy: A handbook for the mental health practitioner.* New York: Springer Publishing Company.

Worden, J. W. (1991). *Grief counseling and grief therapy: A handbook for the mental health practitioner* (2nd ed.). New York: Springer Publishing Company.

Worden, J. W. (2002). *Grief counseling and grief therapy: A handbook for the mental health practitioner* (3rd ed.). New York: Springer Publishing Company.

Wortman, C. B., & Silver, R. C. (1987). Coping with irrevocable loss. In G. R. VandenBos & B. K. Bryant (Eds.), *Cataclysms, crises, and catastrophes: Psychology in action* (pp. 189–235). Washington, DC: American Psychological Association.

Wortman, C. B., & Silver, R. C. (1989). The myths of coping with loss. *Journal of Consulting and Clinical Psychology, 57,* 349–357.

Wortman, C., & Silver, R. (1992). Reconsidering assumptions about coping with loss: An overview of current research. In L. Montada, S. H. Filipp, & M. J. Lerner (Eds.), *Life crises and experiences of loss in adulthood* (pp. 341–365). Hillsdale, NJ: Erlbaum.

Wortman, C., & Silver, R. (2001). The myths of coping with loss revisited. In M. S. Stroebe, R. O. Hansson, W. Stroebe, & H. Schut (Eds.), *Handbook of bereavement research: Consequences, coping, and care* (pp. 405–429). Washington, DC: American Psychological Association.

Wortman, C. B., Silver, R. C., & Kessler, R. C. (1993). The meaning of loss and adjustment to bereavement. In M. S. Stroebe, W. Stroebe, & R. O. Hansson (Eds.), *Handbook of bereavement: Theory, research, and intervention* (pp. 349–366). Cambridge, England: Cambridge University Press.

Wu, Y. (1995). Remarriage after widowhood: A marital history study of older Canadians. *Canadian Journal on Aging, 14,* 719–736.

Zarit, S. H., & Knight, B. G. (Eds.). (1996). *A guide to psychotherapy and aging: Effective clinical interventions in a life-stage context.* Washington, DC: American Psychological Association.

Zarit, S. H., & Zarit, J. M. (1998). *Mental disorders in older adults: Fundamentals of assessment and treatment.* New York: Guilford Press.

Zautra, A. J., Guarnaccia, C. A., Reich, J. W., & Dohrenwend, B. P. (1988). The contribution of small life events to stress and distress. In L. H. Cohen (Ed.), *Life events and psychological functioning: Theoretical and methodological issues* (pp. 123–148). Newbury Park, CA: Sage.

Zick, C. D., & Smith, K. R. (1991). Patterns of economic change surrounding the death of a spouse. *Journal of Gerontology: Social Sciences, 46,* S310–S320.

Zisook, S., & Shuchter, S. (1986). The first four years of widowhood. *Psychiatric Annals, 15,* 288–294.

AUTHOR INDEX

Haring, M., 18
Harris, L., 64
Harwood, D., 90
Hayflick, L. M., 118, 137
Hays, J. C., 56
Hayslip, B., Jr., 70, 105, 144
Heijmans, P., 14, 65
Heinze, H., 122
Helme, R. D., 85
Helsing, K., 67
Helson, H., 143
Henry, R. M., 121
Herzog, A. R., 129
Herzog, R., 90
Hill, R., 52, 53
Hillyard, D., 100
Himmelfarb, S., 83, 84, 150
Hirsch, C., 102
Hobfoll, S. E., 142
Hogan, N. S., 13, 53, 88, 175
Hohmann, C., 149
Holen, A., 19, 36
Holmes, T. H., 157
Horn, J. L., 124
Horowitz, M., 19, 29, 32, 33, 36
Houck, P., 54, 93
Houck, P. R., 85
House, J. S., 98, 99
Hoyer, W. J., 128
Hsu, A. Y. C., 120
Hungerford, T. L., 106
Hurzeler, R., 103
Hutchin, S., 102

Indart, M. J., 144, 146
Ironson, G., 35, 44
Isaacowitz, D. M., 123

Jackson, D. J., 88
Jacobs, S., 14, 18, 39, 90
Jacobs, S. C., 56
Jain, E., 122
Janoff-Bulman, R., 29, 34, 40, 47
Jette, A., 147, 152, 166
Jette, A. M., 147, 148, 149, 151
Johnson, D., 35, 44
Johnson, R. J., 87, 88
Jones, D., 67
Jordan, J. R., 23, 151, 173

Kagan, H., 50
Kahn, R. L., 70, 76, 132

Kaltman, S., 22, 29, 30, 35, 36, 40, 48
Kaminer, H., 39
Kane, R. A., 147, 175
Kane, R. L., 147, 175
Kaprio, J., 67
Kareholt, I., 86
Karel, M. J., 139
Kasl, S. V., 14, 56, 90, 92, 98, 103
Kasl-Godley, J. E., 139
Kastenbaum, R., 61, 157
Keesee, N., 30
Keijser, J., 13
Kelly, A. E., 39
Keltner, D., 36, 38
Kendig, H. L., 85, 101
Kennedy, P., 52, 53
Kessler, R. C., 91, 98, 99, 107
Kiecolt-Glaser, J. K., 101, 150
Klaczynski, P. A., 126
Klass, D., 112
Kleban, M. H., 119, 120, 162
Kleber, R., 33
Knipscheer, K. P. M., 83
Kolarz, C. M., 123
Koskenvuo, M., 67
Kosten, T. R., 56
Kraus, A. S., 66
Kreitman, N., 68
Kuykendall, D. H., 109

Labouvie-Vief, G., 122
Lana, R., 65
Lancee, W., 64
Lang, F. R., 133
Langfahl, E. S., 108
Lansford, J. E., 113, 114
Laren, D. S., 107
Larson, J., 21, 39, 51
Last, J. M., 20
Laungani, P., 16
Lavie, P., 39
Lawrence, R. H., 149
Lawton, M. P., 119, 120, 143, 161, 162
Lazarus, R. S., 25, 26, 29, 31, 32, 43, 56, 58, 71, 132
Leahy, J., 64
Lee, G. R., 111, 112
Lehman, D., 18, 79
Leibowitz, H. W., 137
Leon, I., 10
Lepore, S. J., 40
Levenson, R. W., 121, 122

Tancredy, C. M., 55
Tata, Y., 101, 150
Tedeschi, R., 27
Telonidis, J. S., 92
Terheggen, M., 23, 151, 173
Thompson, L., 15, 21, 65, 80, 100
Thorslund, M., 86
Tsai, J., 120, 122
Tsuang, M., 68
Turvey, C. L., 90
Tweed, R. G., 18

U.S. Department of Health and Human Ser-
    vices, 10, 11, 12, 139
Utz, R. L., 83

Vachon, M., 64, 108
Valkonen, T., 49, 67
van Baarsen, B., 83
van den Bout, J., 13, 14, 23, 51, 52, 53, 65,
    151, 173
van Duijn, M. A. J., 83
van Groenou, M. I. B., 107, 112
van Grootheest, D. S., 107, 112
van Heck, G., 27
Verbrugge, L., 147, 148, 151, 152, 166
Vicario, F., 102
Vierthaler, J., 56
Vincent, K., 64
Vohs, K., 49

Walker, W. L., 64
Wallace, R. B., 90
Walter, T., 29, 30, 43, 52, 112, 170
Walthert, J. M., 149

Ward, C. H., 14
Wayment, H. A., 40, 56
Weiss, D., 33
Weiss, R. S., 15, 54, 169
Wells, Y. D., 101
Whitbourne, S. K., 137, 138, 140
Whittington, F. J., 84
Wi, S., 67
Wijngaards-de Meij, L., 14, 65
Wikan, U., 30, 43
Willetts, M. C., 111
Williamson, J. D., 147, 148
Wilner, N., 33
Winchester-Nadeau, J., 30
Wolinsky, F. D., 87, 88
Worden, J. W., 22, 23, 29, 36, 37, 47, 48
Wortman, C., 18, 21, 25, 30, 40, 51, 52, 62,
    76, 79, 83, 91, 98, 99, 107, 170
Wright, S., 54
Wu, Y., 67

Yesavage, J. A., 82
Yong, H. H., 85
Young, B., 16

Zautra, A. J., 105
Zdaniuk, B., 102
Zech, E., 29, 33, 109
Zick, C. D., 106
Zick, K., 67
Zimmerman, R. S., 88
Zisook, S., 11, 13, 64
Zotti, A. M., 102
Zubenko, G. S., 14, 92

SUBJECT INDEX

caregiver stress, 103
Caregiving
    bereavement outcome factors, 101–102,
        115
    emotional burden, 102–103
    family stress, 108
    for person with dementia, 103–104
    relationship factors, 104–105
    transition to emotion-focused coping
        and, 142
    traumatic exposure in, 103
Cause of death, 11, 67
Changing Lives of Older Couples study, 97–
    98
Child, death of
    bereavement outcomes for older adults,
        78–79
    cultural context of bereavement, 79
    grandparent's grief, 79
    incidence, 10
    parental grief, 65
    survivor mortality and, 20
Child–parent relationships
    emotional regulation in older parents,
        121
    as source of widow(er) social support,
        110–111
Chronic disease
    disablement process, 147–149
    epidemiology, 138–139
    gender differences, 147
    See also Disability
Chronic grief
    depression patterns, 76
    dual process model, 54
    features, 17
    separation anxiety disorder, 15
Circumstances of death
    as bereavement adjustment factor, 98–
        101, 114, 115
    Changing Lives of Older Couples study,
        97–98
    suicide, 100–101
    timing, 20–21, 62, 98–100, 114
Cognitive functioning
    aging effects, 124–128, 161
    assessment with older adults, 174, 176
    caregiving for person with dementia,
        103–104
    cohort differences, 125
    dual process model of coping, 50
    health changes in late life and, 139, 140

individual differences in development,
    125
intelligence, 124–125
life experience gains, 125
life span development, 118–119
postformal thought, 126
protective developmental processes, 7–
    8, 125, 127–128, 130, 161
purposeful selectivity, 127–128
wisdom, 126–127
Cognitive stress theory
    components, 43–44
    conceptual basis, 25–26, 31
    in dual process model of coping, 43–44
    empirical testing, 31–32
    positive emotions in, 37–38
Communication, in grieving couple, 53
Comorbidity
    age-related risk, 139, 147
    depression, 89
    disorders related to pathological grief,
        18
    significance of, in older adults, 136, 147,
        148
Complicated grief
    clinical conceptualization, 18
    depression and, 92–93
    diagnosis, 171–172
    in dual process model, 54
Confrontational grieving, 26, 32, 39–40
Conjugal grief
    mortality patterns, 66–68
    prevalence, 11
    stress of, 11
Coping
    accommodative, 131–132, 141
    age-related physiological declines and,
        8, 135, 136, 140–143
    assimilative, 131, 141
    avoidance strategies, 32, 39–40
    bereavement-specific models, 36–39
    confrontational strategy, 26, 32, 39–40
    course of grieving, 22, 42
    disclosure, 33–34, 39–40
    emotion-focused, 32, 44–45, 131, 141,
        142, 163
    gender differences, 112
    integrative model of, 56–58
    intrusion–avoidance strategies, 33
    in late life, 106–114, 131–134, 141
    life-event models, 31–34
    meaning construction strategy, 34

oscillation between strategies, 48–50, 163–164

problem-focused, 32, 44–45, 52, 131, 141, 146

regulation of emotion in older persons, 36, 163–164

research needs, 162–163

ruminative, 39

secondary (accompanying) adjustments, 42, 47–48

selection, optimization, and compensation strategy, 132–133, 141, 146

shortcomings in scientific analyses of, 41–43

significance of, in grieving, 25–26, 27, 56

social support system, 141–142

See also Adaptive coping; Dual process model of coping; Protective developmental processes

Course of grieving

age differences, 72, 94

among older persons, 80–82

current models, 21–22, 42

depression patterns, 76

dual process model, 47, 49–50

dynamic nature, 11–13, 42

individual differences, 94–95, 165–166

long-term outcomes, 150–151, 165

loss- vs. restoration-oriented stress, 53

resilience among bereaved older adults, 77

suicide bereavement, 100–101

Cultural context

aging, 113

course of grieving, 22

grief work, 30

grieving experience, 112–113

mourning behavior, 16–17

parental grief, 79

protective developmental resources, 118–119

resources for late-life bereavement, 160

shortcomings in current models of grief, 43

social constructionist theory, 170

social support systems, 113

Delayed grief, 17, 18

Dementia, caregiver stress, 103–104

Denial, 39, 40

Depression

associated health risks, 89

bereavement outcomes among older persons, 80, 81, 82, 88–92

caregiving experience as bereavement outcome factor, 101–102, 103

clinical features, 19

comorbidity, 89, 139

complicated grief and, 92–93

epidemiology, 88–90

gender differences, 109, 112, 160

grief patterns, 21, 76

measurement issues, 89–90

normative grief and, 13–15, 19–20, 76

research limitations, 94

social support and, 109–110

Development

cognitive functioning, aging effects in, 124–128

cohort factors, 118

coping strategies in late life, 131–133

diversity among older adults, 70, 76

life span perspective, 7, 31, 117–119

limitations of bereavement research, 70, 71–72, 95, 166

self-concept, 128–130

traditional approach to bereavement studies, 6

See also Physiological declines in late life; Protective developmental processes

Diet and nutrition, 84, 138, 161

Disability

clinical features, 147–148

consideration in integrative model of aging and bereavement, 150–152, 166–168

epidemiology, 138–139, 147

research needs, 148

risk factors, 148

sequential (pathway) model, 148–149

significance of, in geriatric practice, 147

See also Chronic disease

Discharge planning, 147

Disclosure

coping strategy, 33–34

positive vs. negative, 39–40

Dual process model of coping, 7, 154

attachment concepts in, 55–56

cognitive mechanisms in, 50

complicated forms of grief in, 54

conceptual basis, 43–45, 58–59

contextual considerations, 155–156

course of grieving in, 22, 47, 49–50

emotional regulation in, 44

empirical evidence, 51–54

individual and subgroup differences in, 59, 60

integrative framework for outcome prediction, 56–58, 59–60, 97

interpersonal analysis in, 59

interventions based on, 54

late-life developmental perspective, 60

loss orientation in, 45, 46–47, 49, 53

oscillation in, 45, 48–50, 53–54, 126, 164–165

purpose, 45–46, 155

restoration orientation in, 45, 47–48, 49, 53

stressor conceptualization, 44–45, 46

Duration of grief

age differences research, 65–66

among older persons, 80–82

conceptual models, 21–22

depression patterns, 76

normative, 13

Ecological theory of aging, 142, 143

Emotion-focused coping

clinical conceptualization, 32

in dual process model, 44–45

in late life, 131, 141, 163

reduction of social networks in transition to, 142

Emotional functioning

adaptive role of positive emotions in coping, 37–39

assessment, 176

caregiving stress, 102–103

closeness of couple as bereavement outcome factor, 99, 114–115

control over emotions, 119, 120, 162

dampening of emotions, 120, 162, 164

dual process model of coping, 44, 46, 48–50

emotion-focused interventions, 52

four-component model of grieving, 35–36

limitations of bereavement research across lifespan, 71–72

protective developmental processes, 119–124, 130, 161–162

psychophysiological responsiveness, 119, 122

risk factors for bereavement complications, 21

sensation seeking, 120

stability, 119

See also Grief and grieving

End-of-life care, 136

Endocrine function, 138

Environmental docility hypothesis, 143–145

Family functioning

assessment, 176–177

bereavement outcomes, 78, 115

caregiving stress, 104–105, 108, 141–142

child–parent relationships, 110–111

meaning making, 169

research needs, 5

support for widow(er)s, 107

Flexible goal adjustment, 131

Forewarning of death, 20–21, 62, 98–100

Four-component model of grieving (Bonanno and Kaltman), 35–36, 48

Friendships, 110, 111

Functional limitations, 149, 152, 175

Gender differences

bereavement outcomes, 111–112

chronic disease experience, 147

coping style, 112

depression in late life, 109, 112

economic outcomes of conjugal loss, 106–107

emotion-focused vs. problem-focused interventions, 52

grief experience, 53, 116

grief work concept, 43

shortcomings of research base, 64–65

suicidal behavior, 93

widowhood, 107

Genetics, 118

Goal pursuit, 131

Grandparent's grief, 79

Grief and grieving

anxiety and, 15

bereavement-specific models, 36–39

broad-spectrum models, 34–36

cultural differences, 112–113

defined, 13

depression and, 13–15

dosage considerations, 42

duration, 13, 21, 22, 65–66, 76, 80–82

four-component model, 35–36

gender differences, 53, 116

intensity, 13

causes, 11, 67
patterns, 10–11
physical symptoms as risk factor, 87
widow(er) survival, 15–16, 160
See also Circumstances of death
Mourning
cultural context, 16–17
definition, 16
grief and, 16, 17
Musculoskeletal system, 137

Neuroendocrine function, 3
Neurophysiology
age-related changes, 138
compensating skills for declines in, 7–8
Normative bereavement, 6–7, 11–13, 17–18, 21–22, 172
Nursing home, postloss relocation to, 87–88, 159

Oscillation
course of bereavement, 49–50
definition, 48
dual process model, 45, 48–50, 163–164
empirical evidence, 53–54
function, 49, 126
research needs, 164–165
Outcomes of bereavement, 75–76
adaptive coping strategies, 26–27
age-related factors, 164–168
among older persons, 80–93
assessment, 27–28
determinants, 56
diversity among older adults, 76
generational factors, 71
grief work, 25, 30
loneliness, 82–83
long-term, 150–151, 152, 165, 166, 171
mortality, 85–87
physical health, 20, 81–82, 83–87
predictive model, 7, 56–58
scope, 9, 27
significance of coping process, 25–26, 27
sleep patterns, 85
social engagement, 83
See also Age as risk factor for poor outcome in bereavement; Risk for poor outcomes in bereavement
Outcomes research
depression measures, 89–90
dual process model interventions, 51–54

goals, 9–10
shortcomings, 43, 63–66, 93–94
traditional approach, 5–6

Pain
bereavement outcomes of older persons, 85
circumstances of death as bereavement outcome factor, 100
Pathological grief
clinical concpetualization, 17–18
related disorders, 18–20
See also specific type
Personality as risk factor for bereavement complications, 21
Physiological changes in late life
assessment considerations, 173–174
assessment measures, 175
effects of bereavement experience, 3, 152
health risks, 138–139
immune function, 138
implications for adaptive coping, 135, 136, 140–143
implications for bereavement, 136–137, 140, 152, 160–161, 166
physical changes, 137
psychological ramifications, 139
sensory functions, 137
significance of, 135, 136, 137
Population aging, patterns and trends, 4
Posttraumatic stress disorder
bereavement symptomology and, 32–33
clinical features, 19
normative grieving and, 19
pathological grief and, 18
Poverty, 106
Prevalence of bereavement, 10–11
Problem-focused coping
clinical conceptualization, 32
dual process model, 44–45
empirical studies, 52
in late life, 131, 141, 146
Protective developmental processes, 7–8, 69, 130–134, 133
cognitive functioning, 125, 127–128, 130
coping, 161–165
culture-based, 118–119, 160
economic well-being, 106–107
emotional, 119–124, 130
gender differences, 111–112

caregiving experience as bereavement outcome factor, 101–102

concurrent stress in bereavement, 105

loss- and restoration-oriented stressors, 157–158

secondary stressors, 47–48

See also Cognitive stress theory; Coping

Suicide

age patterns, 11, 93

bereavement outcomes, 100–101

gender patterns, 93

risk factors, 93

Task-based models grieving, 36–37, 47

Tenacious goal pursuit, 131

Therapeutic intervention

dual process model, 54

emotion-focused, 52

help-seeking behaviors among older persons, 159

implications of integrative framework, 170–172

indications for, 23

with older adults, 177

problem-focused, 52

role of disability model, 151–152

Trauma exposure in caregiving, 103

Trauma response

bereavement coping theories, 32–34

meaning construction, 34

traumatic grief, 18–19

See also Posttraumatic stress disorder

Vaccinations, 138

Violent death, 11

Vision, 137

Widow(er)hood, 11

age differences in bereavement, 156

bereavement outcomes, 77–79, 81–83, 84, 85

depression outcomes, 90–92, 160

economic outcomes, 106–107

family support, 107

identity issues, 129

marriage quality as bereavement adjustment factor, 99

mortality risk, 15–16, 66–68, 81, 85–86, 160

postloss relocation to nursing home, 87–88, 159

remarriage, 112

social support, 108–111

suicidal behavior in, 93

(un)expectedness of spouse's death, 20–21, 62, 98–100

Wisdom, 126–127

ABOUT THE AUTHORS

Robert O. Hansson, PhD, is McFarlin Professor of Psychology at the University of Tulsa, Oklahoma. He earned his PhD from the University of Washington. His research interests focus on successful aging, aging families, and bereavement. In addition to his previous publications with Margaret S. Stroebe, he is coauthor (with B. Carpenter) of *Relationships in Old Age: Coping With the Challenge of Transition* (1994). He served on the Scientific Advisory Committee on Bereavement for the Center for the Advancement of Health and is a member of the International Work Group on Death, Dying, and Bereavement and a member of the Gerontological Society of America's special interest group on death, dying, and bereavement. He is a fellow of the Gerontological Society of America and has served on the editorial boards of four journals, spanning the fields of aging, relationships, and loss.

Margaret S. Stroebe, PhD, is associate professor of psychology at Utrecht University, the Netherlands. She received her PhD at the University of Bristol, England, and an honorary doctorate in 2002 from the University of Louvain-la-Neuve, Belgium. Her research interests include theoretical approaches to grief and grieving, interactive patterns of coping with bereavement, and the efficacy of bereavement intervention. She is coeditor (with R. O. Hansson, W. Stroebe, and H. Schut) of the *Handbook of Bereavement Research: Consequences, Coping, and Care,* published in 2001 by the American Psychological Association; coeditor (with W. Stroebe and R. O. Hansson) of *The Handbook of Bereavement: Theory, Research, and Intervention* (1993); and coauthor (with W. Stroebe) of *Bereavement and Health* (1987). She received the Scientific Research Award of the American Association for Death Education and Counseling in 2002.